THE RELIGIOUS LEFT AND CHURCH-STATE RELATIONS

Steven H. Shiffrin

PRINCETON UNIVERSITY PRESS   PRINCETON AND OXFORD

Copyright © 2009 by Princeton University Press
Published by Princeton University Press, 41 William Street,
Princeton, New Jersey 08540
In the United Kingdom: Princeton University Press, 6 Oxford Street,
Woodstock, Oxfordshire OX20 1TW

press.princeton.edu

Second printing, and first paperback printing, 2012
Paperback ISBN 978-0-691-15619-4

The Library of Congress has cataloged the cloth edition of this book as follows

Shiffrin, Steven H., 1941–
    The religious left and church-state relations / Steven H. Shiffrin.
        p.   cm.
    Includes bibliographical references and index.
    ISBN 978-0-691-14144-2 (hardcover : alk. paper)
    1. Freedom of religion—United States. 2. Church and state—United States.
3. Liberalism (Religion)—United States. 4. Religion and politics—United States.
5. Religious right—United States. I. Title.
    KF4783.S56 2009
    342.7308′52—dc22   2008054243

British Library Cataloging-in-Publication Data is available

This book has been composed in Sabon

Printed on acid-free paper. ∞

Printed in the United States of America

10   9   8   7   6   5   4   3   2

THE RELIGIOUS LEFT AND CHURCH-STATE RELATIONS

For Neesa, Seana, Benjamin, and Jacob

———————————————————————

Contents

Preface

THIS BOOK HAS BEEN AN adventure. After spending most of my scholarly career writing about freedom of speech and press, I decided it was time to turn to the religion side of the First Amendment. I did not come to the subject unaffected by my past. I have been influenced not only by teaching about the subject for more than thirty years, but also by a checkered theological background, more than two decades of teaching and writing about other aspects of the First Amendment, and by a commitment to progressive politics. I was raised as a Catholic and left the church during college. Subsequently, I became a member of a congregationally independent Protestant church. For many years, I was an agnostic. My wife is Jewish and two of my children have been bar mitzvahed. I have spent my fair share of time in temples. When I began this project, I was a secular humanist attending an interfaith chapel and a Unitarian church. Before I finished the project, I returned to Christianity and thought about becoming a Methodist or an Episcopalian. Instead, I returned (in a sense) to Catholicism. I am very happy with my local congregation and enormously unsatisfied with the all-too-conservative leaders of the Catholic Church. I suppose I am a radical Catholic or a Catholic of conscience, the kind whom those beholden to authority deride as cafeteria Catholics.

Initially, in moving to a different part of the First Amendment, I thought I had broken sharply with the past. But the past has its grip. In writing about freedom of speech, I have inveighed against the systematizers, those who think that it is possible to build a grand theory of freedom of speech in which problems can be solved by resort to a single value or a small set of values. In my view, free speech problems involve the clash of values in too many complicated contexts to be able to hope or imagine that a single value or small set of values could emerge as a talismanic solution. After pursuing that theme for over a decade, I proceeded to argue that the social practice of dissent should receive special weight in determining the outcome of free speech cases. So flag burners are at the heart of the First Amendment; commercial advertisers are not.

Although my theological commitments have varied and my emphasis in writing about the First Amendment has moved around, I have consistently been committed to a pragmatic progressive politics. In the context of religion and the Constitution, this has always meant that I favor strong protection for the free exercise of religion and oppose tight connections between church and state. In arguing for strong protection of the free exercise of religion and opposing cozy connections between religion and the state, I once again oppose the system builders. I do not think the religion clauses of the Constitution should or can be reduced to a single value or a small set of values. In my writings on freedom of speech, I have lobbied for dissenters. Here too I think that laws placing burdens on religious minorities are of special concern. As will be clear, I believe the religious Right has mistaken legal, theological, and political views. I try to show that. But my main concern is to participate in a dialogue with secular liberals concerning how best to think about and defend free exercise of religion and separation of church and state. As I will argue at length, I believe that the religious Left has a more politically attractive argument than that put forward by the secular Left.

With respect to Part I, I have received helpful comments from participants in the Conference on Law and Religion, sponsored by the Program in Law and Public Affairs, Princeton University, February 28, 2003; the Conference on Philosophy and the Social Sciences, hosted by the Institute of Philosophy of the Czech Academy of Sciences, May 16–20, 2003; and the Conference on Feminism and Fundamentalisms, sponsored by the Feminism and Legal Theory Program, Cornell University, April 11–12, 2003. The materials in Part I grow out of an article that appeared in volume 90 of the *Cornell Law Review*, pp. 9–95, entitled "The Pluralistic Foundations of the Religion Clauses" (2004), though they have been updated and revised.

The original idea for Part II was presented as the 2001 Ralph Gregory Elliot Lecture at Yale Law School, although it has taken many twists and turns since that time. Many have responded to various versions including faculty at the Cornell Law School, the University of Texas Law School, and the Yale Law School, as well as participants in the Ethics and Public Life Program at Cornell and the Conference on Philosophy and the Social Sciences at the Institute of Philosophy of the Czech Academy of Sciences in Prague. The materials in Part II grow out of an article in volume 11 of the *Cornell Journal of Law and Public Policy*, pp. 503–51, entitled "The First Amendment and the Socialization of Children: Compulsory Public Education and Vouchers" (2002), as an outgrowth of a symposium sponsored by that journal. Those materials have also been updated and revised.

Part III has benefited from a presentation at the Central Meeting of the American Philosophical Association in Chicago, a plenary address to the Conference on Philosophy and the Social Sciences in Prague, presentations to the law faculties at Cornell Law School, Seattle University, and the University of Utah, and presentations to the Cornell Campus ministers and also to the Campus Ministers of the Ivy League.

I owe special thanks to many people who read or reacted to parts of the book manuscript: Greg Alexander, Fred Appel (who gave me some good early advice about the book's focus), Ed Baker, John Blume, Margaret Chon, Jesse Choper, Christopher Eisgruber, Richard Fallon, Cynthia Farina, Martha Fineman, Richard Isomaki (who did an outstanding job of copyediting), Rick Garnett, Kent Greenawalt, Sheri Lynn Johnson, Lily Kahng, Doug Kysar, Chuck Myers (who also shepherded the book through the Princeton evaluation process, recruiting readers who offered outstanding commentary), John Mitchell, Frank Michelman, Trevor Morrison, Eduardo Penalver, Eva Pils, Margaret Powers, Annelise Riles, David Skover, Gary Simson, Father Robert Smith, Madhavi Sunder, Lee Teitelbaum, Valerie Hans, and Brad Wendel. Nancy Ammons and Jan Rose did wonderful work in getting the manuscript in better form.

I also owe thanks to several members of my family. Neesa Levine set me straight about many things, mainly questioning assumptions I made about the psychology of real human beings. Over the years, Benjamin and Jacob Shiffrin have argued with me about many of the subjects I discuss in this book. I recall with fondness a conversation about the *McCullom* case in Part I in which Jacob was outraged: "Dad, you just can't say that." He was right. Seana Shiffrin read every part of the manuscript and offered outstanding comments, as she always does. I particularly recall her championing Judge Goodwin in Part I; she persuaded me to argue against Court pragmatism; she also compelled me to go deeper in Part III. Benjamin maintained that my views are overly kind to religion. He will say the same thing when he reads the book, but his fingerprints are there, nonetheless. That is true of all the people I have thanked. None of them will agree with all or most of what I say here, but their fingerprints are here in one way or another.

THE RELIGIOUS LEFT AND
CHURCH-STATE RELATIONS

Introduction

FEW PERSONS ARE INDIFFERENT about the role of religion in American law or politics. I have been teaching the First Amendment since 1977. Students have always been excited about issues like obscenity, libel, flag burning, racist speech, commercial advertising, and the role of money in politics. But my students become even more lively when we discuss constitutional issues like a city putting up a religious display during the Christmas season, whether a school rightly included "under God" in the Pledge of Allegiance, whether a state could fund religious schools, and whether the Amish had a right to take their children out of the schools. Often the debates between my students involve a confrontation between those who are hostile to religion and those who favor religion. Those who are hostile to religion routinely favor separation of church and state. Sometimes, however, the debate is between members of the religious Right and the religious Left: The Right favoring tight relations between church and state; the Left opposing such connections.

Although the mass media tend to ignore it, there is a strong religious Left in the United States.[1] The term *left* often is used in a way that is equated with the radical tradition in American politics. But I use the term in a more inclusive way. By *left*, I simply mean to refer to those citizens who are generally on the liberal, progressive, or "left" side of the political spectrum; by *religious* Left, I mean that these citizens arrive at liberal political conclusions in accordance with religious premises whether those premises are thought to be theologically liberal or more traditional. Twenty-four percent of Americans might fairly be classified as belonging to the religious Right, but 18 percent of white Americans belong to the religious Left, and most Latinos and African Americans are politically progressive.[2] The religious Left includes "a large majority of Jews, at least half of Roman Catholics, a growing number of mainline Protestants, most African American churchgoers, a significant minority of white evangelicals, and most followers of traditions other than Christianity and Judaism."[3] As John Green and Steven Wildman conclude, "The Religious Right and the Religious Left are almost exactly the same size."[4] My particular interest here is to focus on those citizens who favor free exercise and oppose tight connections between church and state in accordance with their religious premises. Although Green and Wildman did not ask about attitudes toward church-state relations, liberals typically oppose tight connections between church and state. Whether or not those citizens opposing tight connections between church and state precisely fit into the Green and Wildman data, their data suggests that such citizens are not a marginal group. Given our constitutional culture, this should not be surprising.

Whatever the precise data might be, I maintain that the religious Left's position on church-state relations is superior to and more politically attractive than that of the religious Right or the secular Left. I think this advantage is understood by religious leaders like Jim Wallis and Rabbi Michael Lerner and increasingly by some left-leaning Democratic politicians whose political beliefs fit within a religious framework. But it is not understood by the mass media; it is contested by the religious Right; and the religious Left's argument has not been developed in a sustained way.

My purpose in this book is to develop that argument and to reflect upon how the religious Left should engage the religious Right and the secular Left on the subject of church-state relations. Too often people think that the subject is exhausted by an understanding of the religion clauses of the First Amendment. To be sure, debates about church-state relations in the daily dynamics of local politics are informed and sometimes bounded by the dictates of constitutional law. But much is left open. Tighter connections between church and state may well be permitted by the conservatives on the Roberts Court, but they will never be required. Within the broad limits of the Constitution, decisions about the relationship between church and state will be decided in democratic precincts—well outside the courts.

Nonetheless, an understanding of the religion clauses is crucial to understanding how to think and talk about religion and the state in American law and politics. My project here is to describe and defend a form of *religious liberalism* showing the different, but mutually supporting, forms it should take in the courts and in democratic life.

Religious liberalism is a form of liberalism that reaches liberal conclusions from religious premises. In the context of church-state relations, this means strong free exercise of religion and the avoidance of tight connections between church and state. In the democratic process, I will argue, it is appropriate and necessary for religious liberals to make theological arguments. On the other hand, government in its official actions may not make theological arguments, and that includes courts. Thus the constitutional framework of religious liberalism does not depend upon theological premises or theological arguments, but, as I discuss in chapter 7, it is thoroughly compatible with the theological premises and arguments of religious liberalism. Indeed, in my view, the best legal understanding of the religion clauses is most compatible with religious liberalism. In interpreting the religion clauses, religious liberalism opposes the system builders, those who think that it is possible to build a grand theory of freedom of religion in which problems can be solved by resort to a single value or a small set of values. Instead religious liberalism denies that the religion clauses of the Constitution should or can be reduced to a single value or a small set of values. It believes that the religion clauses should be supported by the full array of relevant values. In supporting religious liberalism, I argue that the religion clauses are supported by pluralistic foundations. For example, I argue that the Establishment Clause serves many functions: (1) It is a prophylactic measure that protects religious liberty and autonomy, including the protection of taxpayers from being forced to support religious ideologies to which they are opposed; (2) it stands for equal citizenship without regard to religion; (3) it protects against the destabilizing influence of having the polity divided along religious lines; (4) it promotes political community; (5) it safeguards the autonomy of the state to protect the public interest; (6) it protects religion from the corrupting influences of the state; and (7) it promotes religion in the private sphere.

Second, the most underappreciated insight in the cases and the commentary is the protection of religion from the corrupting influence of the state. Concern about this influence is not new. It goes back to Roger Williams and James Madison among others. But the Supreme Court in a number of important cases, and some of the most distinguished commentators of the present day, give this concern short shrift. I will insist, however, that a major goal of the Establishment Clause is to protect religions from the state when the state is purporting to help religions. Separation of church from the state should not be considered a reflection of religious hostility or fear of religion. Separation of church and state is our Constitution's way of protecting religions from being dependent upon, co-opted, manipulated, or even strongly associated with political leaders. Government has no credentials to be entrusted with religious leadership. Separation of church and state is our Constitution's method of favoring religion.

These principles of religious liberalism are as important in American politics as they are in American law. But they are not understood by the religious Right and are neglected or rejected by the secular Left. I will argue that religious liberalism is in a far better political position to engage with and combat the religious Right than is the secular Left. Indeed, when it comes to church-state relations, much of the rhetoric of the secular Left is part of the problem, not part of the solution. Of course, Sam Harris should have a constitutional right to maintain that religion, even moderate religion, is "one of the principal forces driving us to the abyss."[5] Christopher Hitchens has every right to claim that religion "poisons everything."[6] But the fear of, or denigration, of religion cannot possibly be conceived of as politically attractive in a country where nearly 90 percent of the people believe in God. So long as the secular Left is believed to dominate the Democratic Party, so long as its religious sensibilities are believed to be suspect, the Democratic Party will be on the defensive.

Simply put, the secular Left is in a poor position to make theological arguments against those put forward by some religious conservatives. As I have said, theological arguments do not belong in courts. But theological arguments are regularly introduced in democratic dialogue. In response, the secular Left bemoans the fact that the religious Right makes religious arguments in American politics. This line of argument may be useful in fund-raising appeals to select groups, but it is otherwise useless. The religious Right will not go away because it has been accused of political bad manners for introducing its arguments in the public square. The arguments of the secular Left in fact are counterproductive. They strengthen the identity of religious conservatives. Rather than arguing that religious arguments do not belong in the public square, it is better to argue against the politics and the theology of the religious Right. The religious Right assumes, but cannot demonstrate, that tight connections between religion and the state are good for religion. The religious Right supposes that the Bible authorizes tight connections between religion and the state. These are deeply problematic assumptions. Despite secular Left misgivings, the great issue in American religious politics is not *whether* religion should be promoted, but *how* it should be promoted. The religious Left believes that religion is best promoted by keeping government away from religion. Thus the secular Left and the religious Left can both agree on separation of church and state, but their paths to this conclusion are quite different. My contention is that the path of the religious Left is far more politically attractive that the path of the secular Left.

I divide the book into three parts. The first part explores the pluralistic foundations of the religion clauses. It argues at some length that Constitution does not simply protect religious equality or equal religious liberty. Deviations from religious equality might or might not violate the Constitution, and respecting religious equality does not necessarily avoid a constitutional violation. In support of this conclusion I discuss many controversial examples (although I leave the important issue of financial aid to religion for Part II) including laws prohibiting the ingestion of peyote and animal sacrifice; the government's use of religious symbols; the government's involvement with monotheistic prayer and the Pledge of Allegiance; the teaching of evolution in the public schools; government protection of conscientious objectors and those who refuse to work on the Sabbath; and government support for religion within the public schools. Given the pluralistic character of the values underlying the religion clauses and the variety of contexts in which questions about the legal status of religion arise, I conclude that equality can best be seen as one, but only one, important value in a rich and evolving tradition.

In doing so, I part company with respected commentators such as Christopher Eisgruber and Lawrence Sager who maintain that the religion clauses are simply designed to protect against religious discrimination and do not imply that religion is valuable.[7] I argue instead that the Constitution values religion. *In God We Trust* on our money is constitutional, not because it is secular, and not because it is trivial, but because our Constitution is embedded in a dominantly monotheistic culture that values religion. It is unfortunate that the people feel a need to use government to express monotheistic views without regard for the views of Buddhists, Hindus, atheists, and agnostics, but it blinks reality to suppose that the Constitution does not favor religion.

One of the important Establishment Clause questions concerns the extent to which the state can provide aid to religious institutions. Part II of the book deepens the analysis of the multiplicity of Establishment Clause values in confronting the question whether law or policy should prevent government from providing vouchers to private schools, including religious schools. Vincent Blasi has referred to this issue as "the most vigorously contested question of church-state relations."[8] I once served on the Ithaca City School District Board of Education. A member of that board wisely observed that school board issues were often bitter and contentious because they involved issues that arouse strong passions: children and money. Vouchers involve not only children and money, but also religion. No wonder that emotions run high. This debate about public and private education raises important questions about the role of the state in promoting a certain kind of person and citizen, which has implications for liberal and democratic theory, the respective rights of children and parents, and the nature of religious freedom in a democratic society.

I am, of course, aware that the Court has spoken on the issue,[9] but I will argue that it glossed over the serious constitutional questions that were raised. Indeed, I argue that the general debate about vouchers has been oversimplified. Too often the argument has been that vouchers are always good or always bad or that vouchers to religious schools either always do or always do not violate the Establishment Clause. I argue that the interests of children and the state in public education have been underestimated; indeed, I argue that there is a surprisingly strong constitutional case for the proposition that government should in many circumstances be able to *compel* adolescents of high school age, but not preadolescents, to attend public schools. No U.S. government is likely to engage in such compulsion, and there are good political reasons not to do so, but analysis of the case for compulsory public education leads to support of a strong presumption *against* vouchers, at least at the high school level. This presumption, however, is more difficult to defend when public schools are relatively homogeneous or are providing inadequate education to poor children. Even if vouchers could generally be supported, vouchers to religious schools raise serious concerns about the appropriate principles of church-state relations in the American constitutional order. The Court has obscured these concerns by failing to recognize the full range of Establishment Clause values. But these concerns might be overcome in certain circumstances. In short, I argue that compulsory public education is sometimes constitutional and sometimes not, that vouchers are generally to be resisted, but sometimes not, and that vouchers to religious schools should ordinarily be considered unconstitutional, but sometimes not.

In Parts I and II, I explore the constitutional framework of religious liberalism, and apply the framework to a wide variety of examples from the Pledge of Allegiance to vouchers. If the conclusions in Part II about vouchers are contingent, the claims of Part III are not. In Part III, I turn from constitutional law (and the policy aspects of vouchers) to the realm of democratic politics. But the turn cannot be complete. Constitutional law strongly influences democratic politics on church-state issues. Religious liberals, however, go beyond the logic of constitutional law in the democratic forum by turning to theology. I develop the thesis that partly because of this, religious liberalism is far better equipped to engage with or to combat religious conservatism than is the secular Left. The secular Left, of course, is not homogeneous. Its attitudes toward religion might be hostile, indifferent, mixed, or cooperative. Nonetheless, its varied attempts to deal with issues of religious liberty, government use of religious symbols, and government aid to religious organizations are politically impoverished. The problem with religious conservatives is not that they participate in the political process. The problem is the substance of their theology and their politics. Indeed the two run together. If religious Americans are politically motivated by theology, then it is important to talk about theology in politics. It is important to combat bad theology with good theology.

Of course, I do not maintain that I have a pipeline to the Holy Spirit. I could be wrong about my theology and my politics. Moreover, believing that the Right is wrong about politics and theology does not suggest that it is evil or intellectually ill equipped or unworthy of respect. Indeed, it is important to identify the circumstances in which the Left and the religious Right can forge common ground (perhaps on helping the poor or protecting the environment). But fallible as my beliefs may be, I do maintain them with conviction. I believe it vital to combat the religious Right's posture on church-state relations (just as they believe it vital to combat the views of the Left).

One should not be deterred by overly precious conceptions of "public reason" or by the politically naive view that religion is a political "conversation stopper." Indeed, I will argue that political candidates rightly entertain religious views in the public forum. I will discuss the Democratic Party and maintain that if it is to be something more than the party to vote for when the alternative has become unpalatable, it must appeal to the spiritual sensibilities of the country without entertaining tight connections between church and state. But it is unreasonable to expect that party candidates would engage in the thick theological dialogue needed to counter the arguments of the religious Right. The country is too pluralistic for candidates to take such risks.

But that dialogue must take place. The religious Right cannot go unanswered, and the religious Left must lead the way. The secular Left is for the most part poorly equipped to talk about theology or to address religious sensibilities. Instead of participating in dreams of a country without religion, the secular Left needs to join with the religious Left in addressing the world that exists now and will exist in the foreseeable future. Although segments of the secular Left may believe that religion is nothing more than superstition, they need to understand that public expressions of religious hostility are politically counterproductive. Instead of dismissing the role of religion in American politics, the secular Left needs to understand that it has much to gain from an alliance with the religious Left.

Part One ————————————————————————————————

THE PLURALISTIC FOUNDATIONS
OF THE RELIGION CLAUSES

Chapter 1

Overview of Part I

ALTHOUGH CLAUSES IN THE Constitution protect the free exercise of religion and prohibit the establishment of religion, debates over the meaning of these clauses are a growth industry in American legal scholarship and throughout American culture. Even the United States Supreme Court, which has been dominated by Republicans for some time, does not toe a party line. Nonetheless, in recent years a theme has broken through. Contemporary Supreme Court interpretations suggest that the religion clauses are primarily rooted in the value of equality.[1] For example, in interpreting the Free Exercise Clause, a majority of the Court has argued that in the absence of *discrimination* against religion or unless *other* constitutional values are present, it is not unconstitutional for a statute to inadvertently burden religion.[2] Similarly, equality values have played a strong role in the Court's Establishment Clause jurisprudence.[3] Many distinguished commentators have argued that the Court's focus on equality results in insufficient attention paid to the value of religious liberty.[4] In my view, these commentators are right in contending that an equality emphasis misses much of importance in religion clause jurisprudence. But their emphasis on liberty or equal liberty[5] is too narrow. Instead, I will suggest that understanding the proper place of equality in religion clause jurisprudence requires appreciation of a broader range of values with regard to both religion clauses,[6] and a recognition that this appreciation is itself independently important. Discussing the failure to recognize the full range of values underlying the Free Exercise Clause is, of course, a necessary theoretical prelude to discussing the Establishment Clause. But it is more than that. The failure to appreciate the breadth of values underlying the Free Exercise Clause is also pragmatically important because a better understanding of the clause could persuade citizens, jurists, and legislators that greater protection is appropriate in particular circumstances.[7] With respect to the Establishment Clause, the failure to recognize the full range of relevant values creates an additional difficulty. By failing to appreciate the value of protecting religion from a government trying to be "helpful," the Supreme Court[8] and distinguished scholars[9] make some Establishment Clause problems appear easier than they are. In reality, too many values interact in too many complicated ways to hope or expect that the clauses could be reduced to a single value such as "equality" or even to a small set of determining values. Failure to appreciate this complexity leads the Court and important commentators to miss the extent to which the values underlying the Establishment Clause conflict with each other.

In exploring these arguments, chapter 1 argues that the Free Exercise Clause is supported by seven values: (1) it protects liberty and autonomy; (2) it avoids the cruelty of either forcing an individual to do what she is conscientiously obliged not to do or penalizing her for responding to an obligation of conscience; (3) it preserves respect for law and minimizes violence triggered by religious conflict; (4) it promotes equality and combats religious discrimination; (5) it protects associational values; (6) it promotes political community; and (7) it protects the personal and social importance of religion.

Chapter 2 argues that the Establishment Clause is also supported by seven values: (1) it protects religious liberty and autonomy, including preventing the government from forcing taxpayers to support religious ideologies to which they are opposed; (2) it stands for equal citizenship without regard to religion; (3) it protects against the destabilizing influence of having the polity divided along religious lines; (4) it promotes political community; (5) it protects the autonomy of the state to protect the public interest; (6) it protects churches from the corrupting influences of the state; and (7) it promotes religion in the private sphere.

In assessing the appropriate relationship between religion and the state, it is vital to draw upon an eclectic mix of resources. No single source of interpretation should be regarded as dispositive. Although original intent is entitled to interpretive weight in some circumstances, it should not be primary for many reasons. Among other things, it is not clear that the original intent of the Framers was for us to follow their intent.[10] Even if it were, the Framers themselves did not agree upon the appropriate relationship between religion and government.[11] And furthermore, even if they had agreed, it is not clear that a legal theory requiring us to be bound in the twenty-first century by the will of a group of eighteenth-century white male agrarian slaveholders would have a lot to recommend it.[12] Moreover, our whole history of constitutional interpretation testifies that precedent is a more important source of interpretation than original intent.[13]

Although precedent may be more important than original intent, it also cannot be of primary importance for our inquiry. Our point here is not to follow the law as if we were lower-court judges. It is not our task to be sheep in the flock of Chief Justice Roberts and his Federalist Society cohorts. Whether or not the Roberts Court moves Establishment Clause analysis (in the area of government symbols) away from an equality approach, as I expect,[14] our goal is to seek to understand religion clause theory and practice in an independent way. Therefore, precedent should not be our primary guide. In determining the value of the religion clauses, we should consult the best thinking on the subject, and that should include the writing of Framers, jurists, political theorists, and commentators. Moreover, we should be influenced by how relationships between church and state have worked in practice, and there the testimony of historians, political scientists, and sociologists is indispensable. In short, my view is that in interpreting the religion clauses, we should act like constitutional scavengers,[15] appropriating the best theory and the best descriptions of how the world actually works in order to arrive at our conclusions. On the other hand, the task is not to produce a "perfect" Constitution,[16] divorced from the values, experiences, and traditions of our nation. Our scavenging must produce insights that comfortably fit within our evolving traditions.[17]

In the end, there is no substitute for practical reason. Indeed, when it comes to applying the religion clauses to concrete cases, I press for the view that there is no pat formula, no single determining principle that resolves them. What is true with the speech clause[18] holds with both the religion clauses: balancing or prudential judgment concerning multiple values in a variety of concrete contexts is unavoidable. By this I do not mean to suggest that ad hoc balancing is always appropriate. The mix of values frequently requires the formulation of rules and standards to apply in specific factual contexts.[19] That these rules or tests may differ need not signal confusion. They may simply respect relevant differences. To have a sense of this, however, it is necessary to consider a range of situations. Accordingly, I discuss many examples, including (1) peyote ingestion; (2) animal sacrifice; (3) the government's use of religious symbols; (4) government involvement with monotheism, including the Pledge of Allegiance; (5) the teaching of evolution in the public schools; (6) government protection of conscientious objectors and those who refuse to work on the Sabbath; and (7) government support for religion within and without the public schools.

In both chapters in this part, I argue that the religion clauses cannot be explained by reference to equality. The equality value is important, but I try to show that many deviations from equality are deeply embedded in the framework of government operations. For example, it will not work to maintain that our Constitution regards religion and nonreligion as equal. Indeed, the religion clauses are best interpreted to protect religion not just because of values such as autonomy, equality, and religious peace, but because religion itself is regarded as valuable. This obviously is a bitter pill for religious skeptics to swallow, and some of the conclusions that follow from it should be a source of regret even for most religious believers. As I will argue, however, it appears to be the best reading of our evolving Constitution.[20] Nonetheless, the foundational view that religion is valuable does not flirt with theocracy. Far from it. The Constitution forbids coercion and the favoring of one religion over another (except when it doesn't—more on that later). Even more importantly, again with some exceptions, the Constitution is best interpreted to curb government intervention in favor of religion, not because religion is a constitutional stepchild, but because the seductions of governmental dependence are great and because government is not to be trusted.

The upshot of these values and principles is that other deviations from religious equality are sometimes permitted. In part, these deviations are influenced by a strong religious presence in American culture, the pluralistic character of American religions, and the plethora of conflicting religious beliefs. For better or for worse, the urge on the part of religious culture to find some expression in governmental activities leads to government engaging in monotheistic prayers. Because of the pluralistic and conflicting character of religious beliefs, government often participates in practices inconsistent with or forbidden by many religions. On a similar note, because religions impact government interests in diverse ways, government can sometimes remove obstacles impeding the practice of some religions, but not others.

Deviations from religious equality are not always fatal, nor should they be. Similarly, compliance with religious equality should not always pass muster under the religion clauses. The kind of formal equality denying liberty to those religiously burdened by a law not aimed at religions is unworthy of respect. As I will discuss in Part II, financial aid afforded to religious and nonreligious schools alike also raises serious Establishment Clause issues despite compliance with equality. The same applies to proposals to permit equal access to classrooms for religious and secular leaders. For those who revel in simplicity, these conclusions will be unsettling. But there is a deeper concern. Complying with equality is seen by many as a proxy for fairness. If equality is not the central meaning of the religion clauses, there is the suspicion that everyone is not being treated fairly. That suspicion is warranted, and improvements can be made, particularly in the direction of substantive equality. I will argue, however, that religious equality cannot possibly be achieved in a diverse society. Given the pluralistic character of the values underlying the religion clauses and the variety of contexts in which questions about the legal status of religion arise, equality is best seen as one important value in a rich and evolving tradition.

Religious liberalism understands this. Both the secular Left and religious Right, however, misapprehend this textured religious tradition. The secular Left does not understand the importance of religion in our constitutional tradition. The religious Right does not understand that government harms religion when it tries to help. Neither understands the complex dimensions of religious equality.

Chapter 2 _____

The Free Exercise Clause

THE MASSACHUSETTS BAY COLONY tried to protect its inhabitants from blasphemers and heretics by banishing them from the colony. If those banished returned, the authorities whipped them, cut off ears, bored tongues with hot irons, and resorted to executions.[1] For minority religions, freedom of religion was the right to keep quiet, the right to be punished, or the right to leave Massachusetts.[2] To stay in Massachusetts was to accept and live by the terms of the Puritan deal.

The fighting legal issue regarding free exercise today is not whether persons are free to hold opinions different from the majority or to express those opinions in the public square, but the extent to which government can restrict religious action.[3] There is general agreement that government may not single out religious action for special adverse treatment.[4] The question is whether a general law that incidentally burdens religious conduct is vulnerable on the ground that it violates the free exercise of religion. Let me begin by giving two examples, analyzing them under the Supreme Court's current approach, under traditional secular liberal approaches, and under communitarian approaches,[5] before developing my own views.

1. The state of Oregon outlaws ingesting peyote regardless of the motivation for doing so. Four persons ingest peyote: the first as part of a religious ceremony of a Native American church; the second as an integral part of an artistic life, believing peyote ingestion is an important part of the creative process; the third as an integral part of a hedonistic lifestyle; and the fourth who tries the drug out of curiosity.
2. Three persons violate a law against the torture of animals: the first as part of a required religious ceremony; the second as a piece of performance art; the third as a part of a sadistic lifestyle.

The Court's Approach

Although the matter is not entirely free of difficulty, it seems that the Court as currently constituted would deny the religious claims in each of the examples mentioned above. Justice Scalia, writing for the Court in

Employment Division v. Smith,[6] argued that a law outlawing the ingestion of peyote could constitutionally be applied to a participant in a religious ceremony of the Native American Church.[7] Justice Scalia did not suggest that the importance of the state interest in the individual case outweighed freedom of religion interest. Instead, he maintained that there was no constitutionally cognizable religious interest in the first place.[8] Any other conclusion, he suggested, would lead to a "system in which each conscience is a law unto itself or in which judges weigh the social importance of all laws against the centrality of all religious beliefs."[9] Ironically, under existing law, the artistic claimant in both examples would have a cognizable speech claim[10] (even though it would undoubtedly be unsuccessful). It seems that the First Amendment is somewhat more solicitous of speech than it is of religion.[11] I believe one would have to rise very early in the morning to justify this differential treatment, and the Court has been sleeping on the subject for some time. In any event, the Court's bottom line would ultimately be the same for all claimants in both examples. One way or another, their claims would be denied; equal protection under the law is not always sweet.

Liberal Theory

Equality of application can be achieved in a different way, however. Followers of Immanuel Kant believe that rights may not be infringed unless the exercise of those rights interferes with the rights of others.[12] So, with respect to the peyote example, a Kantian might argue that the autonomous choice of the individuals involved should be respected because ingesting peyote does not interfere with the rights of another.

The animal torture example is particularly difficult for the Kantian. The Kantian traditionally believes that humans are distinguished from animals in their ability to reason and make autonomous choices.[13] According to this reasoning, animals have no rights because they are not moral creatures.[14] Applying the principle that individuals' autonomous choices should be protected unless they interfere with the freedom of others, a principled Kantian would have to conclude that in a just state, the believer, the artist, and the sadist should each be permitted to torture animals.

Nietzsche once suggested that to have a system is to lack integrity,[15] and I would hope that followers of Kant would lack integrity in this circumstance and not follow his principles.[16] Indeed, Kant himself did not always adhere to his principles. He himself argued that animal cruelty could be proscribed because it brutalized human beings,[17] but this prefers one lifestyle over another and sidesteps the notion that imposing suffering on animals is an independent wrong, regardless of how it impacts human beings.[18]

What the approaches of Scalia and Kant have in common is that neither of them treats religious liberty differently from other forms of liberty. Religion is not deemed to be special, and religious liberty would have no special privilege in these examples.[19]

Communitarian Theory

The approach to religious freedom taken by communitarianism depends on the particular form of communitarian theory. In general, communitarians maintain that liberalism exalts individual liberty at the expense of democracy and self-government,[20] autonomy at the expense of civic virtue[21] or community, and rights at the expense of duties.[22] This cluster of ideas can lead to differing approaches regarding freedom of religion. Distinguishing between participatory communitarians, traditional communitarians, and substantive communitarians should help illustrate this point.

A participatory communitarian would place most emphasis on self-government[23] and the capacity of the polity to change. Rights, on this conception, would not be discarded but would flow from the idea of self-government and the conditions that make self-government possible.[24] On that analysis, it is easy to see how rights of freedom of speech and press would arise. It is, however, more difficult to ground a comprehensive right to freedom of religion.[25] It might be possible to squeeze freedom of religion into the idea of self-government by positing that religion is necessary for the virtues that support self-government. Even accepting this assumption, however, this theory would appear to authorize self-governing citizens to distinguish between and discriminate against those religions that were believed to support civic virtues and those that were believed not to support such virtues. Of course, the notion of self-government assumes equality of persons, but on the communitarian understanding, equality of persons does not necessitate equal respect for the choices people make.[26] The participatory branch of communitarianism, therefore, could support religious discrimination.

On the other hand, Cass Sunstein suggests that religious peace is a precondition for self-government, and that religious persecution, or, more narrowly, government favoritism of religion, endangers religious peace.[27] The necessity-for-religious-peace arguments do not afford a sturdy basis for protecting religions that are unable or unwilling to put up a significant fight,[28] nor do they address other circumstances where violence or instability are unlikely. Moreover, a virtuous citizenry and a citizenry not embroiled in overt hostilities have value above and beyond their support of political deliberation. Finally, the civic virtue and religious peace values do not exhaust the range of values supporting religious freedom. Whether the ingestion of peyote or the torture of animals should be protected, it is unlikely that protection should turn on whether the polity thought the particular religions promoted virtue, or whether they presented a threat of violence.

Perhaps traditional communitarianism can provide a stronger footing for freedom of religion.[29] Traditional communitarians conceive of traditions as the foundation of the national community. One could certainly argue that a substantial part of the American tradition is to protect religion. On the other hand, communitarianism—even on that understanding—justified anti-Catholicism,[30] anti-Semitism,[31] and discrimination against groups such as the Mormons and the Jehovah's Witnesses[32] throughout much of our history, and it is not clear why it would not justify discrimination against Muslims,[33] religions that ingest peyote, and other minority religions in contemporary culture.[34] American ideals honor freedom of religion; American practice protects freedom of religion—except when it doesn't. In interpreting American culture, do we look to the practice or to the theory?[35] If we look to the practice, we ratify violations of religious liberty. If we look to the theoretical ideals, we risk abandoning the rich complications of the community for the abstract liberalism that communitarianism purports to denounce.

Substantive communitarians value religion as a source of moral and civic virtue, as a way of life, and a way of truth.[36] Standing alone, however, these beliefs are not necessarily tied to freedom of religion.[37] After all, the leaders of the Massachusetts Bay Colony were substantive communitarians, yet they banished heretics and blasphemers. Contemporary substantive communitarians presumably would make distinctions of quite a different sort than those of John Winthrop, Cotton Mather, and their fellow colonists. Substantive communitarians value religion as an associational activity and incline against individualism.[38] If the person who ingested peyote for religious reasons was associated with an institutional religion with a history and an association of believers, the substantive communitarian would be sympathetic. The substantive communitarian might have less sympathy for the sincere, but individualistic, New Age pacifist believer who did not belong to a religious group. Nonetheless, the substantive communitarian might be consoled by the fact that the pacifist was following a duty to God rather than making an autonomous choice.

Free Exercise Values

In my view, the approaches taken by the Court, the Kantian liberal tradition, or communitarians are not sufficiently sensitive to the special claims of religious believers. The foundations of religious freedom are more complicated than those approaches assume. Indeed, the Free Exercise Clause is supported by seven different values.

Liberty and Autonomy

Both the religious claimants and the nonreligious claimants in our examples maintain that they have made an autonomous choice to lead their lives in a particular way, and the state is burdening an important aspect of their liberty. Unquestionably, autonomy is a significant value, and it is part of the reason that the free exercise of religion is supportable. Moreover, it should be clear that the *free* exercise of religion implies the liberty right not to practice religion.[39] As we have seen, however, an emphasis on liberty or autonomy does not distinguish religious claims from artistic or hedonistic claims. If liberty or autonomy is the crucial value, one can make a case for all of the claimants, including those in the peyote and animal torture examples.

Obligation and State Cruelty

Unlike the other claimants, the religious claimant maintains that her conduct is dictated by a moral obligation, not pursued according to a choice or preference. To be sure, the religious claimant has made the choice to accept the obligation (or may believe that she has been given the grace to accept the obligation).[40] Nonetheless, it seems particularly cruel[41] for the state to force individuals to do what they are obliged not to do or to penalize them for responding to obligations.[42] That cruelty would seem to be present whether or not the obligation comes from a belief in God, traditional or otherwise.[43] Obligations of conscience should be considered religious for purposes of the Free Exercise Clause.[44] To make no distinction between religious obligations (or obligations of conscience) and lifestyle preferences, however, seems to conflate too much.[45] Whether or not the religious claimant should be punished for ingesting peyote, that claimant has a stronger case than the artist who simply prefers, however strongly, to engage in an artistic project. The point here is not that religion is more important. The religion may be completely wrong. The point is the existential difference in the choice facing the claimants. Nor should it be decisive whether the religious consequences facing a religious claimant for violating the obligation are deemed by the claimant to implicate eternal punishment, though that factor might be relevant to the degree of burden the law places upon an individual.[46] To force someone to do what he is obliged not to do is especially cruel, regardless of the consequences he fears.[47]

Ineffectiveness, Respect for Law, and Mitigation of Violence Triggered by Religious Conflict

Because the claim of the religious person flows from an obligation, apart from cruelty, another reason supports special religious consideration. As John Locke famously argued, persecuting people in an attempt to make them change beliefs might succeed in controlling external conduct, but it is unlikely to be effective in controlling beliefs.[48] To be sure, modern impositions upon religion are designed to control conduct, not belief. But the existence of a law does not eliminate the perception of an obligation. Attempted enforcement of laws against religious claimants might not even succeed in controlling external conduct. In fact, it can frequently promote disrespect for law.[49] For example, persons drafted to serve in the military despite religious objections will often refuse to serve. The military will not get another soldier, but the state will be forced to support another inmate whose crime consists of following his or her perception of God's will over that of the state. It would push this argument too far to suggest that the absence of religious exemptions generally presents a serious risk of violence, but the goal of religious peace is certainly a compelling reason to ground a constitutional opposition to more general forms of religious persecution.[50]

Equality and Antidiscrimination

As Christopher Eisgruber and Lawrence Sager[51] and more recently Martha Nussbaum[52] have argued in detail, enhanced judicial scrutiny for religious claimants is appropriate because of the possibility of discrimination on the basis of religion. As we have discussed, American colonists fled from and then imposed religious inequality. The Constitution was designed to put an end to such discrimination.[53] In a sense, as Jack Rakove puts it, "the religion question occupied a position similar to that of the race question in mid-twentieth-century America."[54] Of course, adopting the Constitution did not usher in a nation of religious equality. Discrimination against many religious groups stains our history.[55] Although much of this discrimination has been in civil society, the Supreme Court has played a role in reflecting the religious prejudices of American society.[56] Nonetheless, the Court is well prepared to stamp out clear cases of discrimination. Thus, when the City of Hialeah outlawed animal sacrifice as part of a religious ritual while permitting it in other circumstances, the Court unanimously struck the ordinance down.[57] Although the question of what counts as discrimination and the question whether discrimination is sometimes justified can sometimes be complicated, equality is generally regarded as an important free exercise value.

Associational Values

Association is a significant value, independently supported by non-religious aspects of the First Amendment, but it is also one of the values underlying free exercise.[58] The importance of association to freedom of speech is not often noted,[59] but it seems absolutely vital.[60] Suppose the government outlawed the telephone book. The telephone book seems crucial to interpersonal communication and association. Secular associations nurture friendships, beliefs, controversies, ways of life, identities, and often affect the wider social and political sphere. Religious associations do all these things as well. Finally, the freedom of religious association warrants greater protection than freedom of association generally not only because religious associations are more likely to be discriminated against, but also because, as I shall subsequently argue, religion has special constitutional value.

Promotion of Political Community

Free exercise promotes political community in many ways. First, equal liberty with its implications for preventing violence is a necessary prerequisite for the maintenance of a tenable political community. Nations divided by the prospect or the reality of religious persecution can hardly nurture a defensible political community.[61] Second, the pluralistic character of American religion allows for Madisonian checks and balances, thereby stabilizing the political community.[62] Third, protecting free exercise has symbolic implications that reach beyond its nonsymbolic functions. One of the defining characteristics of the United States is its commitment to religious liberty. That the country has been at the forefront of offering such protection is a substantial part of the pride of being an American citizen.[63] There are grounds to question whether a commitment to rights is enough to bind together a strong political community,[64] but it seems inescapable that the commitment to religious liberty is an important ingredient in binding our political community together.[65] Finally, as I will discuss in chapter 3, one can argue that the protection and promotion of religious liberty supports the kind of civic virtue necessary for the maintenance of a viable political community.

The Value of Religion

Religion itself can be regarded as independently valuable. Like autonomy, this consideration alone could support free exercise. Moreover, it is possible to argue that religion is deemed to be constitutionally more valuable than other forms of the good life[66] (not merely as a hedge against discrimination, for example) even though the Constitution rightfully imposes severe limits on governmental attempts to promote religion. I will consider these contentions in the course of treating the underlying purposes and functions of the Establishment Clause. For the present, however, it is enough to conclude that even if one assumes that religion has no special value under the Constitution, even if the values of the Free Exercise Clause were confined to liberty, autonomy, avoiding cruelty, stability, association, community, and the like, religious claimants would deserve special attention when the state imposed a burden on their conduct.

Applying the Free Exercise Clause

Special attention need not mean inevitable victory, however.[67] A prudential judgment weighing the appropriate facts and circumstances is warranted. As Donald Giannella suggested nearly forty years ago, the relevant factors include the importance of the secular governmental interests involved, the relationship of the governmental means to its interests, the impact that an exemption would have on the government interests, all balanced against the impact on religious liberty including its importance in the particular case.[68] In addition, religious equality interests should be taken into account.

A prerequisite to invoking the Free Exercise Clause, of course, is determining that a *religious* interest is burdened. In most cases this does not involve a difficult judgment. As Kent Greenawalt maintains, "Only a small percentage of actual claims about religion raise a serious question whether something is religious or not."[69] Nonetheless, in those outlier cases, the question can be vexing. Indeed, Winnifred Sullivan argues that the inquiry about the presence of religion is so fraught with difficulty that the inquiry should be abandoned.[70] Sullivan offers an extended discussion of *Warner v. Boca Raton*[71] to support her contention, a case that involved a municipal prohibition on vertical grave decorations.

If Sullivan was out to find a case involving crabbed judicial insensitivity, she was certainly on the mark. The plaintiffs had decorated the graves of their loved ones with religious symbols and with some symbols that were not obviously religious (unless grave site symbols are inherently and obviously religious).[72] One would think in a country that purports to honor freedom of speech and freedom of religion that the plaintiffs would have an easy day in court. One would think that the city's interests involving (its particular brand of) aesthetics, efficiency, and wildly implausible safety concerns could hardly be seen to outweigh deeply held speech and religious interests. But the courts were prepared to privilege bureaucratic interests over important liberties.[73] As to the speech issue, the courts recited the state interest, assumed without argument that the plaintiffs' needs could be met by horizontal displays,[74] announced that the municipality's regulation was "reasonable," and called it a day.[75] In addition, the Florida Supreme Court declared that it was not enough that the conduct of the plaintiffs was in observance of sincerely held religious beliefs. For protection to be extended, the conduct had to be *mandated* by the religion.[76] It makes sense that it is particularly problematic for government to forbid conduct mandated by a religion or require conduct that is forbidden. But it is not at all obvious that conduct motivated by religious beliefs should be entirely bereft of protection just because it is not mandated. Moreover, as Sullivan well demonstrates, on the question of what was mandated, the *Warner* district court disregarded the popular religious understanding of the plaintiffs simply because it was out of step with the elite understanding of the tradition.[77] Many of the plaintiffs, in fact felt obligated to place religious symbols on the graves of their loved ones.[78] Their beliefs were religious despite their lack of conformity with religious texts and traditions. Their beliefs could not reasonably be dismissed as mere "personal preferences."[79]

Warner presents a more difficult question regarding the placement of materials on a grave that might or might not be religiously motivated in a traditional sense. For example, think of flowers placed on a grave site. Assuming the flowers symbolize the honoring of a dead person, the easy solution to this issue is to turn to the speech clause and decide that religious and nonreligious symbols are protected (as they should be). An alternative approach would be to contend that the flower placement should be protected under the Equal Protection Clause if religious expression were protected, especially if that religious expression was not mandated by the religion. The religious claim regarding the flower placement, on the other hand, might depend on the view that personal honoring of the dead at a grave site is an inherently religious activity. One can see from this example that difficult issues involving the definition of religion can arise. I am attracted to the view of Kent Greenawalt that in difficult cases involving the definition of religion no single standard is plausible, that a variety of factors are relevant to the decision (including concern with fundamental problems, claims to comprehensive truth, and formal signs, not all of these being required in particular cases), and that one should reason by analogy from those beliefs, practices, and institutions that are recognized as religious in determining whether something unfamiliar should count as religious. As in the conscientious objector context,[80] when the dead are honored at a grave site, I would think that the specific reasons and philosophy behind the action should matter in the determination.

Making the decision as to the religious character of an action frequently requires inquiries into the sincerity of the litigant and the precise nature of the litigant's beliefs. State inquiries into religious beliefs are privacy-invading in troublesome ways, but they are justified by the need to establish that a religious claim is present. In the *Warner* case, however, no such need was present. Upholding the free speech claim would have ended the inquiry. Although I concur with Sullivan that the determination of whether a belief or practice or institution is religious can be difficult, I do not believe it is any more difficult than a host of other legal concepts, and, in any event, the problem arises in a small number of cases. In addition, abandoning the inquiry and relying exclusively on equality (as Sullivan suggests)[81] would afford no possibility of relief to plaintiffs like those in *Warner*.[82]

In any event, once the requirement of determining that a religious claim is implicated has been satisfied, a court should apply the kinds of factors isolated by Giannella. If we apply those factors to the peyote example, in my view, the religious claimant should win. Even conceding that the state interest in regulating peyote is significant, it would not be sacrificed in any significant way by a compelled religious exemption. The law against peyote consumption burdens religion in a significant way; and there are good reasons to believe that it discriminates against a minority religion. For example, if the Protestant majority ingested peyote as part of a communion service in Oregon, the law against peyote ingestion would surely have exempted religious ceremonies.[83] The *Smith* case thus reeks of insensitivity to the plight of a religious minority.[84] This is not to say that the Court believes that the equality value has no role to play in free exercise analysis, but the Court's conception leaves much to be desired. As to the nonreligious claimants, whether or not it is good policy to outlaw their conduct, there is surely no constitutional barrier. We do not live in a Kantian country. To be sure, the artist might raise a free speech claim, but even assuming his conduct fell within the scope of the First Amendment, the artist would—and should—lose.

The animal sacrifice case, however, is more difficult.[85] On the one hand, the state interest is important—animals deserve protection.[86] Surely, they deserve to be protected from the nonreligious claimants. On the other hand, the law may seriously burden religion if it prohibits people from fulfilling spiritual obligations. Moreover, there are some equality concerns. Animals are treated horribly in this society so that our meals will taste better.[87] If the state permits such vile treatment of animals for culinary reasons, might it not be hypocritical to outlaw similar treatment for religious purposes? Another equality concern is exposed by asking whether there would be a similar prohibition if majority religions employed animal sacrifice as a part of their ceremonies. The question answers itself, but too much should not be made of the point. What if human sacrifice were an occasional part of our majority religious ceremonies?[88] Presumably, such sacrifices would not be outlawed if that were the case. But that counterfactual should not justify the inhumane practice of a minority religion.[89] Equality is an important value, but it is not all important.

In the end, one is forced to choose between vindicating religion and stopping the inhumane treatment of animals in this context. If we suppose that the religious treatment of animals is no worse than that employed for culinary purposes or for medical research,[90] I would conclude that the equality concerns should militate toward the invalidation of a law prohibiting animal sacrifice. On the other hand, if the religious ceremony involved treatment that is worse than that employed for other, "legitimate" purposes, I would uphold the law.

These examples highlight two objections to invoking heightened scrutiny of religious burdens. The first is that the process of making such decisions is subjective. Supporting this objection is the fact that honest and intelligent people disagree on how to resolve these cases. Those justices who employed heightened scrutiny in the peyote case were divided over the resolution.[91] The Constitutional Court of South Africa was also deeply divided over the issue in a similar case.[92] That subjectivity is involved does not necessarily mean that the decisions are arbitrary. If they were arbitrary, the justices would be flipping coins rather than engaging in argument about recurring decision-making factors. Moreover, controversy frequently permeates the outcome of constitutional decisions. The underlying logic of the subjectivity objection is that if there are no obvious objective answers to legal questions, the decisions should be in the hands of the legislatures.[93] To fully canvass this issue, we would need to replow the ground unfurled in the debate over judicial review. We are not going there.

The second and more serious objection is that judicial review of this type violates the Establishment Clause. The idea is that the Establishment Clause forbids the favoring of religious claimants over nonreligious claimants.[94] While exploring the purposes of the Establishment Clause in the next chapter, I will argue that this objection is misconceived. One of the purposes of the Establishment Clause is to protect religious liberty. It would be odd to say that protecting religious liberty in the Free Exercise Clause violates a clause also designed in part to protect religious liberty. Protecting religious liberty in the Free Exercise Clause promotes the interest of both religion clauses. Even more directly, I will argue that the Establishment Clause in fact favors religion over nonreligion, but that favoritism should be limited in ways congenial to religious liberalism.

Chapter 3 ————————————————————

Establishment Clause Values

THE TWO MAIN ISSUES CONFRONTING the Establishment Clause involve government's relationship to religious messages and government's financial aid to religious institutions. Chapters 3 and 4 explore the purposes of the Establishment Clause and government's relationship to religious messages. Chapters 5 and 6 in Part II explore government's financial aid to religious institutions in the form of vouchers to religious schools. A good starting point[1] for exposing the clash of perspectives surrounding the Establishment Clause is *County of Allegheny v. ACLU*,[2] where a nativity scene was centrally placed in a public building during the Christmas season.[3] The Supreme Court invalidated the display as a violation of the Establishment Clause, but four justices led by Justice Kennedy dissented.[4] Justice Kennedy argued that as long as there was no coercion or proselytizing, government should be able to recognize and accommodate the role that religion plays in American society. Justice Kennedy thus echoed themes espoused by the religious Right. In a sense he suggested that instead of recognizing a high wall between church and state, the government should be permitted to build bridges.[5] Justice Kennedy pointed to many government practices recognizing the importance of religion, from the prayer opening Supreme Court sessions to Thanksgiving proclamations by numerous presidents, as well as the existence and support of legislative chaplains and a prayer room for members of the House and Senate. To block Allegheny County from cooperating with this display, argued Justice Kennedy, would show hostility toward religion.

Justice Kennedy and his concurring justices clearly promoted a communitarian line. From their perspective, the state should be able to cooperate with those forces of society that promote virtue; the state should not alienate itself from the views of the people; indeed, in the absence of coercion, the majority of the community ought to be able to express themselves through local governments without rigid constitutional intervention. Ironically, several of the justices who voted "for" religion in the *Allegheny County* case form a crucial part of the majority of the Court in the peyote case that not only denied the rights of the religious claimants in that case, but also would deny it in any and all cases in which a statute incidentally impacts religion even in a severe way, at least in the absence of some other constitutional interest.[6] This looks like hostility to religion in the free exercise context. It may not be pretty, but what unites the perspective of these justices is a communitarian perspective favoring majority religions over minority religions because the majority is deemed entitled to express their religious views through the state.[7]

The majority of the Court, however, disfavored the communitarian approach. Instead, the prevailing justices in *County of Allegheny* took an egalitarian line. Using an approach offered by Justice O'Connor in an earlier case,[8] Justice Blackmun inquired whether the display involved an endorsement of religion.[9] An endorsement of religion was deemed problematic because it "sends a message to nonadherents that they are outsiders, not full members of the political community, and an accompanying message to adherents that they are insiders, favored members of the political community."[10] Justice Blackmun concluded that viewers may fairly understand that the purpose of the display was to endorse religion, and was therefore invalid. Taking *Smith* together with *County of Allegheny*— not to mention other cases—it would be easy to conclude that equality is the central value of the religion clauses. In *Smith*, religion and nonreligion are treated equally, and the law is upheld; in *County of Allegheny*, religion is seemingly endorsed by the state, and the law is invalidated. A proper reading of the Establishment Clause cases, however, leads to the conclusion that equality is neither a necessary condition in some cases to avoid a constitutional violation, nor a sufficient condition in other cases.

Establishment Clause analysis should take a page from the methodology employed in free speech cases.[11] That is, it should evaluate the challenged state action against the full range of Establishment Clause concerns, and it should proceed to determine if the state's promotion of particular interests sufficiently justifies the impingement on Establishment Clause concerns.[12]

Clearly, then, it is important to identify the full range of the Establishment Clause values. I argue that the clause serves many functions. It is a prophylactic measure that (1) protects religious liberty and autonomy, including the protection of taxpayers from being forced to support religious ideologies to which they are opposed; (2) as we have discussed, the clause stands for equal citizenship without regard to religion; (3) it protects against the destabilizing influence of having the polity divided along religious lines; (4) it promotes political community; (5) it safeguards the autonomy of the state to protect the public interest; (6) it shelters churches from the corrupting influences of the state; and (7) it promotes religion in the private sphere.

Liberty and Autonomy

A long-standing claim about the relationship between the Free Exercise Clause and the Establishment Clause is that the Free Exercise Clause protects liberty directly and the Establishment Clause protects liberty indirectly.[13] Thus, if the state sponsors school prayer, the sponsorship pressures little children to participate in the prayer. Indeed, the Supreme Court has held that a prayer at a high school graduation has this effect.[14] From the liberty perspective, those who voted for the claimants in the peyote case and against Allegheny County in the crèche case were voting to protect religious liberty in both cases. This interpretation also addresses the objection that preferring religious claimants over nonreligious claimants in the peyote case would violate the Establishment Clause. To the contrary, if the Establishment Clause is interpreted to protect religious liberty, favoring the religious claimants in the peyote case would advance the objectives of both clauses.[15]

A particular liberty interest raised when government seeks to fund religious institutions is the right of taxpayers not to be forced to support religious ideologies to which they are opposed.[16] It is not clear to me that this interest is entitled to the weight attached to it by opponents of vouchers and other subsidies of religious institutions. If taxpayer liberty were the key issue, the appropriate remedy would be refunds, not prohibitions.[17] Nonetheless, this concern is worthy of some weight in an Establishment Clause balance.

Equality

If a state is permitted to endorse a particular religion, formally creating insiders and outsiders on the basis of religion, there is good reason to fear that this formal marginalization will carry over to the social and economic spheres.[18] Discriminating on the basis of religion would be subtly encouraged. In addition, complying with formal equality does not always address issues regarding substantive equality. Equality of form can be accompanied by inequality of effect. Politicians were not blind to the impact of state establishments at the outset of our history. As Leonard Levy points out in his excellent history of the Establishment Clause, "the American multiple establishments were nonpreferential in law and theory but not necessarily in fact. In the four New England states that maintained establishments, the Congregationalists dominated overwhelmingly, as was expected when they adopted the system of tax-supported nonpreferential aid."[19] This inequality of effect was a vital factor in the movements to eradicate the state establishments.[20]

One of the failures of the *Smith* case was its refusal to take inequality of effect seriously enough to expose the state action to serious constitutional scrutiny.[21] As we shall discuss in chapter 6, a similar insensitivity accompanies the Court's treatment of vouchers.[22] Nonetheless, I will argue that deviating from equality might sometimes best accommodate the interests at stake in particular contexts. Moreover, deviations from formal equality may sometimes be justified in the interests of substantive equality.

Stability

Religious wars have plagued the world for many centuries. If the state is open for capture by religious groups, the potential for intolerance, ugly confrontation, and violence is multiplied. Nonetheless, it goes too far to suggest that a significant purpose of the Establishment Clause is to assure that the polity is not divided politically along religious lines. The stability of our country does not depend upon keeping religious arguments out of public life.[23] Indeed, churches have made many progressive contributions to the political life of the country.[24] William Brennan famously wrote in *New York Times v. Sullivan* that our nation has a "profound national commitment to the principle that debate on public issues should be uninhibited, robust, and wide-open."[25] It mocks that commitment to say that we believe that debate on public issues should be uninhibited, robust, and wide-open, except when it comes to religious speech. The religion clause does not contradict the speech clause. The First Amendment is not at war with itself.

Although the Establishment Clause should not be read to limit the role of religion in public debate, the concern that religious divisions can lead to violent conflicts is supportable. We live in a country in which Catholics have been beaten over disputes about the role of the Bible in the public schools,[26] Muslims have been particularly victimized since the attacks on the World Trade Center,[27] and the Ku Klux Klan has spread a reign of terror designed to produce a white "Christian" America. The potential for violence is sufficiently serious to warrant caution regarding governmental actions that embrace some religions and exclude others. It may well be that the existing religious divisions in our country have been substantially less violent because the Establishment Clause has precluded state capture for religious purposes.[28]

Promoting Political Community

It is possible to maintain a political community with an established religion.[29] The dangers to a political community from an established church are not as significant as those that are triggered by religious persecution. Religious persecution predictably triggers responsive hostility, but using government symbols to mark some religions as outside or at the margins of the political community is also risky. Symbolic affronts themselves undermine the kind of reciprocal respect that is helpful in supporting political community. A government that treats all citizens as insiders regardless of their religious beliefs helps to foster a more inclusive political community.[30]

Protecting the Autonomy of Government

Another historical concern is that religions will use the government to further their own sectarian ends.[31] The colonists, after all, had fled from a situation in which they believed that religions had used the machinery of the state to their disadvantage. Moreover, in the pre–Vatican II age, Protestant Americans worried that if Catholics came to power they would threaten liberties and institute the type of religious persecutions all too prevalent in Europe.[32] That these concerns were exaggerated and fueled by class and ethnic prejudice does not negate the legitimacy of a concern that religions might use government for their own ends. Indeed, Protestants captured the public school system and used it in an attempt to instill their own religious views.[33] That they called this hegemony "nondenominational" did not successfully paper over the fact that Protestants were using government to further their own religious ends. This concern need not mean that the Establishment Clause precludes religious participation in political life. It does, however, exhibit concern that particular forms of legislation make government an instrumentality of particular religions. If government adopts a civil rights law or abolishes capital punishment in response to lobbying by religious believers, there is no Establishment Clause problem.[34] If it places a crèche in a prominent public place, it is reasonable to be concerned that religion is using government to further its own sectarian ends.

Protecting Churches

In *The Garden and the Wilderness*, Mark De Wolfe Howe emphasizes an aspect of Roger Williams's contribution to the analysis of freedom of religion.[35] According to Howe, Williams warned that close connections between church and state would work to the detriment of religion. If the church is the garden and the state is the wilderness, Williams worried that the state would ruin the garden and transform it into the wilderness.[36] In fact, Williams was even more pessimistic than Howe let on. Williams fled England because the Church of England was impure, and he was subsequently banished to Rhode Island after he criticized the Puritans of Massachusetts for maintaining impure churches. He ultimately came to believe that all churches were impure—even his own.[37] One need not fear that the wilderness might corrupt the garden because there was no garden to be corrupted.[38]

Nonetheless, Howe was right to emphasize the argument he understood Williams to make.[39] Williams, as Howe understood him, like Madison[40] and Jefferson,[41] and a movement of eighteenth-century Christian evangelicals,[42] argued that God was not so stupid as to place the fate of religion in the hands of politicians.[43] He argued that politicians had historically operated in ways that did not benefit religion.[44] This should hardly be surprising. Politicians operate with many motives. They are probably far more motivated by a desire to further the public interest than they are ordinarily given credit. But they are also often corrupted by the desire for reelection, by the need for campaign funds, and by the various foibles of human character. We have witnessed numerous cases in which *religious* leaders have violated the trust placed in them to advance the cause of religion. How much less should one expect politicians to act on behalf of religion?[45] Indeed, when politicians combine with merchants to commercialize Christmas,[46] and when they invoke the name of God to justify unjust wars (often God is invoked on both sides of a conflict),[47] it becomes obvious that religion is being used to serve politics, not the other way around.[48]

Even more serious, the reliance of religious organizations upon the state for evangelical purposes tends to undermine their own integrity.[49] Indeed, there is considerable evidence that the Roman Catholic Church, the church with the historically strongest ties to the state in Europe and Latin America, has compromised its commitment to social justice in its effort to maintain its privileged position in many countries.[50] At least prior to Vatican II, Catholic support for dictators in some countries and opposition to them in others followed a relatively consistent pattern. If the dictator supported religious privileges such as subsidies for Catholic education, the church did not oppose the dictator.[51] If the dictator opposed Catholic privilege, the church opposed the dictator.[52]

There were, however, exceptions on both sides.[53] For instance, the church was relatively quiet about Hitler despite his suppression of religious freedom because it calculated that its best interests were nonetheless served by keeping quiet.[54] On the other hand, strong church forces criticized Latin American dictators despite their support for the church because these forces felt morally obliged to do so[55] (though the Vatican has since made strong efforts to cut back on the political involvement of priests and bishops).[56] Although the recent popes have been willing to take unpopular positions (particularly on moral issues involving gender and the family), the church has historically muffled its stance in favor of social justice when it thought its evangelical interests were served by doing so.[57] Indeed, for centuries, it permitted political leaders to play a major role in the selection of religious leaders.[58] As Alister McGrath observes, "A church which scents the powerful fragrance of power and influence shows a worrying ability to become accommodating and flexible on matters which some might regard as non-negotiable."[59] There are strong reasons to believe that many Christian evangelicals in the United State have compromised their views in order to walk in the corridors of power.[60] If it is desirable for religious voices to play a role in the democratic process,[61] providing incentives for them to remain silent is not helpful.

In any event, it is really quite wrong to claim that those who are concerned about tight relations between church and state are necessarily antireligious. When Justice Kennedy complains that those who seek to prevent the nativity scene display are hostile to religion,[62] he ignores not only non-Christian religious believers, but also concerns about tight church-state relations within the Christian tradition that stretch back for centuries. Justice Kennedy's brand of name-calling has no place in Establishment Clause jurisprudence.

Promoting Religion

Many argue that separation of church and state has served to promote religion.[63] Assuming this is correct, the next question would be whether promotion is a good thing or a bad thing, or, more precisely, whether promotion of religion is a constitutionally cognizable value. Before deciding this issue, we must first determine if separation of church and state has actually promoted religion.

Separation Positive for Religion?

Whether or not it is a good thing to promote religion, substantial evidence suggests that the absence of established churches in the United States has been positive for religion.[64] Most scholars, for example, conclude that Americans are more religious than their counterparts in European countries, where established churches persisted for centuries.[65] As Everett Ladd writes, "by just about every measure that survey researchers have conceived and employed, the United States appears markedly more religious than its peers in the family of nations, the other industrial democracies."[66] James Madison seems to have been prescient when he argued that state-supported churches become dependent, compliant, lazy, bloated, and corrupt.[67] They lose the vitality necessary to attract and retain loyal committed followers. As suggested earlier, the Roman Catholic Church in particular seemed to lose a grip on its commitment to offer a moral voice in substantial parts of European society. The church may have done itself no favors when it sided with Franco in Spain,[68] Salazar in Portugal,[69] the Vichy regime in France,[70] the Christian Democrats in Italy,[71] or when it was quiescent[72] in Hitler's Germany.[73] Similarly, the Anglican Church could hardly have benefited from its control by the English government.[74] Nor is it likely that the Church of Sweden has benefited from its association with the Swedish government.[75] In each of these countries, religiosity is now relatively low.[76] By contrast, the Roman Catholic Church sided with the Irish against England, the Poles against the Communists, and with the people against many Latin American dictators.[77] Catholicism continues to be deeply tied with the national identity in Ireland[78] and Poland[79] and is strong throughout Latin America.[80]

Citing such evidence, Jose Casanova argues that the church's decision to oppose separation of church and state in many circumstances precipitated religious decline.[81] Moreover, Roger Finke and Rodney Stark argue that religiosity is stronger in the United States than in Europe precisely because of the separation of church and state.[82] Nonetheless, any claim that the relationship between church and state is invariably the decisive factor for the rise or fall of religiosity would be difficult to sustain. Religion has thrived during and after many dictatorships. Consider the Constantinian dictatorship and the many that followed.[83] I suspect that Nicholas Burns goes too far when he writes, "Without Constantine, we might not even remember Jesus' name in the twentieth century."[84] Nonetheless, the extent to which repression has enhanced some religions and diminished others may not be fully appreciated in much of the religion clause literature.[85] Indeed, Christianity flourishes in Central and South America[86] as well as Africa[87]—regions where dictatorships and support for Christianity have often been intertwined. Equally significant, if religions flourish when the church is separated from the state and protections for religious freedom are in place, one might expect that religion would now be flourishing in Europe.[88] Yet Europe has emerged as the poster child for secularism.[89] It might well be that separation is helpful to religion at one stage and not another.

Clearly factors other than the relationship between church and state play a significant role in the sociology of religion. Some are specific to specific religions; some are more general. Corruption, or perceived corruption, in the clergy has diminished support particularly for the Catholic Church[90] in France;[91] vivid reminders of the existence of evil fuel the perception that a loving God does not exist;[92] attendance is stronger in rural areas than in urban areas;[93] women are more likely to be religious than men[94] (though the Catholic Church's position on the role of women has taken a substantial toll);[95] poor people are more likely to be religious than the wealthy; the Catholic Church's position on birth control has troubled millions;[96] and the Enlightenment, with its emphasis on reason and science,[97] has rocked the faith of many.[98]

It is not clear, however, that these factors vary significantly between European countries and the United States. One factor that might be significant in the United States is that it was largely founded by religious dissenters who were intense in their religiosity and prone to form new sects rather than compromise[99] their individualistic integrity.[100] The existence of freedom of religion and believers' concomitant ability to form many different churches might have had a particularly strong impact in the United States given the religious demographics of the population. Despite the multiplicity of factors relevant to the sociology of religion, then, there is support for the view that the prohibition of tight connections between church and state has served to promote religion in the United States.

The Value of Religion

The question remains whether promoting religion is a good thing, and whether the religion clauses of the Constitution should be interpreted to favor religion over nonreligion. The debate over the utility of religion, of course, is long-standing. In his Farewell Address, George Washington maintained that "[o]f all the dispositions and habits which lead to political prosperity, religion and morality are indispensable supports."[101] By contrast, John Stuart Mill conceded the importance of morality, but denied the utility of religion.[102] Mill maintained that a belief in the supernatural served useful purposes in the early stages of human development, but was now dispensable. He suggested that religion continued to be significant because of authority, education, and public opinion, and that a supernatural foundation was no longer needed for moral beliefs. Indeed, he argued that a supernatural foundation was positively harmful in that belief in religion discouraged criticism of some flawed beliefs. Mill admitted that "so long as human life is insufficient to satisfy human aspirations, so long there will be a craving for higher things. . . . So long as earthly life is full of sufferings, so long there will be need of consolations, which the hope of heaven affords to the selfish, the love of God to the tender and grateful."

Nonetheless, Mill thought an alternative to "baseless fancies" existed.[103] Just as human beings have been willing to sacrifice all for their countries, Mill believed, they could be enticed to play their part in the destiny of the human race, a role in which they need not sacrifice themselves to the whole, but would accommodate freedom and duty. He believed that they would be consoled by living the kind of life that would be admired by family or friends, dead or living.

Many have been moved by humanistic ideals like Mill's. Moreover, it is hard to deny the force of public opinion. If religion were authoritatively regarded as superstition in a society, socialization against religion would be powerful, and it might be possible to organize a society around the humanistic appeals of Mill.[104] Indeed, those humanistic appeals are present in any religion worthy of the name. As Reinhold Niebuhr puts it, "morality is as much the root as the fruit of religion."[105]

But we do not write on a clean slate. For millions of citizens, religion fills a need that humanism does not fill. For those citizens, the dominant religions in the United States provide an explanation of the mysteries of the universe,[106] a ground for the importance of personality in an impersonal world,[107] a sense of obligation and mission not provided by humanism,[108] and a "guaranteed security against the forces of nature."[109]

Moreover, religious institutions regularly maintain rituals and other events that create opportunities for moral reflection and encourage believers to come together. This makes religiously based moral practice less lonely than humanism and provides more social support for its burdens. Such community-centered events are not incompatible with secular humanism, but they are relatively rare, particularly outside educational settings. By comparison, then, secular humanist moral agency is rather isolated.[110]

Measuring the extent to which religion promotes altruism, however, is tricky business.[111] To the extent there is a case for religion in this regard, it lies among the group that is religiously active in significant ways. Nonetheless, the overall impact of religion on altruistic behavior is arguably suspect. For example, as Mary Ann Glendon observes, "Crossnational studies repeatedly show that the proportion of children in poverty in the United States is greater than in other countries with which we frequently compare ourselves."[112] Moreover, the United States ranks last among developed countries in foreign aid as a share of our economy, and taking private charity into account does not make us look any better.[113] If altruism were connected with religion, one might have expected the "religious" United States to take better care of its poor children than secular Europe. On the other hand, Europeans remain influenced in their values by a prior religious history,[114] and they are more comfortable with a strong government welfare role. Nevertheless, some sociologists wonder whether, as Europe continues to secularize, its commitment to humane values will wane.[115] In any event, whatever the comparative dimensions with Europe, it is hard to ignore the substantial role played by religious associations in directly assisting the poor.[116]

Even if religion does not promote altruism, there are grounds to believe that religious associations promote civic participation[117] and provide moral and political criticism uncontaminated by the profit motive.[118] I will argue in chapter 8 that religion has on balance been a positive political force in the United States, but there are substantial points to make on the other side.

The Constitutional Value of Religion

Conceding that there are arguments on both sides on the civic value *vel non* of religion, the question remains whether it is reasonable to interpret the religion clauses to favor religion.[119] Of course, part of the motivation for the Establishment Clause was unconcerned with the value of religion. The Establishment Clause was designed to ensure, among other things, that the federal government did not interfere with the then-reigning state establishments of religion.[120] This does not mean that the Framers favored tight connections between church and state, however. Far more likely, the Framers respected the autonomy of states to conduct their own affairs. They plainly did not believe that tight connections between church and state at the federal level would be good for religious liberty.[121]

Beyond federalism, a substantial theme of the Framers favoring separation of church and state emerged from religious reasons. The notion was that some things belonged to God and others to the state.[122] Moreover, the Framers seemed generally to value religious commitments over nonreligious commitments, with many like George Washington believing that the nurturing of religion was necessary for the promotion of civic virtue.[123] On the other hand, Thomas Jefferson did not favor promoting institutional religion.[124] He believed, among other things, that it was unnecessary. From Jefferson's perspective, God had already supplied us all with a moral sense.[125] Indeed, Jefferson hoped that traditional religion would fade away.[126] The presence of the Enlightenment theme in the foundation of the republic cannot be ignored.[127]

Moreover, there are serious grounds to question whether it is reasonable to interpret the religion clauses as proceeding from a religious foundation in the more pluralistic and skeptical age in which we live.[128] One approach to this might be to say that an overlapping consensus of the religious (more precisely, most of the religious) and the nonreligious support freedom of religion,[129] and that the clauses should not be interpreted to favor one side over the other. From this perspective, if the separation of church and state promoted religion, the Constitution would be indifferent. The promotion of religion might be a fact; it might be valued by many; but it would not be a constitutional value.[130]

Although many might well regard the overlapping consensus approach as an attractive ideal, it is not a persuasive constitutional interpretation. It simply does not fit the Establishment Clause view that protecting religions from the corrosive effects of state interference is of constitutional importance. From the perspective of the nonreligious, compromising the garden of religion might or might not serve civic purposes. From a religious perspective, protecting the garden of religion from the wilderness is of overriding importance.

In addition to the Roger Williams value, the Constitution has permitted government to favor religion, at least to a limited extent, throughout our constitutional history. As I will discuss below, the presence of *In God We Trust* on coins, for example, is a nontrivial indication that government can favor religion in some contexts without violating the Constitution. One way to look at this is that the Constitution favors religion over nonreligion, but that there are limits to which the government can promote religion both out of respect for nonbelievers and for reasons that appeal to many religious believers including religious liberals. Alternatively, one could posit that the Constitution is indifferent about the fate of religion, but compromises supporting religion have been made along the way. As I will suggest in connection with discussion of the Pledge of Allegiance and "In God We Trust," I think the latter perspective is at odds with our constitutional history. It seems reasonable to interpret the religion clauses as favoring religion, but with significant limitations on how that favoritism may be expressed. Such a position does not undercut the protection of free exercise for nonbelievers. If there is one proposition unanimously favored in religion law, it is that the decision to accept or reject religion should be a voluntary matter.[131] Moreover, the Free Speech Clause, Article VI, clause 3, prohibiting religious test oaths for public office,[132] and the Equal Protection Clause also make clear that our Constitution does not tolerate governmental discrimination against the nonreligious.

Nor does such a position do much to endorse general governmental involvement in the religious sphere to promote religion. Favoring religion ordinarily counsels *against* government action designed to favor religion. Distrust of politicians is not only a mark of our system of checks and balances; it is a fundamental ingredient of the religion clauses.[133] Nonetheless, the Establishment Clause cannot fairly be read to preclude all actions by politicians that favor religion any more than the Free Exercise Clause precludes all state actions with a negative impact on religion.

Although there are easy cases, applying the Establishment Clause frequently calls for nuanced practical judgments that cannot be reduced to
simplistic formulas. In chapter 4, I apply the Establishment Clause to a
variety of questions, most involving government's connection with an explicit or implicit religious message. In the course of the discussion, I show
the ways in which the equality value is compromised by the Constitution,
sometimes because it should be; sometimes not.

Chapter 4

Applying the Establishment Clause

APPLYING THE ESTABLISHMENT CLAUSE is more difficult than applying the Free Exercise Clause. When government burdens religious liberty directly, all the values underlying the Free Exercise Clause are potentially in play, and they all point in the same direction. Unlike the Free Exercise Clause, however, Establishment Clause values frequently come into conflict with each other. Recall from chapter 3 that the Establishment Clause is supported by seven values: (1) it protects religious liberty and autonomy, including the protection of taxpayers from being forced to support religious ideologies to which they are opposed; (2) it stands for equal citizenship without regard to religion; (3) it protects against the destabilizing influence of having the polity divided along religious lines; (4) it promotes political community; (5) it protects the autonomy of the state to protect the public interest; (6) it protects churches from the corrupting influences of the state; and (7) it promotes religion in the private sphere. Equality plays a particularly complex role in the interaction of these values. The character of the interaction of Establishment Clause values forces a more extended discussion of applications than was necessary with the Free Exercise Clause. But in many ways Establishment Clause applications are more interesting than Free Exercise applications, partly because of the greater richness produced by conflicts between values, partly because they force deeper inspection of the relationship between religion and government, and partly because so many of the cases arise out of controversies affecting our children in the schools. In this chapter, I primarily focus on questions involving government's relationship to explicit or implicit religious messages. In Part II, I will discuss financial aid to religious institutions.

Perhaps there is a natural human tendency to transform the complex into the simple, and the *Allegheny County* case is a model case for those who would reduce the Establishment Clause to a simple equality model. The county's action favors Christianity. This it may not do. End of case. If equality were the sole value underlying the Establishment Clause, one would expect that governmental deviations from religious equality would invariably be unconstitutional and that government conformity with equality would invariably be constitutional. But the world is not that simple. Government deviations from equality are frequently constitutional.

cal perspective is not on display in the Rehnquist opinion. Nor does he offer any reason to support the view that the law contains two fixed categories that cannot overlap: the patriotic and the religious. On his own analysis, the pledge seems to be *both* a patriotic and a religious exercise fused together.

Justice O'Connor's concurring opinion elaborated more on the claim that religion is not present, but is equally unpersuasive. Her main line of argument focused on whether the "reasonable observer" would think that the pledge was religious.[17] This reasonable observer is "deemed aware of the history of the conduct in question and must understand its place in our Nation's cultural landscape."[18] Of course, children, including the children of atheists, agnostics, and Buddhists to name a few, are quite unlikely to be aware of this history or the pledge's "place." Assuming their views match their parents, they are overwhelmingly likely to think that they are "outsiders, not full members of the political community,"[19] and they would regrettably be right to think so. But on Justice O'Connor's rendition of the Establishment Clause these children's reasonable reactions are of no moment. In other words, she formulated a test that can achieve equality for a group of elite insiders, not for American parents and children. This, she maintains, is prompted by the "dizzying religious heterogeneity of our Nation."[20] The alternative, she suggests, is anarchistic subjectivity threatening nearly every government action. In support of this claim, one might conjure up the fundamentalist who maintains that the public school curriculum establishes a religion because it does not mention God. As I will argue, there is a solution to that problem, but it does not require imaginary people with insider information.

Let us suppose, however, that we are stuck with the O'Connor test. Does it follow that the pledge is not religious? Justice O'Connor says yes because the pledge is used for secular purposes, has not engendered significant national controversy, does not involve worship or prayer, and is a minimal part of the pledge. The notion of using religious language for secular purposes ought itself to raise constitutional eyebrows. Religion is already damaged by using it for secular purposes; the damage is compounded by denying that religion is not involved. And it is a non sequitur to say that reasonable observers would think that they were not outsiders because a religion they oppose was only used to consolidate secular objectives. On the other hand, even from a secular perspective, one might imagine the honoring of the Puritan contribution of democratic thought or of Martin Luther King and the role religion played in his life as a part of recognizing the role of religion in American life. Such honoring would be quite different than the use of God in the Pledge of Allegiance unless one indulges the fiction that it exists only to recall a historical "fact" about the founding of the Republic.

mote religion. President Eisenhower, during the act's signing ceremony, stated: "From this day forward, the millions of our school children will daily proclaim in every city and town, every village and rural schoolhouse, the dedication of our Nation and our people to the Almighty."[11]

Persons from very different traditions could support the Goodwin opinion. Obviously, strong followers of the Enlightenment tradition would find the opinion congenial. If you think that belief in God is just superstition, believed because of fear or ignorance, then the idea that children should be encouraged to pledge allegiance to a flag "under God" is difficult to swallow.[12] But traditional religious believers could also support the opinion on the ground that, among other things, the mixture of politics and religion works to the detriment of religion.

Whether viewed from a nonreligious perspective or a religious perspective, then, the Goodwin opinion had much to recommend it. Nonetheless, one need not have been a constitutional lawyer to predict that the Court would find a way to reverse the Ninth Circuit, and in *Elk Grove United School District v. Newdow,* reverse it did.[13] Six justices found a procedural ground, arguing that Newdow did not have standing to bring the action. Three justices, however, namely, Chief Justice Rehnquist and Justices O'Connor and Thomas disagreed with Judge Goodwin on the merits.

Analyzing Judge Goodwin's opinion requires separation of two issues: First, is the pledge a *religious* exercise, and, second, can a government actor constitutionally require that the pledge be part of the official public school day? Chief Justice Rehnquist and Justice O'Connor both denied that the pledge was a religious exercise and, therefore, concluded that it could be a part of the official public school day. Justice Thomas conceded that the pledge was religious, but, for reasons I will not explore here, argued it was constitutional nonetheless.[14] My view is that the pledge is clearly religious and that it is constitutional for Congress to encourage its use, but that it should not be considered constitutionally permissible to use the pledge in public school classrooms.

How does one argue that the pledge with its "under God" language is *not* religious? Chief Justice Rehnquist argued that the pledge is a patriotic exercise, not a religious exercise. On one reading of the opinion, the chief justice was suggesting that under God simply refers to what he regards as a historical truth, namely that "our Nation was founded on a fundamental belief in God."[15]

Elsewhere in the opinion, however, he stated that under God "might mean several different things: that God has guided the destiny of the United States, for example, or that the United States exists under God's authority."[16] These are quite obviously theological claims. Why it would violate the Establishment Clause to encourage prayer, but would not violate the Establishment Clause to encourage a pledge embracing a theological perspective is not on display in the Rehnquist opinion. Nor does he offer any reason to support the view that the law contains two fixed categories that cannot overlap: the patriotic and the religious. On his own analysis, the pledge seems to be *both* a patriotic and a religious exercise fused together.

Justice O'Connor's concurring opinion elaborated more on the claim that religion is not present, but is equally unpersuasive. Her main line of argument focused on whether the "reasonable observer" would think that the pledge was religious.[17] This reasonable observer is "deemed aware of the history of the conduct in question and must understand its place in our Nation's cultural landscape."[18] Of course, children, including the children of atheists, agnostics, and Buddhists to name a few, are quite unlikely to be aware of this history or the pledge's "place." Assuming their views match their parents, they are overwhelmingly likely to think that they are "outsiders, not full members of the political community,"[19] and they would regrettably be right to think so. But on Justice O'Connor's rendition of the Establishment Clause these children's reasonable reactions are of no moment. In other words, she formulated a test that can achieve equality for a group of elite insiders, not for American parents and children. This, she maintains, is prompted by the "dizzying religious heterogeneity of our Nation."[20] The alternative, she suggests, is anarchistic subjectivity threatening nearly every government action. In support of this claim, one might conjure up the fundamentalist who maintains that the public school curriculum establishes a religion because it does not mention God. As I will argue, there is a solution to that problem, but it does not require imaginary people with insider information.

Let us suppose, however, that we are stuck with the O'Connor test. Does it follow that the pledge is not religious? Justice O'Connor says yes because the pledge is used for secular purposes, has not engendered significant national controversy, does not involve worship or prayer, and is a minimal part of the pledge. The notion of using religious language for secular purposes ought itself to raise constitutional eyebrows. Religion is already damaged by using it for secular purposes; the damage is compounded by denying that religion is not involved. And it is a non sequitur to say that reasonable observers would think that they were not outsiders because a religion they oppose was only used to consolidate secular objectives. On the other hand, even from a secular perspective, one might imagine the honoring of the Puritan contribution of democratic thought or of Martin Luther King and the role religion played in his life as a part of recognizing the role of religion in American life. Such honoring would be quite different than the use of God in the Pledge of Allegiance unless one indulges the fiction that it exists only to recall a historical "fact" about the founding of the Republic.

Chapter 4

Applying the Establishment Clause

APPLYING THE ESTABLISHMENT CLAUSE is more difficult than applying the Free Exercise Clause. When government burdens religious liberty directly, all the values underlying the Free Exercise Clause are potentially in play, and they all point in the same direction. Unlike the Free Exercise Clause, however, Establishment Clause values frequently come into conflict with each other. Recall from chapter 3 that the Establishment Clause is supported by seven values: (1) it protects religious liberty and autonomy, including the protection of taxpayers from being forced to support religious ideologies to which they are opposed; (2) it stands for equal citizenship without regard to religion; (3) it protects against the destabilizing influence of having the polity divided along religious lines; (4) it promotes political community; (5) it protects the autonomy of the state to protect the public interest; (6) it protects churches from the corrupting influences of the state; and (7) it promotes religion in the private sphere. Equality plays a particularly complex role in the interaction of these values. The character of the interaction of Establishment Clause values forces a more extended discussion of applications than was necessary with the Free Exercise Clause. But in many ways Establishment Clause applications are more interesting than Free Exercise applications, partly because of the greater richness produced by conflicts between values, partly because they force deeper inspection of the relationship between religion and government, and partly because so many of the cases arise out of controversies affecting our children in the schools. In this chapter, I primarily focus on questions involving government's relationship to explicit or implicit religious messages. In Part II, I will discuss financial aid to religious institutions.

Perhaps there is a natural human tendency to transform the complex into the simple, and the *Allegheny County* case is a model case for those who would reduce the Establishment Clause to a simple equality model. The county's action favors Christianity. This it may not do. End of case. If equality were the sole value underlying the Establishment Clause, one would expect that governmental deviations from religious equality would invariably be unconstitutional and that government conformity with equality would invariably be constitutional. But the world is not that simple. Government deviations from equality are frequently constitutional.

For example, governmentally sponsored monotheistic prayers are ordinarily constitutional, at least outside the context of public schools;[1] government frequently acts in ways that breach religious doctrine without violating the Establishment Clause; and government ordinarily may remove obstacles from religious practice in ways that discriminate against or burden nonreligious actors. Similarly, conforming with equality does not immunize government from Establishment Clause liability. For example, government may not permit religious teachers in public school classrooms even on an equal basis. Equality's explanatory power is thwarted precisely because of the pluralistic foundations of the Establishment Clause.

Acceptable Deviations from Equality

Monotheistic Prayer and the Pledge of Allegiance

Justice Kennedy's claim that those who oppose the action of Allegheny County are hostile to religion[2] is widely shared. Many worry that the absence of religious symbols from public life would create the impression that religion is unimportant, not part of the lives of the American people, and not something that should be part of the lives of children. They worry about the consequences of a political culture devoid of religious symbolism. They worry about the consequences of maintaining a "naked public square."[3]

Much public ceremony, however, contains reference to or prayers to God, countering any claim that the United States is a godless government.[4] The formulation and use of the Pledge of Allegiance is one of many governmental actions that pay homage to God. Some such efforts have been declared unconstitutional. For example, the Court struck down prayer[5] and Bible readings[6] in public school classrooms some four decades ago. Nonetheless, Supreme Court justices have routinely suggested that the Pledge of Allegiance is not constitutionally problematic. These statements were finally challenged.

Shortly before the Fourth of July 2002, Judge Goodwin of the Ninth Circuit Court of Appeals wrote an opinion declaring that the words "under God" in the Pledge of Allegiance violate the Establishment Clause.[7] It was not a hard argument to make. Far from being a lasting tradition reaching to the beginning of the Republic, the words had been added to the pledge by Congress in the 1950s.[8] The Supreme Court had clearly stated that it was unconstitutional for the state to promote religion.[9] But, as Goodwin pointedly observed, the "under God" amendment not only endorsed religion over nonreligion, it endorsed monotheism over polytheism.[10] Indeed, its unmistakable purpose was to endorse and pro-

Justice O'Connor argues that the absence of litigation over the last half century and the absence of public controversy show that the reasonable observer would recognize that the pledge is secular. I would think it shows the contrary. I would think it shows that atheists, agnostics, and Buddhists knew they were outsiders and knew they had no chance of winning a lawsuit. It is hard to imagine that atheists, agnostics, and Buddhists have been happy to send their children to schools that sport the pledge. That they have not set themselves up as targets for reprisals and have instead quietly accepted a public insult does not infuse the pledge with a secular character.

Justice O'Connor also finds it significant that the pledge is not a prayer. To prove this, she would have the reasonable observer consult the California Education Code to determine that the pledge is characterized as a patriotic exercise and also notice that the pledge is led by a teacher rather than a religious leader. Fair enough. But then she walks into outer darkness.

She insists that the constant repetition of the pledge in a patriotic context has removed religion from the pledge: "[A]ny religious freight the words may have been meant to carry originally has long since been lost."[21] Similarly, Justice Brennan once wrote that the phrase *In God We Trust* on coins had lost religious meaning.[22] I have always thought that such an argument was ironic. When government puts a prayer on a coin, it cheapens the prayer. When government makes Christmas a commercial holiday by cooperating with merchants in putting Christmas lights all over town, it cheapens Christmas. And when I hear the phrase "under God" in the Pledge of Allegiance, I think of cynical and sanctimonious politicians currying favor with their constituents.

Perhaps Justice O'Connor means to suggest that the pledge does not instill religious values. If that is what she means to say, I am inclined to agree. There are grounds to wonder whether significant numbers of children have become religious or stayed religious longer because they mouthed the magic words on school-day mornings. It seems unlikely that brief ceremonies of that character have any significant religious influence.[23] Indeed, in the nineteenth century, religious promotion was far more conspicuous in the public schools than it is today.[24] Yet many argued that the effort was ineffective. Indeed my colleague R. Laurence Moore strongly argues that the "importance of religion to intellectual development in the nineteenth century had almost nothing to do with what happened in public school classrooms."[25]

But neither this, nor the fact that the pledge fails to induce spiritual attitudes,[26] nor the fact that the reference to God is circumscribed,[27] or that it is only two of the pledge's thirty-one words[28] in any way makes the *under God* phrase nonreligious. Citizens may have forgotten that the name of the city of Los Angeles has a religious meaning, but any English speaker knows that *under God* and *In God We Trust* carry theological meaning. Indeed, Justice O'Connor states that the phrase is "merely descriptive; it purports only to identify the United States as a Nation subject to divine authority. That cannot be seen as a serious invocation of God or as an expression of individual submission to divine authority."[29] I am not sure why individuals are not subject to divine authority if the United States is, but I am sure that a pledge identifying the United States as subject to divine authority is asserting the existence and authority of the divine.

Justice O'Connor may be suggesting that even if there is some minimal religious content, it is basically noncontroversial and, therefore, not an endorsement. But Justice O'Connor knows this to be false. It is not clear why atheists and agnostics do not matter in her analysis, but she does respond to the contention that Buddhism is not based on belief in a separate Supreme Being: "[O]ne would be hard pressed to imagine a brief solemnizing reference to religion that would adequately encompass every religious belief expressed by any citizen of this Nation."[30] True, but it is no more satisfying to be told that the pledge is not an endorsement than it is to be told that it is not religious.

Nor does it work to suppose that the God amendment represents a trivial conflict with Establishment Clause values. As I have just discussed, one cannot persuasively claim that it is bereft of religious meaning. Rehnquist and O'Connor aside, the history leading to the adoption of *under God* makes its religious purpose clear.[31] Moreover, the firestorm following the Ninth Circuit's opinion itself demonstrated the religious character of the message and the tenacity with which it is held.[32] To claim that it is just a patriotic ceremony is to pretend that it was not converted into a patriotic/religious ceremony by the God amendment. To claim that the God amendment is de minimis tells those who are marked as outsiders to pretend that they are not marked as outsiders. In contrast, the ideal of those who oppose the insertion of *under God* in the Pledge of Allegiance is one of equal citizenship. Their constitutional vision sees a nation in which one's religion or lack of religion has no bearing on one's identity as an American citizen.

But, unfortunately, they see a nation that does not exist. It never has, and it never will. Certainly, government has been deeply involved in promoting religion over nonreligion for the whole course of American history, and, for the greater part of that history, it has supported Protestantism over other forms of religion.[33] The public schools were formed in large part to support Protestant values.[34] Indeed, for most of our history, reading from the Bible in the public schools was considered constitutional[35] at the same time that financial aid to private schools was considered unconstitutional.[36] Perhaps some fine mind can reconcile these two positions on the basis of some neutral principle, but the fact is that the reading was from a Protestant Bible unaccompanied by commentary,[37] and the private schools were largely Catholic. Supporting the Protestants was considered neutral, commonsense promotion of morals; supporting the Catholics was establishing a religion.[38]

Although the Court, in the landmark case of *Everson v. Board of Education*, said that "[n]either a state nor the Federal Government . . . can pass laws which aid one religion, aid all religions, or prefer one religion over another,"[39] it is hard to take this language seriously. This is a country in which *In God We Trust* appears on the currency, the Supreme Court begins its sessions with "God save the United States and this Honorable Court," and Congress has ordained a National Day of Prayer. In theory, of course, these and other practices could be rolled back.[40] In practice, it is inconceivable that they will.[41] Moreover, pretending they are not religious is simply insulting.

What does this hard reality mean for Establishment Clause interpretation? It seems inescapable that the Establishment Clause should be interpreted in light of precedent along with the values of the American people, that the high wall between church and state should be respected as a regulatory ideal, and that when these considerations clash, the justices should come as close to the ideal as our evolving traditions permit. From that perspective, it seems clear that generalized governmental endorsements of monotheism are consistent with the Establishment Clause. This need not mean that Justice Douglas was correct when he said that our institutions presuppose a divine being.[42] The Constitution deliberately does not mention God, and that omission was fought over at the time of the founding. Nonetheless, it seems clear that, despite all the lip service to equality, the United States Constitution is best interpreted to be consistent with monotheistic ceremonial prayers that do not involve coercion. Now, of course, it need not be that way. Indeed, given the pluralistic character of our people, it seems to me that we would have a better Constitution if we did not have what amounts to a monotheistic established religion, and, it should be noted, a monotheism of a specific type—one that, among other things,[43] puts *In God We Trust* on the coins, not *In Allah We Trust*.[44]

Of course, we need not be bound by the dead hand of the past. Of course, we should remember that it is *a constitution* we are interpreting, one designed for ages to come and to be adapted to varying conditions.[45] We, however, have also been counseled to recognize that it is *this* Constitution we are interpreting,[46] and *this* Constitution cannot plausibly be understood to foreclose the engraving of *In God We Trust* on coins and the like.[47] At least, not yet; and probably, not ever.

How does this apply to the issues put forward by the pledge? On this analysis, Congress could legitimately put forth a model as to how citizens might honor the flag if they wished.[48] On the other hand, the use of the pledge in public school classrooms should not be defended. If the Court could strike down prayer and Bible readings in public school classrooms, it is a short step for it to recognize that encouraging public recitations of the existence of God by children in public school classrooms is not consistent with the Establishment Clause.[49] If the Court could hold that prayers in graduation ceremonies were coercive in that members of the audience might feel compelled to stand, as it did in *Lee v. Weisman*,[50] how much more coercive is the daily recitation of the pledge in public school classrooms?[51] There is plenty of room under this Constitution to hold that the coercive atmosphere of peer groups in public school classrooms cannot constitutionally function to induce recitals of belief in God.

There is a strong case for an alternative path to the conclusion I have set out, but I do not believe it is ultimately persuasive. This alternative path strives to be pragmatic. It would suggest that justices should make decisions on the basis of what would best protect religious liberty overall. To declare unconstitutional the engraving of *In God We Trust* on coins under this approach would be thought futile because it would trigger a quick constitutional amendment to the contrary.[52] Aside from the symbolic damage created by amending the Bill of Rights, there is no assurance that a new amendment would be narrowly crafted or that it would be narrowly interpreted.

Certainly, one argument for a pragmatic path would be that it has more integrity than pretending that monotheistic ceremonies do not violate equality, or are not really religious, or that the public affirmations of and prayer to a deity are trivial.[53] On the other hand, one might object to this approach on the ground that it sacrifices minority rights on the altar of the intense majority, and so it does, but only when thought to be necessary. One might also object that the Court sacrifices its reputation as a court of law when it resorts to pragmatism. But this would not be the first time that the Court's constitutional decisions have been influenced by pragmatic assessments of its own power. Indeed, if concern about the Court's reputation as a legal actor were primary, a decision finding *under God* constitutional would be mandatory given the swift condemnation that greeted the Ninth Circuit Court of Appeals when it invalidated the pledge.

But some might argue that this, too, misses the point. The point is not the Court's reputation, but the fact that the Court is supposed to be a legal institution immune from political pressure. The Constitution, on this understanding, requires that the Court interpret the Establishment Clause according to the high-wall understanding even if the reading is contrary to our history, even if the reading would swiftly be circumvented by a constitutional amendment that might make matters even worse, and even if the reading would do great damage to the Court as an institution. I do not agree with that high-minded objection. I do not believe that vague slogans or deep analysis of the "rule of law" yield the result that justices are required to render decisions that threaten to undermine critical constitutional values and institutions.[54]

My concern about the pragmatic approach is pragmatic. I fear that if such an approach were legitimized in defining rights,[55] the Court would not be as aggressive as it should be. It is not clear that a Court armed with pragmatic concerns would have had the nerve to desegregate schools, outlaw prayer in schools, or recognize the burning of flags to be protected freedom of speech. Despite occasionally exceptional appointments, the process of appointing justices is not calculated to produce those who are vigilant in supporting civil liberties. Offering a pragmatic excuse to enforce civil liberties strikes me as a political mistake.

It could, for example, lead to upholding the pledge in classrooms. To be sure, the prospect of a constitutional amendment in this situation is not as sure as it would be if the Court invalidated *In God We Trust* on coins. After all, Governor Jesse Ventura vetoed a bill that would have required the pledge to be used in all Minnesota public school classrooms,[56] and only half the states have any such requirement. One could argue that the American people may have no patience for removing *In God We Trust* from coins and the like, but doubt that there is enough of a consensus to underwrite a constitutional amendment requiring the pledge in American classrooms. On this analysis, the religious liberty of third graders might fall victim to political demagogues, but it is a stronger cause than flailing against inequalities like engraving *In God We Trust* on coins.

Nonetheless, the political risks are substantial. Obviously, government could function quite effectively without parading religious symbols in a ceremonial way. The intense desire to use these symbols may just show that Americans are a religious people who believe that prayer or the recognition of religion is an important part of public life. There is a lot of that involved. But I am sure there is something else, too, and it is revealed by the intensity of the outrage responding to the suggestion that the Pledge of Allegiance presents a problem. There is a desire on the part of many to marginalize those who do not agree, to show who the insiders are, and to send a loud, clear message as to who the outsiders are.[57] And thus a pledge purportedly designed to unite a people divides a people into the "good guys" and the "bad guys." The risk that politicians would pander to these currents might be too much for a pragmatist to swallow.[58]

If the use of the pragmatic consideration would enhance civil liberties, I would not hesitate to endorse it, but judges are already too cautious. In the case of the pledge, it could cause judges to consign our children to religious coercion in the classrooms even if they believed it was unconstitutional. That is too much of a price to pay.

Acting Contrary to Religious Doctrine

Government frequently speaks and acts in ways that *implicitly* seem to contradict religious doctrine, and these communications and actions have not been thought to violate the Establishment Clause. Indeed, the Constitution allows governments to act in ways that violate doctrines of Quakers, Roman Catholics, Christian fundamentalists, Muslims, and Jews. The military is not unconstitutional despite the Quakers; capital punishment is not unconstitutional despite the Roman Catholics; state teaching about gender roles and homosexuality in ways that are contrary to the teachings of Muslims, Christian fundamentalists, and other religions is not unconstitutional; state support of medical care is not unconstitutional despite the Christian Scientists; and public high school Friday night football games do not violate the Constitution despite the Jews.

One could attack parts of this list. The Friday football game example to me shows the unthinking hegemony of Christianity, but attempting to change it would trigger enormous anti-Semitism. In many circumstances, it should be permissible to excuse children from objectionable instruction, though this is very different from abandoning the instruction altogether. Capital punishment should probably be unconstitutional on other grounds.[59]

Nonetheless, such government policies raise troubling theoretical issues. Christian fundamentalists, for example, faced with a secular school system ask why they are not the kind of outsiders who should be protected under the Establishment Clause.[60] When fundamentalists believe that God created the world in seven days, why isn't the teaching of evolution an establishment of religion? Fundamentalists rightly believe that the majority is treating them as outsiders.

One response to the fundamentalists is that government could not effectively function if it were forced to avoid contradicting religious doctrine in its communications and actions. Indeed, in a pluralistic society it may often be impossible to act without contradicting one religious doctrine or another. For religions divide upon how governments should be organized and how the church should relate to the state; any organizing action will contradict some religion. Nonetheless, it is not clear this shows that in every case government must be permitted to contradict religious doctrine. Perhaps permitting religious claims on this basis would overwhelm government and the courts, but the empirical foundation for that claim depends upon the process for adjudicating the claims and the degree of scrutiny applied.

A more fundamental response to the fundamentalists is that the Establishment Clause prohibits the establishment of *religion* and the teaching of evolution is not the teaching of religion. A central message of the Establishment Clause is that government has no jurisdiction to determine what God has to say about any subject[61] or to "measure religious truth."[62] It cannot make theological judgments with respect to any policy including capital punishment or support of medical care. The teaching of evolution does not violate this precept. Indeed, a teacher of evolution in the public schools might believe that the best scientific evidence pointed to the truth of evolution, that the Bible pointed in the other direction, and that the Bible was right. The teacher also might think that it is her job to teach science, not religion. From this perspective, the teacher or the school has taken no position on the interpretation of the Bible or the weight to be given to it.

Imagine how different it would be if the science teacher taught the science of evolution and explicitly proceeded to say, "And this shows that the fundamentalists are wrong." Clearly she would have left the realm of science and entered the realm of religion. Despite the example of monotheistic prayers, in the overwhelming majority of cases, when government speaks or acts it does so for civic reasons, not because God has something to say about the subject. Such actions do not deny the existence of God or suggest that God has nothing to say about evolution or any other subject. Despite the fact that fundamentalists reasonably experience the teaching of evolution as a contradiction of their religious views, such teaching is not religious within the meaning of the Establishment Clause.[63]

Arguments such as these, however, are hardly satisfying to fundamentalists. But what is the alternative? Should public school teachers teach what God has to say about evolution and other subjects? Should school board meetings resolve the question of God's word or whether there is a God? There may be a compromise to some of these questions. I see no reason why public school teachers should be disabled from teaching that various religions question the views that are being expressed in the classroom—whether those views involve evolution, the legitimacy of war, capital punishment, abortion, or what have you. Nothing in the Constitution has been interpreted to prevent teachers from talking about religion. Students need not be deprived of information about strongly held views. Indeed, I would argue that fairness demands that students be provided with this information. Without suggesting that judges should police this aspect of education, I would maintain that this dimension of fairness could ground a constitutional obligation to include such material in the curriculum. Public school authorities, who take oaths to defend the Constitution, may undertake constitutional obligations that are rightly regarded as judicially unenforceable.

The ultimate fundamentalist position ranges far beyond examples like evolution. The fundamentalist claim is that the public schools teach a religion, namely secular or ethical humanism. But this claim is simply wrong. The doctrine of secular or ethical humanism, according to this claim, holds that no God exists. God, from this account of the secular humanist, is simply superstition.[64] But so understood, no such thing is taught in any public school in America. Moreover, the public school bureaucracy, including masses of schoolteachers, is filled with a substantial portion of religious believers.[65] Indeed, if any school did teach agnosticism or atheism, the Establishment Clause would clearly be violated. From the fundamentalist perspective, however, the failure to teach religion in the public schools violates the religious rights of many religious believers because they believe that religion should permeate the educational process. From their perspective, the failure to advocate religious beliefs is itself a religious position.[66] The difficulty with this argument is apparent. Religion permeating education in the public schools would clearly violate the Establishment Clause. To close down the public schools in order to accommodate the religious beliefs of some would also violate the religious beliefs of others. However church-state relations might be structured, the religious beliefs of many millions of Americans will be contradicted.[67]

It bears emphasizing that I have been discussing the question of whether teaching evolution and the like violates the Establishment Clause, not a free exercise claim. Suppose, however, that the parents of a child in the school and the child complained that she was exposed to instruction that contradicted her religion. Suppose she asked to be excused from the instruction rather than demanding that the state not teach evolution or the offending subject. This would present the question whether her free exercise rights were being violated, and there would be no question that her religious interests were involved. Ordinarily, in my view, the free exercise claim should prevail when children are compelled to attend lectures that contradict their religion.[68] But I see no room for compromise if parents insist on separating their child from other children on grounds of intolerance or depriving their child of vital information or critical thinking skills—skills necessary for democratic citizenship and for adaptability in a changing marketplace. I think that evolution falls in the "vital information" category, and I would not uphold the free exercise claim. Nonetheless, it is useful to contrast the different issues under the religion clauses. Teaching evolution is not religion for purposes of the Establishment Clause, but forcing a child to hear a lecture teaching evolution does raise a free exercise issue.

Removing Obstacles to Religious Practice

Government frequently removes obstacles to religious practice. For example, many states make exemptions to their drug laws to permit Native Americans to ingest peyote at religious services. The *Smith* Court stated that legislative exemptions of this sort were not constitutionally required, but were constitutionally permitted.[69] This obviously favors religious peyote users over nonreligious users. But, for reasons I have canvassed earlier, preferences of this type seem reasonable.[70]

More complicated in terms of analysis are provisions like the federal draft law that exempted those who were conscientiously opposed to *all* wars "by reason of religious training and belief."[71] This, too, favored religious objectors over nonreligious objectors and raises no new issues in that respect, but it favored some religious objectors over other religious objectors, and that should rarely be countenanced. The Court maintained that determining the sincerity of those who object to all wars would generally be easier than determining the religious sincerity of those who object only to particular wars.[72] True enough. But when serious liberty values (forcing someone to kill when their religion commands otherwise) and fundamental equality values (favoring one group of religions over others) combine in the same case, more serious justification needs to be offered. It has also been suggested that permitting such general conscientious objection opportunities would compromise the government's ability to raise the kind of fighting force it needs.[73] If one takes a democratic perspective, the desire of elites to fight a war lacking strong democratic support should undercut the importance of the governmental interest. If the interest is sufficiently grave, a democratic perspective would suggest a less restrictive alternative: justify the war effort to the people.

A final objection to permitting conscientious objection is that it does not just remove obstacles to religious practice; it may offer powerful incentives for people to join a religion.[74] I do not doubt the psychology that lies behind this argument. I believe that many persons joined the Quakers in an effort to avoid the Vietnam War. These side effects, however unintended, are offensive to the values of the religion clauses. But violating liberty and equality values in such a severe way by not allowing conscientious objection seems even more problematic.[75]

Commentators such as Ira Lupu have powerfully argued that permitting discretionary accommodation risks discrimination against minority religions.[76] But one intriguing feature about the conscientious objector example is that the statute favored minority religions like the Quakers over more powerful religious constituencies such as the Catholics and mainline Protestants. A partial answer to Lupu's worries is that courts should extend the benefits of legislation intended to protect religion to minority religious groups.

Another concern frequently raised about such accommodation provisions is that they impose burdens upon others.[77] For example, *Estate of Thornton v. Caldor*[78] invalidated a Connecticut statute guaranteeing workers an absolute right not to work on the day they observed as the Sabbath. The Court was especially concerned about the sweeping character of the statute, and that it did not permit exceptions when honoring the Sabbath would cause a substantial economic burden on the employer or the imposition of significant burdens on other employees. Too be sure, some burdens in some circumstances could be undue (though it is not clear this was one of them).[79]

Significantly, the *Thornton* Court did not object to the state's concern with the interference with free exercise by private actors.[80] If it had, the religious aspect of Title VII of the 1964 Civil Rights Act would have been endangered.[81] Of course, the Constitution does not protect free exercise against private interference. As Michael McConnell observes, "The legislature should have as much latitude to protect the exercise of religion [as] it has to protect other important values in life."[82] The state has a substantial interest in protecting its citizens' free exercise of religion, just as it has an interest in protecting them in a wide variety of other spheres.

Unacceptable Conformity with Equality:
Equality in the Public School Classroom

If the complexity of the Establishment Clause means that some deviations from formal equality are permissible, it should not be surprising that complying with formal equality is not sufficient in other circumstances. Although conservatives have argued that exceptions should be permitted in favor of religion in particular legislative schemes, they have pressed the view that compliance with formal equality should otherwise be sufficient to meet Establishment Clause standards. Conservatives, for example, have been arguing for many years that school voucher programs should be deemed constitutional under the Establishment Clause so long as the standards for their distribution do not discriminate against religious or nonreligious schools.[83] We will consider that issue in chapters 5 and 6.

But the issue need not be confined to vouchers. Suppose, for example, that a school board thinks it inappropriate to provide nonreligious education without providing religious education. Imagine that it sets a couple of hours per week to permit priests, ministers, rabbis, other religious teachers,[84] and nonreligious humanists[85] to enter the public schools to give religious or nonreligious ethical instruction, that students (with parental permission at earlier ages) are free to enroll in the class of their choice, and that nonreligious electives are available at the same hour.

A similar arrangement was declared unconstitutional by the Supreme Court in *McCollum v. Board of Education*[86] in 1948, but it might be argued today that the school board was merely rectifying inequality. Notice precisely what would be at stake. It is already permissible to teach *about* religion in the public school curriculum.[87] The Constitution does not require that students be uninformed about the religious diversity of the American people. Schools are free to inform future citizens about the religious values and positions that inform many of the most controverted policy issues in the Republic. Such instruction allows students "to *think other people's thoughts* instead of ignoring them and fearing them (which does not mean thinking *as others do*)."[88] Moreover, there are clear circumstances in which religious proselytizing can take place in the public schools. For example, suppose a public school allows private organizations in the community to use its classrooms in the afternoons after school or other times when school is not in session. If the school is generally open to organizations, religious organizations may not be excluded even if they are engaged in proselytizing.[89] When a limited public forum has been opened, content discrimination is rarely permitted. In such a circumstance, the public school honors freedom of speech; it does not endorse religion.

On the other hand, if a school board in a predominantly Catholic community approves a course in Catholicism taught by a practicing Catholic whose goal is to make Catholicism appealing, the arrangement would clearly exceed constitutional bounds. It is not the business of the public schools to endorse Catholicism. The example we are considering involves none of this. It does not endorse a particular religion as in *Allegheny County* and it does not endorse religion over nonreligion. The school board would argue that it just gives religion a fair place at the table.

If formal equality is the sole Establishment Clause value, the board has a strong case. After all, the arrangement need not favor one religion over another,[90] and it does not favor religion over nonreligion. Moreover, the size or existence of particular religious classes would depend not upon the decision of the state, but the decisions of numerous private actors. The state might reasonably argue that it had not endorsed any particular religion. In addition, it would be plausible for the state to deny a religious purpose if it offered nonreligious classes at the same time it offered religious classes.

If formal equality is the predominant Establishment Clause value, the result in *McCullom* is open to question. And perhaps it should be. Public schools in England, Northern Ireland,[91] Spain,[92] Portugal,[93] Italy,[94] Germany,[95] and Poland[96] typically teach religion.[97] Indeed, in Germany, children have a constitutional right to receive a religious education in the public schools.[98] Perhaps these countries have come to a better reasoned conclusion about the place of religion in the educational process.[99]

Perhaps, but there are substantial grounds for believing otherwise. First, formal equality in this circumstance promises to lead to substantial substantive inequality. Suppose the system is adopted in school districts in Mississippi, Utah, and Minnesota. Classes will be overwhelmingly Southern Baptist in some districts in Mississippi, Mormon in some districts in Utah, and Lutheran in some districts in Minnesota. This inequality in itself is problematic.[100] But suppose such a proposal is enacted in a more heterogeneous district. It might be supposed that such a system could arguably serve an important multicultural purpose. Having children attend religious classes in the public schools makes it more difficult to paper over difference, and arguably might foster genuine reflection and dialogue about the character of those differences and the extent to which there is unity in those differences. Students who attend to those differences on this line of thought need not abandon their faith tradition, but by empathic engagement with those of other traditions, may learn more about themselves and the traditions of which they are a part.[101]

Nonetheless, there is good reason to worry that segregated religious education in the schools would promote separatism, marginalization, and intolerance. Multicultural goals might better be achieved in the context of teaching about religions generally. In those contexts, students are not formally marked out as separate, and dialogue can arise out of the experience of subject matter taught to all. The presence of segregated religious education in the schools functions to emphasize difference in a visible way that would seem to lead students away from the recognition of unity in difference. This kind of state involvement seems contrary to the toleration values embedded in the religion clauses of the First Amendment.

Moreover, the burden of these disadvantages could fall with particular weight on the children whose religions are small minorities in the district. In addition, there are good reasons to believe that some of the religious teaching in the schools would be contrary to public goals. Such teaching might be racist, sexist, homophobic, and more generally intolerant; that is, we are saved and they are not. The potential for stigmatization and denial of liberty is not inconsiderable.

These concerns are not rescued by substantial state interests. Perhaps the best argument sounds in equality. Nonreligious subjects are taught, but not religious subjects. In addition, although the schools do not teach secular humanism, the failure to communicate the existence of God in the public schools unwittingly communicates a secular humanist message[102] and discourages religion.[103] One might argue that the public schools contributed to religious life for most of our history, but the Supreme Court ended all this by excluding prayer from the schools. In support of the view that the public schools discourage religion, one might point to the slow, but steady rise of nonbelievers in the United States.[104] On the other side, the failure effectively to teach the existence of God in the public schools can also seen for what it is: an acceptance of the separation of church and state. Moreover, outside the public school curriculum, religious clubs flourish; moments of silence or the Pledge of Allegiance exist at the outset of classroom day; prayer groups frequently meet before the beginning of school. At the same time God is absent from the public school curriculum, sociologists marvel at the religious character of the American people.[105] There are also grounds to doubt the extent to which the public schools have played a significant role in religious socialization. It is hard to believe, for example, that the existence of a ritualized prayer at the outset of a school day had any substantial spiritual effect.

Indeed, assuming that it is worthwhile for the state to promote religion, one could reasonably wonder how much would be accomplished by the small amount of classroom time involved in such programs. The European experience would suggest not much. Of course, it is all a matter of perspective. Perhaps in Spain religious participation would be even lower if religion were not taught in the public schools; perhaps religiosity in the United States would be even higher if religion were taught in the public schools.

Perspective matters on how many personal conversions count as a success. From the perspective of many religions, every soul counts. Forty conversions might be a success. From the perspective of government, we are supposing that religiosity of the people as a whole matters in a democratic society. From a civic perspective, affecting the views of only forty students would not be worth pursuing. But government has to adopt a civic perspective, not a religious perspective, and from the perspective of public goals, evidence that religion in the schools has substantial effects is hard to come by.[106] There does not seem to be evidence that would outweigh the Establishment Clause concerns.

Perhaps even more to the point, in the end, the issue is not whether children get religious instruction; the issue is whether they get it in the schools. If children do not get religious instruction in the public schools, they can get religious education in their churches, mosques, or temples. Indeed, the Court in *Zorach v. Clauson*[107] upheld released time programs that could, if properly structured, mitigate, but not liquidate, the Establishment Clause concerns. Regrettably, the program upheld in *Zorach* was doubly defective. First, the program in essence suspended the duration of the school day by not holding classes for those who were not released and requiring them to stay in study hall. Justice Jackson in dissent characterized this as a "temporary jail for a pupil who will not go to church."[108]

Hyperbolic as this may be, the failure to provide elective classes seems to take the program beyond accommodation into using the compulsory machinery of the state to encourage religion.[109] Similarly, the *Zorach* program provided that teachers were to receive written reports from churches to confirm attendance. This, too, seems to cross the line. Excusing students on religious grounds is one thing; using state machinery to enforce religious attendance is quite another.[110] Nonetheless, released time programs not containing the objectionable features of *Zorach* strike me as a reasonable compromise. Although concerns about secular or ethical humanism have been overstated, the underlying equality concern is legitimate. The state is paying students to be educated in a nonreligious way. Accommodation of the equality concern in this manner allows parents to use time for their children for religious education in a religious atmosphere. To be sure, the accommodation may cause some stigmatization, but stigmatization would likely be more serious if the children removed themselves to segregated classrooms on public school premises. Of course, the released time solution is not perfect, but no solution can be perfect when the values of the religion clauses conflict with each other.

Concluding Observations about Part I

The attempt to explain the religion clauses by reducing their support to a small set of values—most commonly equal liberty—is too narrow. The Free Exercise Clause is supported by seven values: (1) it protects liberty and autonomy; (2) it avoids the cruelty of forcing an individual to do what he or she is conscientiously obliged not to do or to penalize an individual for responding to an obligation of conscience; (3) it preserves respect for law and minimizes violence triggered by religious conflict; (4) it combats religious discrimination; (5) it protects associational values; (6) it promotes political community; and (7) it protects the personal and social importance of religion. The failure to appreciate this array of values is not only of theoretical importance, but also of pragmatic importance. If free exercise is to be given its full weight in a constitutional balance, the full range of values needs to be considered.

The attempt to reduce the religion clauses to equal liberty is even less convincing with respect to the Establishment Clause. The Establishment Clause is supported by seven values: (1) it protects religious liberty and autonomy, including the protection of taxpayers from being forced to support religious ideologies to which they are opposed; (2) it stands for equal citizenship without regard to religion; (3) it protects against the destabilizing influence of having the polity divided along religious lines; (4) it promotes political community; (5) it protects the autonomy of the state to protect the public interest; (6) it protects churches from the corrupting influences of the state; and (7) it promotes religion in the private sphere.

In this part we have seen that the Court has placed too much emphasis on formal equality by failing to protect Native Americans in their worship service. In addition in the Establishment Clause context, we have considered a variety of cases involving government's connection to explicit and implicit government messages about religion as well as cases removing obstacles to the practice of religion. The attempt to reduce the Establishment Clause to formal equality works well in a case in which the government appropriates religious symbols to celebrate Christmas, as it did in *County of Allegheny*. Moreover, the liberty and equality values explain why government-sponsored prayer does not belong in the schools. But deviations from equality are sometimes permitted. The equality value does not explain why it is permissible to put *In God We Trust* on coins and currency. It does not explain why government can engage in actions that violate the doctrines of specific religion such as the teaching of evolution in the schools. It does not explain why government may sometimes remove obstacles to free exercise imposed by private employers without removing obstacles to secular practices. Nor does equality explain the complexity of the question of whether government can permit religion in the schools on a formally equal basis. Such permission advances religious liberty and treats religions equally, at least from a formal perspective. But it would often support a dominant religion, threaten toleration values, and risk stigmatizing children of minority religions.[111]

The reasons for the attempt to simplify religion clause analysis are undoubtedly complex. Of course, a part of the simplification project is result-oriented. As we will see in the next chapters, if one favors vouchers, it makes things more difficult if the values of the clauses range beyond equal liberty or if the conceptions of liberty or equality are problematized. But the drive to simplify the analysis often goes beyond the likely consequences. There is an aesthetic appeal to analysis[112] that proceeds as if it were a form of legal geometry.[113] Moreover, there is a psychological appeal to security in having firm foundations.[114] And there is an appeal to the rule of law in avoiding the kind of messiness and discretion that follows when values come into conflict. There is a sense of rationality, objectivity, and integrity accompanying a method that minimizes subjectivity.[115] And there is the appeal to fairness that pulls toward an ideal of formal equality.

In the end, however, the simplification project cannot be endorsed. It asks too much of theory in a context in which theory can have little resolving power. The pluralistic values underlying the religion clauses conflict with multiple governmental interests in a culture with a strong, diverse, and conflicting religious presence. The complications of these interactions are enormous. Theory can help to reveal the factors that should be relied upon to resolve problems in concrete contexts, and theory can help explain why particular problems are difficult. But the power of theory to dictate results in concrete contexts often runs out. Then we must rely on prudential judgment to make decisions and on practical experience to revise those decisions when they fail to work on the ground.[116] It makes for a messier world, but it is the world in which we live.

Part Two

THE FIRST AMENDMENT AND THE
SOCIALIZATION OF CHILDREN:
COMPULSORY PUBLIC EDUCATION
AND VOUCHERS

Chapter 5 _____

Compulsory Public Education

IN PART I, I ADVANCED what I consider to be the best understanding of
the constitutional framework of the religion clauses, a framework that
fits with religious liberalism. It is not a perfect fit with religious liberalism.
As I mentioned in chapter 4, religious liberals wished we lived in a country
where the American people did not feel it necessary to discriminate
against Buddhists, Hindus, agnostics, and atheists by putting *In God We
Trust* on the coins and currency and under a Constitution where such
discrimination would not be permitted. But we do not have a perfect Constitution. Nonetheless, it is arguably the best constitution in the world on
the subject of religion. It is unfortunate, however, that the Supreme Court
does not live up to the Constitution's values. I trust I have said enough
generally to demonstrate that the religion clauses are supported by many
values, and, in particular, that the religion clauses cannot be reduced to
a concern for formal equality. Regrettably, the Supreme Court has not
assimilated this message. Perhaps its greatest failure has been the reduction of the Free Exercise Clause to formal equality in its handling of the
Smith case discussed in chapter 2. But its privileging of formal equality
also has substantial implications for one of the most significant of Establishment Clause issues: the controversy surrounding school vouchers.

That controversy arouses significant passion and energy because it concerns three matters of great concern to the American public: children,
money, and religion. Almost 90 percent of American children attend public schools. Most parents on the whole are satisfied with the education
their children receive. But criticism of the public schools has been a cot-
tage industry since the nineteenth century.[1] In recent years the criticism
has gone to the roots.[2] Critics charge that to leave children imprisoned in
the public school monopoly[3] is to risk the standardization of our children;[4] it is to socialize them in the preferred views of the state. So, they
argue, it would be better to adopt a system of vouchers or private scholarships to support a multiplicity of private schools. A multiplicity of such
schools, it is said, would enhance parental choice,[5] would foster competition,[6] and would promote a diversity of views,[7] which in turn would bring
the kind of independent perspective needed for the sort of robust private
and public debate needed in our constitutional democracy.[8] A narrower
argument for vouchers arises in reaction to the context of those public

schools that do not serve poor children well. The latter argument is attractive to many liberals,[9] particularly to those concerned about the state of public education in many of the central cities.[10]

This debate about public and private education raises important questions about the role of the state in promoting a certain kind of person and citizen, which has implications for liberal and democratic theory, the respective rights of children and parents, and the nature of religious freedom in a democratic society. In addressing these issues, I will argue that the debate about vouchers has been oversimplified. Too often the argument has been that vouchers are always good or always bad or that vouchers to religious schools either always do or always do not violate the Establishment Clause. I will argue that the interests of children and the state in public education have been underestimated; indeed, I will argue that that there is a surprisingly strong constitutional case for the proposition that government should in many circumstances be able to *compel* adolescents of high school age, but not preadolescents, to attend public schools. No U.S. government is likely to engage in such compulsion, and there are good political reasons not to do so. Nonetheless, there is a payoff. Analysis of the constitutional case for compulsory public education leads to support of a strong presumption *against* vouchers, at least at the high school level. This presumption, however, is more difficult to defend when public schools are relatively homogeneous or are providing inadequate education to poor children. Even if vouchers could generally be supported, vouchers to religious schools raise serious concerns about the appropriate principles of church-state relations in the American constitutional order. But these concerns might be overcome in certain circumstances.

In short, I argue that compulsory public education is sometimes constitutional and sometimes not, that vouchers are generally to be resisted, but sometimes not, and that vouchers to religious schools should ordinarily be considered unconstitutional, but sometimes not. In making these arguments, I do not maintain that my analysis is consistent with that of the Supreme Court. Rather I make claims about how the Constitution should be interpreted despite the Supreme Court. Moreover, because the issue of vouchers and compulsory public education raises constitutional concerns beyond the Establishment Clause, I will need to consider them as well.

I begin this chapter with criticism of the reasoning in *Pierce v. Society of Sisters*,[11] the first case to consider compulsory public education. I then present the strong purposes supporting public education, weigh those interests against the claim that parents have the right to direct the upbringing and education of their children, and conclude that compulsory public high school education should be constitutional in many circumstances, although not in the years prior to high school. The same conclusions follow in the face of First Amendment speech, association, and religion claims, but they are vulnerable in some circumstances against a claim for a right to a good education. Although compulsory public education should be constitutional in many cases, I do not recommend it as policy. But the strength of the case for compulsory public education has implications for the debate over vouchers that I directly address in the next chapter.

Pierce v. Society of Sisters: *A Landmark Case*

Pierce v. Society of Sisters stands for the general proposition that children may not be forced to attend public schools. *Pierce* involved an Oregon law, the Compulsory Education Act of 1922. The law required virtually all children to attend public schools through the eighth grade. Two operators of private schools, the Society of the Sisters of the Holy Names of Jesus and Mary and the Hill Military Academy, sought and secured injunctions against the act's enforcement. Pierce, the governor of Oregon, ultimately appealed to the Supreme Court. The Supreme Court struck down the specific Oregon law, and *Pierce* is routinely read to support the right of parents to send their children to private schools throughout the adolescent years.[12] In the voucher debate, most scholars have taken *Pierce* for granted. A few have raised serious questions about it.[13] My position is that *Pierce* as generally read is half right; it is right for the pre-high school years (which I will refer to as the preadolescent years even though pre-high school students include early adolescents), but typically wrong for the high school adolescent years.

Pierce may be half right, but its analysis is shallow. The Court primarily relied on two arguments: first, that the Oregon law interfered with the right of parents and guardians to direct the upbringing of their children;[14] second, that the "fundamental theory of liberty upon which all governments in this Union repose excludes any general power of the state to standardize its children[15] by forcing them to accept instruction from public teachers only."[16]

Both of these contentions are overblown. Of course, parents and guardians have a right to direct the upbringing and education of children under their control, but even the *Pierce* Court recognized that any such right was not unqualified. It referred to parental obligations toward their children, and it suggested that the right of parents to send their children to private schools was qualified by the power of the state to require compulsory education[17] and to regulate private schools, requiring that some things be taught, that some things not be taught, and that teachers be of good moral character and patriotic disposition.[18]

If those qualifications of parental rights are acceptable, and assuming parents have at least a limited right to send their children to private schools, it is fair to ask whether the scope of that right should extend through the high school, adolescent, years. Consider the question in even more loaded terms: Should parents have a constitutional right to hermetically seal off their children from the views of others through their adolescent years? Do children have a right to be exposed to alternative points of view? It is one thing to say that parents have a right to direct the upbringing and education of their children; it is quite another to say that they have a right to monopolize their children.[19] Mandatory public education in the high school years would not erase the right of parents to raise their children. By the time of high school age, parents and their agents will have devoted tens of thousands of hours in communicating values to their children,[20] and public schools do not preclude continuing parental input. Even assuming that *Pierce* itself is rightly decided—as I do—when we focus instead on the high school years, the Court's assertion that it is "entirely plain that [compulsory public education] unreasonably interferes with the liberty of parents and guardians"[21] is open to serious question.

But what about the Court's companion pronouncement: "The fundamental theory of liberty upon which all governments in this Union repose excludes any general power of the state to standardize its children by forcing them to accept instruction from public teachers only."[22] Would mandatory public education for high school adolescents entail the standardization of our children?[23] The picture called up by this argument is that of an efficient monolithic government armed with a goal of homogenizing children coupled with a means of achieving this objective. But this picture ignores the multilayered character of the educational system. It does not take into account the federal system, the thousands of school boards, the different administrators of school districts, and, most important, the hundreds of thousands of teachers whose capacity for passive-aggressive behavior in the face of administrative mandates should never be underestimated. The notion that the message in public schools is monolithic from Holly Springs, Mississippi, to San Francisco, California, is really quite preposterous.[24]

Of course, there are exceptions. Despite the pleas of some liberal philosophers to be neutral about the good life,[25] public and private schools routinely take positions about the good life. They uniformly reject the view of living life to the fullest in terms of immediate sensory gratification. They teach our children not to take drugs (even marijuana—despite those who believe that the taking of marijuana is a valuable part of the good life), not to drink too much alcohol (despite those whose lifestyle includes guzzling large amounts of beer while watching football games),[26] not to smoke cigarettes (despite an army of smokers),[27] and, although the message varies, not to have sex[28] or, alternatively, not to have sex without a condom. Despite these teachings, teenagers, and sometimes young children, use drugs (including tobacco),[29] abuse alcohol,[30] and engage in unprotected sex in massive numbers.[31] Of course, millions of children do not do these things. The health curriculum is not wholly ineffective.

The picture of the standardized child, however, is hard to take seriously. As I mentioned, nearly 90 percent of American children already attend public schools.[32] They attend these schools at the same time the popular press is full of talk about the dangers, challenges, or opportunities posed by the nation's diversity.[33] American children are wildly different from each other in ways that escape the imagination of most school boards and superintendents. Indeed, the frequent claim that public schools discourage religion with their secular message[34] is hard to reconcile with the reality that Americans are among the most religious people in the Western world,[35] this despite massive public school attendance.[36] Even if public schools wanted to produce a standardized child, they would have had no prospect of success.[37]

This is not to deny the socializing effects of education and the wider culture. Americans are successfully socialized to believe in the greatness of their country and are steered toward a narrower political spectrum than Europeans. Effects such as these, regrettable or not, are promoted in public and private schools and the broader culture. They warrant no special indictment of compulsory *public* education. The public school system is not bereft of other socializing tendencies. I shall argue that public education tends to produce some important socializing effects, but these effects do not properly call up a picture of a totalitarian state or a standardized child. For example, I will argue that some of the socializing effects include the promotion of autonomy, empathy, creativity, imagination, respect, and tolerance. If it is standardization to promote autonomy, empathy, creativity, imagination, respect, and tolerance, we need to know what is wrong with standardization.

The standardization language—with all of its negative implications—in *Pierce* is understandable, however, because the dreadful briefs submitted by the Governor of Oregon and its attorney general opened themselves up to just such a response. The briefs expressed concern over "ignorant foreigners, unacquainted with and lacking in sympathy with, American institutions and ideals."[38] The briefs worried that private schools might emerge that were hostile to American ideals. Governor Pierce argued that if the Oregon law were declared unconstitutional, "[O]ur country will be dotted with elementary schools which instead of being red on the outside will be red on the inside."[39] The briefs declared war on difference and emphasized the need to produce American patriots.[40] They were truly susceptible to the interpretation that Oregon was trying to produce a homogenized public—built upon standardized children.

In this respect, Oregon mirrored the dark side of the movement to establish the public schools. Moreover, Oregon's motivation included a pungent dose of anti-Catholicism. The major private schools were Catholic,[41] and anti-Catholic sentiment was rampant.[42] The Oregon initiative was strongly supported by the Ku Klux Klan,[43] at a time when the Klan exerted substantial power in the Oregon legislature,[44] and Governor Pierce was a nativist who thought that Catholics should not be able to hold public office.[45] Barbara Woodhouse's brilliant rendition of the *Pierce* case insightfully argues that anti-Catholicism alone could not account for the Oregon law,[46] but even Woodhouse does not deny that anti-Catholicism played an important role.[47] Despite the overwrought rhetoric of the *Pierce* decision, the Court had good reason to strike down the Oregon law, but compulsory public education should not invariably be deemed unconstitutional in all contexts.

The Purposes of Public Education

Public education is supported by a number of strong purposes, including interests in democratic education, autonomy, empathy, creativity and imagination, respect and tolerance, social skills, equality, and justice.

Democratic Education

A major purpose of public education is to promote democratic values.[48] Although most would admit that this suggestion could form a part of the case for compulsory public education, it can be maintained that the argument cannot stand by itself. Thus, it would not do to tell children that they will be compelled to attend public school simply because it would be good for the society, as if it were appropriate to use them as mere instruments to a social end.[49] Even if it were appropriate, it would take a strong theory of democracy to show that compulsory public education could make a significant democratic difference. Such an argument would have to show that it is not enough to educate 90 percent of the nation's children—that the last 10 percent is important to democratic success. If we can figure out how to produce democratic citizens, we will have a rich supply without compelling the rest to attend public schools.[50]

Nonetheless, citizens have an obligation to participate in the process of combating the injustices of the society of which they are a part. To do this requires an understanding of the character of the society, with appreciation for its just aspects and concern about those aspects that cannot be defended. Persons have no right to be free riders on the work of others in a well-functioning democracy.[51] Thus, democratic education need not consider children as pawns in the process of social reproduction; democratic education honors the moral obligations of its citizenry.

Yet another obstacle to the success of this argument remains. The argument assumes that public education is democratic education and that private education is not.[52] In one sense that is tautological. The content of public education is controlled by democratic processes to a far greater extent than is the case in private schools.[53] The issue, however, is whether the democratic content of public education is substantially different from that of private education, regardless of the process of arriving at the content. There are grounds for believing this to be true, but it should not simply be assumed. We will return to this issue at the end of the next section.

A Diverse Student Body

A hallmark of public education is its commitment to educate children of all classes, races, and religions together.[54] This commitment to integrated education fosters autonomy, empathy, creativity and imagination, equality, respect and tolerance, social skills, justice, and democratic education.

AUTONOMY AND LIBERAL EDUCATION

Everyone has autonomy in a narrow sense. That is, everyone makes choices about some things from the trivial—deciding which part of an item of food to eat first or deciding which foot to put forward—to the substantial—for example, whom to befriend. But schools promote a thicker conception of autonomy.[55] A liberal education provides children with an understanding of the physical and social environment of which they are a part. Such an understanding is fundamental to a rich human life. Such an understanding (which is never complete) also assists children in making choices and in determining the range of choices to be made.[56] Bringing children of different backgrounds together fosters autonomy in the same way that the study of history and anthropology fosters autonomy. Exposure to people of different backgrounds and lifestyles makes vivid alternative conceptions of how to lead a life. If one of the purposes of education is to show children the range of choices that might be available to them and to teach the skills and habits of mind in making choices,[57] public education's commitment to integrated education makes a valuable contribution. The alternative of being educated with people of similar backgrounds and perspectives masks the available choices and encourages the view that the backgrounds and perspectives one was in a sense "born into" are given—are natural.[58]

Some argue, however, that it is not the business of the state to promote autonomy. A standard line of argument maintains that promoting autonomy violates the respect that should be shown to alternative ways of life.[59] Another line of argument, put forward by William Galston, concedes that the state has interests in toleration and "in developing citizens with at least the minimal conditions of reasonable public judgment. But neither of these civic requirements entails a need for public authority to take an interest in how children think about different ways of life."[60] Galston argues that there is a right to live unexamined as well as examined lives[61] and that the greatest threat to modern liberal societies is "not that [children] will believe in something too deeply, but that they will believe in nothing very deeply at all."[62]

The argument from respect has considerable merit in contexts where the state tells consenting adults that they cannot engage in otherwise harmless behavior because the state disapproves of the conduct, for example, same-sex sexual relations.[63] In the educational context, however, the state is not prohibiting conduct but encouraging it; the child is free to reject the values promoted by the state. More important, the child is forming values, so that to encourage the value of autonomy may disrespect the views of some parents[64] (indeed, the very point may be to offer an alternative to the views of the parents), but it does not disrespect the child. Finally, it is impossible to run a school without offending the beliefs of some. Individual teachers by their comportment endorse one model of a way to live. Coaches of athletic teams and drama directors explicitly endorse attitudes toward competition and cooperation and the relationship between them. The curriculum will invariably teach that racism is wrong, much to the chagrin of white supremacists. A value-free educational institution is not feasible;[65] it is neither necessary nor desirable.[66]

Even if everyone in an educational institution could be squeaky-clean neutral about the importance of values like autonomy, Galston's view that fostering autonomy is not important to democratic education is both contestable and beside the point. A citizen in a vigorous democracy needs more than minimal conditions of public judgment. Citizens, if they are not to be free riders, need to be able to contest public attempts at manipulation. They need to be independent, critical thinkers, capable of autonomous thinking.

Of course, citizens have a right to live unexamined lives; but if they are to be good citizens, they will not live a life in which their society goes unexamined. Perhaps it is possible to train citizens who would examine society closely but not their own lives; but that kind of compartmentalization has little to recommend it. Wholly apart from democratic justifications, a child who in the parental lottery draws parents opposed to the development of autonomy inherits limited choices. Autonomous development promises liberation from the parental monopoly, which in turn produces broadened choices. Of course, to broaden choice may be to forego the choice of blind acceptance, but the state reasonably makes the judgment that the child will be better off when presented with the choice to choose.

Finally, autonomous development is not inconsistent with deep beliefs (Galston himself has those), nor is it inconsistent with deeply held religious beliefs.[67] But, "when believing 'deeply' is just a function of believing ignorantly,"[68] it is hard to endorse such beliefs as protective of a liberal society.

EMPATHY, CREATIVITY, AND IMAGINATION

One of the features of literature is to introduce students to characters they might not otherwise encounter. Meeting such characters opens one to new worlds. These worlds reflect back on one's own. It not only opens one to new possibilities, but the making of new connections sparks the imagination and ignites the creative process.[69] Similarly, literature forces one to empathize with the problems and lives of others.[70] Integrated education also forces one to bump up against the other, to imagine what their lives are like, and to explore the connections between their lives and one's own, to empathize with others.[71] Education is not just the stuff of books; the varied character of the students one encounters is a rich source of enlargement and understanding.[72]

RESPECT AND TOLERANCE

Segregated education breeds fear of those who are different. It is all too easy to believe that those outside one's circle are different, strange, and even evil.[73] This was one of the many evils of racially segregated education. Although integrated education is not a panacea, it combats the fear of difference. It gives a human face to the other. It demagnetizes the strangeness. The possibilities of respect and toleration are thereby increased.[74] The lived experience of diversity presents a broader understanding of the culture in which one participates and encourages the student to feel at home in a pluralistic world.[75] When Governor Pierce spoke in favor of the Oregon law, he combined the themes of equality and toleration: "Every one of our six children was educated in the public schools from the primary to the college and university. . . . I believe we would have a better generation of American free from snobbery and bigotry if all children . . . were educated in the free public schools of America."[76] The idea was that respect and toleration would be encouraged if children of all races, classes, and religions were educated in the same common school.[77]

The data strongly supports the conclusion that intergroup contact reduces prejudice[78] and that these contact effects "hold equally well for groups other than races and ethnicities."[79] A meta-analysis of more than 750 studies involving more than 250,000 participants in more than 75 countries support the conclusion that the reduction of prejudice results from decreased anxiety, increased empathy, and, to some extent, increased knowledge.[80] Toleration and integration are companions. To tolerate, however, is not to abandon contrary beliefs. Nor should toleration be absolute. Toleration need not involve respect for the oppressive or discriminatory aspects of a culture.[81] In the end, toleration is based on respect for the humanity of persons, not on respect for the equality of all views.[82]

SOCIAL SKILLS

Autonomy, empathy, creativity and imagination, and respect and tolerance are skills or virtues that are valuable for individuals in a variety of contexts as well as important traits for democratic citizens. But they are also valuable for the ability of different children to relate to each other. Segregated education limits the exposure of children to other children who are different. Of course, segregated education does not entirely rob children of the ability to develop social skills. But integrated education affords broader exposure and greater opportunities.

JUSTICE

A good education nourishes a sense of justice and a commitment to playing a role in making a better world. Yet students are exposed to many clashing views about justice in the public schools. The effect of this for many will be to open their minds; some will change their minds; perhaps most will cling to previously considered views, but few will be entirely unaffected by the interpersonal dynamics of the common school. The public school's promotion of autonomy will itself promote critical reflection upon the various perspectives. And this is also important from the perspective of encouraging lively dissent.[83] John Stuart Mill rightly contends that the most effective dissenters are those who understand the perspective of their opposition and have engaged with it in a serious way.[84] There is a place for dogmatic dissenters, but a system committed to social justice needs savvy dissenters. Sealing off children from the views of others is a prescription for insularity, not a method for cultivating a robust democratic citizenry.

As Henry Levin observes, "It would be unrealistic to expect that Catholic schools will expose their students to both sides of the abortion issue; that evangelical schools would provide a disinterested comparison of creation and evolution; that military academies would debate the value of disarmament and peace movements; that leftist schools would provide a balanced presentation of the positive and negative aspects of capitalism; or that white academies would explore different views toward race in the United States. Their curriculum and faculty would be selected in order to make them efficient competitors in a differentiated market for students in which the views of parents would be reinforced and others excluded or derided."[85]

CLASS EQUALITY

Integrated education promotes class equality.[86] When the wealthy are permitted to enroll their children in private schools, the schools suffer in many ways. They typically lose well-prepared students; they lose important parental involvement; and they lose vital political activity and support for the financial resources needed to sustain high-quality schools.[87] The children of the wealthy lose the opportunity to socialize and learn from people in a more diverse setting. If parents were assured that similarly situated parents would be required to send their children to public schools, many of them might feel less of a need to send their children to private schools. Whether or not that is the case, the proponents of the Oregon law considered in *Pierce* had a point when they submitted this argument to the voters: "When every parent in our land has a child in our public school, then and only then will there be united interest in the growth and higher efficiency of our public schools."[88] Or as one of the slogans of the universal common schooling movement put it, "Free Public Schools—Open to All, Good enough for All, *Attended* by All, All for the Public School and the Public School for All."[89]

DEMOCRATIC EDUCATION

Conservatives complain that education in the public schools is liberal and multicultural.[90] This is by no means universally true, but, from a liberal perspective, a commitment to educating the children of all classes, races, and religions tends to press the schools in salutary directions. Such a commitment not only inclines the schools to denounce racial prejudice, but also leads them to celebrate the contributions of individuals from diverse cultures.[91] Similarly, that commitment inclines the schools in a direction that is far less patriarchal than might be expected in many of the nation's private schools.[92] Girls may be taught in many private schools that a women's place is in the home,[93] and they may ultimately decide that is best for them, but few public schools would suggest it as a given.

Many private schools will condemn homosexuality, and though they may tell students to hate the sin and not the sinner, homophobia is a serious problem. Breaking it down requires effort. Only the rare public school would teach that heterosexuality, homosexuality, and bisexuality are on a par (the politics of the public school environment would not permit it). But the public schools are far more likely than the private schools to stress the importance of toleration and respect regardless of sexual orientation. Of course, a commitment to educating all students is not a guarantee of a multicultural approach. Oregon sought to solve the "problem" of immigration and diversity by homogenizing its students,[94] but today most public schools castigate discrimination and salute diversity[95] while recognizing our common humanity and our common constitutional heritage.[96]

I conclude that very substantial interests underlie the interest in public school attendance. If *Pierce* is made to stand for the proposition that no level of government can require children in their adolescent years to attend public schools, and if the constitutional basis for that proposition is the right of parents to direct the upbringing and education of their children, *Pierce* just goes too far.

One might argue, however, that the due process right to choose where to go to school might properly belong to the adolescent child, particularly if vouchers accompanied that right of choice.[97] Let us assume for purposes of argument that the right of the child should supersede that of the parent in those years. There are, nonetheless, strong grounds to believe that the parents would successfully pressure the child to attend the private school of the parent's choice. Alternatively, if the child chose to reject the parents' advice and decided to attend public school, the conferring of the choice upon the child would end up throwing a dagger in the middle of the family. In most cases, however, adolescents will want to go to school where their friends go, and this would cause them to stay where they are, though some of their friends might leave for the public school. Although a system of compulsory public education would compel many adolescents to leave the comfort of what they have been used to, it would ordinarily ensure that adolescents could stay with their friends while providing the benefits of integrated education.

The Limits of Compulsory Public Education

In considering compulsory public education, the distinction between high school adolescents and preadolescents is crucial. Parental expectations of a right to control the upbringing of their children are strongest in the preadolescent years. It is one thing to say that high school children can be forced to attend public high schools and quite another to tell parents that their little first-graders must attend schools run by the state. Preadolescents generally have a substantial need to live in a coherent world.[98] If the value systems of the parents and the school are in conflict, the preadolescent child will be caught in the middle. This could be an extremely difficult situation for the preadolescent child.[99] We know enough about the importance of parental support in the educational process to recognize that such a conflict could be deleterious to the child's educational and emotional development. By contrast, adolescents have begun the process of separating from their parents; they are notoriously skeptical. They have acquired and are acquiring not only critical skills and problem-solving skills,[100] but also greater empathic abilities[101] and increased tolerance.[102] In short, they are ready to be challenged with diverse perspectives.[103]

On the other hand, some might argue that the case for compulsory public schools is even stronger in the preadolescent years. These are the formative years, the years in which children are most easily influenced. Some would say that if you do not get to children in these years, you never will. Of course, the formative years are important, and much that is learned then persists for a lifetime. But adolescents also use their growing cognitive and empathic abilities to reflect upon, adjust, and change their views.[104]

Similarly, although an important goal of public schools is to teach democratic values, private schools meet this need to a substantial degree. Such schools typically address issues of justice from a particular perspective. With some exceptions, there is time enough for the public perspective of justice to be introduced in the adolescent years. In the exceptional cases, either private schools can be regulated to provide the needed perspective or alternative arrangements can be made to educate the children in particular areas. Moreover, to the extent the goal of the state is merely to *expose* children to alternative views, the adolescent years suffice just as well as the preadolescent years. Although the state interests are all present in the preadolescent years, I conclude that the state should not be able to mandate compulsory public education at that time.

Finally, I do not contend that compulsory public high school education should invariably be immune from constitutional attack. The case for compulsory high school education rests to a large extent on the existence of a population more diverse than that which is present in private education.[105] Although a substantial goal of public education is to bring children of all races, classes, and religions together, the flight to the suburbs has often undercut this goal in substantial ways. Certainly, racial diversity has been substantially compromised. Class diversity is often undercut and, in some areas, religious diversity as well. One should not exaggerate the degree of homogeneity in the suburbs, however. Political diversity by American standards is ordinarily present, and in most areas religious backgrounds are diverse as well. Even class diversity in the suburbs is greater than commonly realized. For example, 36 percent of the poor live in the suburbs.[106] Moreover, many school districts are quite diverse, certainly offering more diversity than that afforded to the growing number of children in home schooling.[107] I conclude that the argument for the constitutionality of compulsory public high school education, when pitted against a due process attack, must overcome a defense that in particular areas private school options are more diverse than the public schools.[108]

The constitutional case against compulsory high school public education, however, is not confined to the right of parents and guardians to direct the upbringing of their children. Claims of freedom of speech and association, of equality, and of free exercise of religion also need to be considered.

Freedom of Speech and Association

The freedom of speech argument can be framed in two ways. First, parents may want to send their adolescent child to the Hill Military Academy because they are ideologically opposed to the messages communicated by the school district. The parents might believe in strong allegiance to authority and might be committed to unswerving and uncritical patriotism. Let us suppose that they are right in thinking such values are promoted by the particular military academy. Second, parents may claim that they have an unqualified right to speak to their children or that they have a right to select the agents who will speak to their children.[109]

The freedom of association argument is similar. It claims a right of family association. It extols the virtues that follow from being a part of an intimate association of the like-minded. Included in this might be a sense of comfort and security, and the concomitant ability to try out new intellectual efforts in an atmosphere of relative safety. Intervention from this perspective intrudes the state into the middle of the family.[110]

Each of these objections, however, depends upon the rights of parents to direct the upbringing of their children. If the parents had no such right, they would have no legal claim against anything the state did to their children. Thus, if the parents' right to direct the upbringing of their children is not absolute, if they have no right to seal their children off from opposing perspectives, then their free speech or association rights are not infringed by compulsory public education.

Yet a different free speech argument does not trade on a personal or natural right of parents to raise their children. Instead, the argument posits that we are better off placing decision-making power in the hands of parents because it will produce diversity and encourage the robust dissent needed in a democratic society.[111] But the easy assumption that diversity yields dissent deserves to be qualified. Despite enormous publicity about the Christian Right, it has been true for most of our history and it remains true today that most conservative Christians believe "My Kingdom is not of this world," and are not active dissenters, at least in the political realm. Similarly, the Amish exhibit dissent, but are not engaged in the political process. Diversity is not an end in itself, though Mark Yudof has rightfully argued that alternatives to public education might employ different methods of education that could influence public schools and vice versa. As an abstract proposition, this makes sense, but the empirical extent of the cross-fertilization is speculative, and the dependence of new pedagogy on private administration is also unclear.[112] Conceding that there is substance to this view, producing such diversity and competition is achieved by compromising not only the interest of the state in democratic education but also the interest of children in being exposed to differing perspectives, which in turn would compromise the cultivation of their imagination and undermine the quality of their dissent.

The Right to a Good Education

Even if children might be compelled to attend public high schools in some circumstances, it might not be constitutionally permissible to require children to attend such schools in all circumstances. This might especially be the case when the public school does not provide a good education, as is certainly true of many public schools. In those circumstances, compulsory public education might well be regarded as constitutionally and morally objectionable.[113] Notice that this argument does not depend on an overbroad conception of parental rights. Indeed, the right claimed in this context is not the right of parents to direct the upbringing of their children; it is the right of children to a good education.

One difficulty with this argument is that of definition. It requires determining the constitutional content of bad education. Assuming that this difficulty can be overcome (as I do), the objection may prove too much. It may violate the Constitution to force children to attend bad schools instead of better private schools, but the maintenance by the state of bad schools should itself be regarded as a violation not only of equality of opportunity, but of the minimum requirements of due process. Allowing children to attend private schools (if their parents can afford it) does not solve the basic constitutional difficulty. All children attending such schools should be afforded a public remedy.

Free Exercise of Religion

Because of the antireligious purpose present in *Pierce*, the legislation as applied to religious schools should also have been invalidated on religious grounds.[114] But suppose that no antireligious purpose is present, and parents who, for example, want to send their children to Catholic schools say that the compulsory school law violates their free exercise of religion. Beyond this argument from personal freedom, there is arguably a group right, the interest of the Catholic religious community. Compulsory public school laws would have an adverse and disproportionate impact on religious schools in general and Catholic schools in particular.

The first question about the personal right set forth is whether it is vulnerable to the retort employed against the liberty right and the freedom of speech and association rights, that is, it seemed unreasonable to maintain that liberty, speech, and association rights were relatively absolute and unqualified throughout the adolescent years of the child.[115] Stephen Carter, no opponent of religious rights, himself questions the scope of the personal religious right: "Compulsory attendance laws bind the parents, but it is the children who are most directly affected. The parents remain free to be Catholic (or anything else) no matter what the state does to the children. In other words, if the children are weaned from the religion of their parents, that does not change the parents' religion."[116] Carter's comments speak to the degree of the religious burden, but they cannot support the position that no burden exists. Parents may maintain their religion even if their children do not; nonetheless, parents may believe they have a religious obligation to raise their children in a particular religious faith, that such an obligation includes sending their children to religious schools, and that compulsory public education would make it impossible to fulfill that obligation.

Compulsory public education, however, would not prevent parents from continuing to educate children in a religious tradition. Indeed, 80 percent of Catholic children do not attend Catholic schools at any point of their elementary or secondary education, yet religious education outside the public schools seems to have been effective.[117] Indeed, only 29 percent of a child's waking hours take place in school.[118] Moreover, the picture of the public school as a space where religion is excluded ignores the thousands of religious clubs in school districts across the country.[119] This is not meant to deny the existence of a free exercise interest but to suggest that the burden has frequently been exaggerated. On the other hand, the interests of the state in exposing children to different perspectives and to an integrated environment are at their highest when the children have previously been educated in a relatively sheltered environment.

Here, again, it seems appropriate to distinguish between the preadolescent and the adolescent years. In the preadolescent years I think the parental upbringing argument, the free speech argument, and the religion arguments interpenetrate. In those years, where children are less independent, parents are particularly entitled to direct the upbringing of their children; moreover, because the tie between parents and children is stronger in the preadolescent years, the concern about children being exposed to ideologies that their parents are attempting to combat is more salient, and this seems especially true of religious views. Even if the impact on the Catholic religion would be insubstantial if all Catholic children could be forced to attend public schools in their elementary years, parents should have a religious right to send their children to religious schools in the preadolescent years.

Such a right should not extend to the adolescent years, where the adverse impact on religion would be less substantial and the state interests greater. With respect to Catholics, the major problem would not be the curriculum. With the exception of the health curriculum, secular public school curricula are unlikely to contradict Catholic doctrine, and to the extent they did, it would be unlikely to undo years of Catholic schooling. Certainly a major cause of loss of faith in the church in the adolescent years is the adolescent's confrontation with Catholic views on nonmarital sexuality.[120] That confrontation will take place whether the child attends Catholic or non-Catholic schools. For many children, if the church's position on sexuality is emphasized in the private school, the prospects for long-term allegiance to the church might in fact diminish.[121]

The incursion on religion of compulsory public education is somewhat greater for fundamentalist Christians. Some fundamentalist Christians object to their children interacting with nonfundamentalists; some object to teaching critical thinking and to other aspects of the curriculum. Their objections could be handled by excusing their children from some forms of objectionable instruction, though I do not think that is constitutionally required in the high school years.[122] But, as I suggested in chapter 4, I see no room for compromise with their insistence on separating their children on grounds of intolerance, or depriving their child of vital information, or for depriving their child of critical thinking skills, skills that are necessary for democratic citizenship and for adaptability in a changing marketplace.[123] Parents have no general right to monopolize their children through the adolescent years, even when they wish to do so for religious reasons. A religious desire to deny the basic interests of children by attempting to rob them of the ability to choose between ways of life should not be enforced by the law.[124]

On this principle, the Amish should have lost in their effort to resist compulsory high school education.[125] This conclusion applies particularly strongly to Amish girls who are locked into a patriarchal tradition and, at least, need to be exposed to other options. Once again, compulsory public education would not prevent the child from living in the Amish community while attending school or remaining in it thereafter. Compulsory public education opens doors to a world that the Amish child may or may not choose to enter.[126] Even assuming, however, that such policies would enormously damage the Amish as a group, their freedom of association cannot rightfully be maintained by denying their children an adequate education.[127]

In the end, my position on *Pierce*, in the absence of an antireligious purpose, is that government should ordinarily be permitted to compel children to attend public schools, except that parents should have a right to send their children to private schools in the preadolescent years. This does not mean that compulsory public education is wise or practical policy, however.

Constitutional? Sometimes. Good Public Policy? No.

Government should constitutionally be permitted to compel public high school attendance in many circumstances, but I believe it would be unwise policy. For example, the existence of private schools is financially advantageous to public schools in many areas. Public schools are in a financial crisis that promises to get worse. As the population ages, taxpayer opposition to generous funding of public schools is likely to grow, and higher salaries are needed to attract talented people into a market lacking enough certified teachers. To close the private schools and cast their students into the public schools could be financially catastrophic in many localities.

More important, compulsory high school public education is not a politically practical proposal. There is no constituency for it, and no state or locality anywhere is likely to adopt it. Even if there were a locality that tried to adopt it, strong political reasons counsel against it. If a locality succeeded in imposing compulsory public education against constitutional challenge, conservatives would have a strong vehicle for organizing against the public schools. They already have a strong motivation. Conservatives strongly believe that contemporary society is in serious decay, and, given their belief system, it is not surprising that they do. At least since the inception of the distribution of birth control pills in 1960, gender roles and sexuality practices have profoundly changed. Shortly after the pill became available, childbirths dropped significantly.[128] Women entered college and the workforce in vastly accelerated numbers.[129] Premarital sex rose significantly.[130] The number of unmarried couples who lived together increased eightfold in the 1960s.[131] The 1960s brought a sea change in attitudes toward sex, gender roles, and the family that flies in the face of traditional religious values.[132] If change challenged the faith of many, it strengthened the faith of others.[133] Traditional conservatives look on the current social scene with horror, and it is not surprising that they believe a greater emphasis on religion is necessary. It is understandable that they would regard the Supreme Court's decision in the 1960s authorizing the removal of prayer in the schools with dismay, that they would press for vouchers, and that they would participate in a movement for home schooling. A decision upholding compulsory public education would unleash a firestorm. Whether or not it is appropriate to take such consequences into account as a constitutional matter, it is surely appropriate to consider them as a policy matter. Although I believe that compulsory public high school education would be sometimes be desirable in the absence of such a backlash, the prospect of such a political reaction makes a proposal for compulsory public education a noble thought experiment, but a political nonstarter.

Chapter 6

Vouchers

IN THE LAST CHAPTER I ARGUED that the idea of compulsory public education was a noble thought experiment, but a political nonstarter. Thought
experiments are not worthless, however. Recognition of the strong purposes supporting public education and the interests of children should
ordinarily lead us to a presumption *against* vouchers, at least in the high
school years. Although the system of educational organization in the
United States does not compel attendance at public schools, it does lever-
age attendance in powerful ways. Indeed, as I have suggested, nearly 90
percent of American children are educated in public schools. Simply put,
the United States has a predominantly socialized system of education, and
the idea of dismantling that system is not popular. We should understand
that it would be possible to compel education without having state-run
schools. It would also be possible, while compelling education, to refuse
to pay for the education of rich and middle-class children.[1] Not even the
Republicans favor any such approach. The live issue is whether the state
should pay tuition for children in the form of vouchers to attend private
schools, including religious schools. Some argue that vouchers are constitutionally required; others maintain that they are not constitutionally permitted for religious schools.

Given the case for public education I have already outlined, my contention is that vouchers at the high school level should generally be resisted. The advantages of public education for children and the extent to
which its quality is enhanced by widespread attendance is underappreciated. But this does not directly address the constitutional issues, and it
leaves open the issue of preadolescents. Below I consider the argument
that vouchers should be constitutionally required, the argument for
vouchers in the preadolescent years, and the Establishment Clause questions raised by vouchers to religious schools.

Are Vouchers Constitutionally Required?

Some argue that vouchers are constitutionally required because the public
schools themselves violate the Establishment Clause. The claim is that the
public schools adopt the religion of secular humanism, and that this turns

children away from more traditional religions. As we have already seen, the latter claim is unsupportable. Beyond that argument, some argue that if *Pierce* was properly decided, then vouchers should be constitutionally required.[2] For example, the argument goes that if progressives believe that the right to an abortion entails the conclusion that states may not subsidize childbirth without subsidizing abortions, then the right of parents to send children to private schools entails the judgment that the state may not subsidize public education without subsidizing private education.[3] It is hard to justify denying poor women the funds to secure an abortion, particularly when abortion is generally permitted. But there is a difference between criminalizing abortion and refusing to subsidize it. One is a negative liberty simply requiring the state to stay out; the other is a positive liberty demanding resources from the state. The state may not criminalize the making of a movie, but it need not subsidize everyone who wants to make one.[4]

The case for subsidizing abortions need not deny the distinction between negative and positive liberty, and that case need not lead to support of vouchers.[5] The case for subsidizing abortions best rests upon the assumption that all people have a right to the resources that meet their basic needs: food, clothing, child care, housing, employment, a good education, and medical care, including abortions.[6] But the ability to send a child to private schools is not a basic need[7] unless the public schools are failing and will not be fixed, and it is the case that poor children's education overall will be improved by the existence of vouchers. In those circumstances, it should be especially troublesome for progressives when rich people have a constitutional right to send their children to private schools, but poor people do not have an effective right to do so. Even in those circumstances, however, it does not necessarily follow that the solution should come in the form of vouchers any more than the right to food necessitates food stamps. The solution may simply be to provide the poor with sufficient income to permit them to secure adequate food, clothing, child care, housing, and the rest of it, including the ability to send their children to private schools. Indeed, progressive principles mandate even greater redistribution.[8]

Wise Policy for Preadolescents?

Although vouchers in most circumstances should be resisted for adolescents, the question of vouchers for preadolescents is more difficult.[9] A substantial part of the difficulty is that the evidence of the academic impact of vouchers is not easy to untangle. Some scholars maintain that vouchers yield significant academic benefits for children,[10] particularly for disadvantaged children.[11] Others maintain that there is no substantial evidence to support this contention.[12] In particular, they typically argue that the measurement problems are formidable. For example, Jeffrey Henig maintains that:

> The thorniest problem plaguing efforts to empirically determine the educational consequences of school choice, however, concerns selection bias. . . . Those who choose to choose likely differ from those who fail to take advantage of choice opportunities, in such factors as motivation, ambition, and capacity. These factors, rather than choice and its consequences, may account for any higher levels of academic achievement that choice students subsequently reveal, and standard statistical controls for family background may not be sufficient to take this into account.[13]

Others concede that there is statistically significant evidence that children attending choice schools show academic gains but contend that the size of the gains is not significant enough to justify policy change.[14] Still others maintain that the evidence of significant gains is largely confined to Catholic schools and that other private schools do not share the successful ingredients that apply in the Catholic school context.[15] Finally, there are grounds to suspect that the present Catholic schools are sufficiently different from prior Catholic schools as to cast doubt on the continuing relevance of the previous studies showing a "Catholic school effect."[16]

My assessment of the studies is that there is good reason to believe that choice students have some academic gains from vouchers and that sometimes these gains are significant, particularly in Catholic schools.[17] At a minimum it seems clear that the parents of choice students are typically pleased with the choice schools.[18] On the other hand, it is not clear whether children overall benefit from vouchers—taking into account the resources lost to the public schools when students leave.[19] If children leaving the public schools are benefited to some extent, but children left behind are damaged, it would be hard to claim that a voucher program was successful.[20] More important, it is not at all clear whether quality claims on behalf of choice students can be sustained as more schools are created to meet the increased demand for choice schools.[21] The extent to which Catholic schools could expand while maintaining quality is unclear.[22]

What is clearly unacceptable is the maintenance of bad public schools in the central cities.[23] Even assuming that vouchers were a part of the answer to this problem, it would seem a major mistake to imagine that it is a panacea. Certainly the unequal distribution of financial resources, the downsizing of the gargantuan urban districts,[24] and the modification of teacher assignment policies need to be addressed in the public schools. Nonetheless, a voucher program with details sensitive to the problems of the students left behind in the public schools might yield academic gains in some circumstances.

Beyond the academic issues, an advantage of vouchers for preadolescents is that attendance at schools with a point of view different from that
of the public schools and more in keeping with the views of the parents
might assist the child in acquiring a secure sense of identity. In addition,
a program of vouchers would promote a diverse marketplace of ideas
developed in settings where like-minded people work together. Assuming
it were available to all, it would afford parents greater opportunities to
educate their children as they think best.

One concern about the voucher alternative is its potential cost.[25] Close
to 10 percent of children currently attend private schools. Although there
are offsetting considerations,[26] providing vouchers for all would increase
the cost of education because government would be paying the costs of
educating substantially more children at a time when dollars are scarce
and when any increase in funding might be put to better use, for example,
for salaries to attract more teachers into the profession. This objection
would have less force if vouchers were confined to the poor or the relatively poor, but, if it were so confined, the identity and diversity advantages of vouchers might reach fewer children.[27]

Another concern relates to the funding of schools that do not adequately promote democratic values. Take, for example, schools that teach
racist ideology. Racist speech is protected under the First Amendment,[28]
but, hopefully, the state could refuse to issue vouchers for schools that
taught racism.[29] Racism is not the only example, however. One might
question whether tax dollars should support the teaching of sexism, homophobia, and various other forms of intolerance. Assuming the absence
of a First Amendment problem in refusing to fund such schools, a political
problem remains. There are grounds to question the political will and the
political skill of the state in its regulation of the content of education. The
state has a sorry record in its regulation of private education.[30] Many
fundamentalist schools have no certified teachers. Instead children are
taught from workbooks with precious little social interaction.[31] A state
interested in not offending a group that knows how to make noise ignores
the failure to adequately educate these children. A similar scandal applies
to some, but by no means all, home schooling, where the state looks the
other way as many children are deprived of an adequate academic and
social education.

An additional concern is that vouchers could aggravate racial segregation in education.[32] Although racial segregation is already a substantial
problem in the United States, racially integrated schools are more prevalent than is commonly appreciated. The standard stereotype pictures
blacks in the central cities and Anglos in surrounding suburbs. But 69
percent of African American students attend schools outside the central
cities, and 44 percent of those enrolled in central city public schools are

neither black nor Hispanic. Nonetheless, one-third of minority children attend segregated schools. Vouchers will aggravate this situation because parents tend to choose schools that are close to home, that do not include a majority of another race,[33] and that are religious.[34] To the extent vouchers offer incentives for new schools to be created, organized churches would have both the motivation and the organizational resources to respond. From an integration perspective this is problematic because churches are notoriously segregated. What Martin Luther King Jr. said many years ago remains true today: the most segregated hour in America is eleven o'clock on Sunday. Millions of children raised in racially segregated churches and families attend racially integrated schools. Vouchers would make the segregation complete for all too many children.[35] Beyond racial segregation (and class segregation),[36] funding for vouchers would obviously enhance religious segregation in the United States, hardly a boon for toleration.

A fourth concern is that vouchers entrenched at the preadolescent level could create a strong political constituency to expand them to the high school level. The analysis I have offered suggests that any such expansion would be bad for children and bad for the promotion of democratic education. Even if the best world included vouchers at the preadolescent level and compulsory or financially leveraged public education at the adolescent level, it might not be possible to have vouchers at the preadolescent level without threatening the system of public education at the adolescent level.

Finally, as I will argue later, any large-scale system of vouchers could entail a significant gamble. Ninety percent of children currently attend public schools, and similar percentages have been the rule for decades. If such attendance plays a strong role in holding a pluralistic society together and promoting civic values, a radical shift in enrollments to less ecumenical schools could aggravate societal tensions in substantial ways. Concerns such as these have prompted even strong proponents of vouchers to call for them only on a limited basis.[37] I remain open to the view that vouchers might be worth trying on a limited basis in particular contexts. Vouchers to religious schools, however, raise independent constitutional questions.

Should Vouchers Be Constitutionally Permitted for Religious Schools?

Assuming that vouchers are appropriate in limited circumstances or are adopted in circumstances that are appropriate, should vouchers to religious schools be permitted under the Establishment Clause?[38] Doctrinal discussion of this issue, however sophisticated it may have been, for years ended up guessing about what Justice O'Connor, the swing vote, was likely to do when the issue was presented.[39] We found out in the landmark case of *Zelman v. Simmons-Harris*, where she joined the five-to-four majority opinion of Chief Justice Rehnquist.[40] The case involved the constitutionality of Ohio's system of providing funds primarily to poor children to attend private schools. The overwhelming majority of recipient families used the funds to send their children to religious schools.[41] The system seemed to present the Court with a hard choice: either accept substantial intrusions on serious Establishment Clause interests or invalidate an important effort to help poor children enmeshed in a failing urban public school system.

For the Court led by Chief Justice Rehnquist, however, it made no difference that the recipients of Cleveland's largesse were poor, nor did it matter that the public schools were in sorry condition.[42] For the chief justice, it was enough that the program was formally neutral with respect to religion[43] and that the choice of which school to attend was a private and independent parental choice, not a decision of the state. As a result of the private choice element, Rehnquist determined that no reasonable observer could believe that religious schools were endorsed by the state. Similarly, Rehnquist found no purpose to advance religion.

Since the Ohio program, at least on its face, was not designed to advance religion over nonreligion or to favor one religion over another, the Court maintained that the program met Establishment Clause standards. As the dissenting justices observed, this form of analysis is too fast; indeed, it is utterly impoverished. *Zelman* can serve as a poster child for the proposition that Establishment Clause analysis has been unduly narrow. The difficulty is that other Establishment Clause values were burdened in *Zelman*. Failing to give them adequate consideration was a naked exercise in constitutional hubris. As I have suggested, the Establishment Clause serves multiple functions: it is a prophylactic measure that protects religious liberty; it stands for equal citizenship without regard to religion; it protects churches from the corrupting influences of the state; it protects the autonomy of the state to protect the public interest; it protects taxpayers from being forced to support religious ideologies to which they are opposed; it promotes religion in the private sphere; and it also protects against the destabilizing influence of having the polity divided along religious lines. Vouchers in Cleveland forced many taxpayers to support religious ideologies that they opposed,[44] had unequal impact, favored one religion in a substantial way,[45] and ignored "the risk that religion can be neutralized, homogenized, and secularized when it participates in governmental programs."[46]

Liberty and Autonomy

It has long been understood that compulsory support of religious instruction by taxation was unlawful under principles of religious freedom. In commenting on state limitations protecting religious freedom in the nineteenth century, Thomas M. Cooley observed that the prohibition on any such funding was nearly universal.[47] Despite this historical pedigree, I do not think this consideration is the heart of the constitutional objection to funding religious schools. Many fellow progressives argue, however (citing James Madison), that taxpayers should not be forced to support religious institutions to which they are opposed because it impinges upon their freedom of conscience.[48] But I have been forced to support wars to which I was religiously opposed without any constitutional recourse. If vouchers were public policy, I would be forced to support some religions I deplore. But if I could be forced to support what I regarded as murder by my government, I do not think it obvious that an alleged right not to support religious education should have a more privileged position.[49] In addition, since when did it become the position of progressives to attach their identity to their money? If the evil of vouchers were harmful to dissenting taxpayers, the appropriate remedy would be refunds, not voucher prohibitions.

Nonetheless, however easy it may be to exaggerate the issue, it seems clear that taxpayer compulsion presents an Establishment Clause concern. People do feel some identity with the uses to which their money is put, and when it is used for uses that contradict their freedom of conscience, that usage is more problematic than uses that present mere policy disagreements. The war example in that respect underscores the point. If my opposition to war is moral, rather than strategic, it takes on a religious dimension. It might be administratively impractical to separate the conscientious from the pragmatic objecting taxpayer, but support for religion presents a brighter line. Taxpayer compulsion then seems to be a legitimate concern.

Even more fundamental, however, is the question whether it is within the appropriate jurisdiction of government to provide funds to religious schools either directly or indirectly by giving the money to parents who then give it to the schools.[50] Liberty is not the paramount issue.

Equality

Vouchers do not constitute a formal violation of the conception of equal citizenship. Nonetheless, a serious equality concern is implicated because vouchers in many, if not most, jurisdictions would have a substantial disproportionate impact in favor of some religions. It is no answer to point to the neutrality of form in which the voucher program might be cast. Politicians are not blind to the impact of a voucher system.

In addition, one can be legitimately concerned that the voucher dispute threatens to corrupt our political debate, corrupt in the sense that illegitimate equality-denying purposes will inevitably be implicated on both sides. Consider this argument: Our children are being socialized by the mass media, socialized into becoming consumers, not citizens, socialized to believe that the good life depends on acquiring a bewildering variety of products. Education in a faith-based tradition is a better way of combating this socialization than the secular emphasis of the public schools. This argument is surely right for many children, but it is inappropriate under the Establishment Clause for the state to advance religion in order to serve even secular ends.[51] Yet there is no way to keep this argument out of the debate over vouchers, and it would be difficult to show that this illegitimate purpose was decisive in the passage of legislation.

There is also no way to keep antireligious considerations out of the debate. Those who think that religion is a security blanket for the superstitious or think that particular religions are crazy or dangerous might balk at vouchers for just these reasons.[52] Nonetheless, some antireligious purposes appropriately play a role in the voucher debate. James Madison argued in his remonstrance that support of all religions would inevitably lead to the support of false religions. From a religious perspective, such support is indefensible. False religions need to be driven from the marketplace on the merits, not artificially supported by governments. To support all religions, preferring none, is to endorse a form of religious relativism. It is odd that proponents of vouchers, who know how to play dark chamber music about the dangers of relativism, should join happy hands singing in favor of a proposal that rings of relativism from start to finish. The Framers took religion seriously; supporting all religions trivializes religious difference. Alternatively, many religious people believe that there are many paths to the same God. But supporting ecumenical religious views over antiecumenical views is obviously not the legal answer. The way out is well known; it's called the Establishment Clause. In any event, anti- and proreligious considerations permeate the voucher debate, but it might be difficult to show that particular religious considerations either caused vouchers to be passed or not to be passed or caused them to be withdrawn or restricted in some way.

Stability

Determining which policies might undermine stability on an ad hoc basis is surely difficult. Nonetheless, the concern that religious divisions can lead to violent conflicts should not be entirely read out of the Establishment Clause. As I discuss in the conclusion of this chapter, it may well be that the religious division in our country has been substantially less violent than that in other countries because of the religious integration of our public schools.[53]

Protecting the Autonomy of Government

Equally important, vouchers abuse the precept that religions should not be able to use the government to further their own sectarian ends. Vouchers threaten a serious form of entanglement. For example, about half of the children who attend private schools are in Catholic schools,[54] and those schools exist primarily to maintain or to increase the membership of the church.[55] If vouchers are constitutional, the church would have an interest in lobbying and making campaign contributions to make sure they are enacted, to maintain their existence after enactment, and to affect the nature of the voucher program. Similarly, politicians would have an interest in extracting contributions with respect to the same issues. This just cannot be the kind of relationship between church and state that is appropriate under the Establishment Clause. Of course, churches have lobbied politicians for many decades on issues like poverty, nuclear weapons, civil rights, and abortion. The state inevitably will be involved in issues upon which churches take a stand.[56] But church-state negotiations about the money that will go to help churches propagate theological doctrines in their schools seems quite different.[57] Negotiations about state money for proselytizing purposes involve improper use of the state for religious ends.[58]

Protecting Churches

Such negotiations also risk compromising the independence of churches. Churches play an important role in political debate, and it is important that their moral voices not be silenced or compromised.[59] Yet it is clear from the discussion in chapter 3 that significant compromises have been made by churches seeking to retain government benefits.[60] Issues surrounding the conditions of a voucher program are independently problematic.[61] For example, should a state be able to limit vouchers to schools that do not discriminate on the basis of religion in their admissions policy or that require students to participate in religious exercises against their will?[62] If not, the state would be prevented from assuring that governmentally funded schools operate in accordance with basic principles of equality and freedom.[63] If these conditions were permitted, however, religious schools would be offered a state-backed financial incentive to compromise the religious integrity of their institutions.[64] Similarly, should a restriction that recipients of public funds not be permitted to discriminate on the basis of religion, for example, be applicable to religious schools? If so, freedom of association and religion are both impinged upon. If not, and if a voucher program is extensive, teachers who otherwise would have free access to jobs in the public sector will be denied access to publicly funded positions on the basis of their religion.[65] Could the state require that democratic values be taught at all schools receiving vouchers even when the state's conception of democratic values, for example, a position on gender equality, is counter to the religious beliefs of a school?[66] None of the positions associated with such conditions to voucher schools is attractive[67]—which again suggests that the Framers of the Establishment Clause might have been on to something.

Even without conditions, as Vincent Blasi suggests, a voucher program could shift the priorities and practices of a denomination toward education and away from what it would have otherwise chosen.[68] He also worries that voucher schools might hire popular teachers over the most devoted and skilled teachers in order to compete for students and voucher dollars.[69] I would add, as I mentioned before, that any significant expansion of voucher schools might come at the cost of quality.

State Interests

Vouchers to religious schools seem to impinge seriously on important Establishment Clause concerns. Under conventional analysis this would complete the case against them.[70] Interest balancing has ordinarily not been employed in the Establishment Clause context. But interest balancing is frequently employed in the free speech context,[71] and it seems to me that the same arguments commending interest balancing in the free speech context, apply in the Establishment Clause context.[72] There is just no reason to assume that Establishment Clause interests always outweigh the interests on the other side. So despite the Establishment Clause concerns, I would argue that vouchers might nonetheless be upheld if the state were able to show that vouchers promoted a sufficiently substantial interest. What the state would need to show is that the public schools were failing poor children, that measures less restrictive of Establishment Clause values would not be effective, that vouchers would substantially help children overall (or that vouchers offered a reasonable prospect of success), and that some impingement on Establishment Clause values was justified at least for a trial period. I believe that such a showing might be made in some circumstances, but I do not believe the evidence can support any wholesale abandonment of the public schools.

Voucher advocates have typically relied on two lines of argument. One is that public schools fail poor children and that vouchers can alleviate the problem. I have just suggested that we should be sympathetic to such a claim if it can be made out. The other line of argument is that parents have an absolute right to control the values taught to their children and that the public school system necessarily undermines that right.[73] Funding the public schools instead of a full-scale system of vouchers for all parents discriminates against other value systems, or so this argument goes. As I suggested in chapter 3, pluralistic values underlie the Establishment Clause. I believe that maintaining the independence of churches is particularly important in the voucher context. But I also think the interest in stability is particularly important in confronting the radical character of the values argument. In concluding this part, I want to explain why.

Justice Jackson once wrote that if there is any fixed star in our constitutional constellation, it is that no official high or petty can prescribe what shall be orthodox in politics or nationalism.[74] Justice Jackson's rhetoric was formulated in the service of a worthy cause. But in an important sense, Justice Jackson's star does not belong in our constitutional sky. We have a national orthodoxy. The First Amendment is a major part of it along with many other features of our Constitution. People are free to challenge the existence of the First Amendment, of course, and they need not salute the flag, but our schools daily socialize our children into accepting the principles of our Constitution, from the Bill of Rights to the Equal Protection Clause. Our schools celebrate the birthday of Martin Luther King Jr., and in the process they create and nurture what shall be considered orthodox in politics. The irony is that in nurturing the orthodox they nurture dissent. In part, this is because dissent is a major part of our orthodoxy. Moreover, the gap between our constitutional ideals and the country in which we live is stark, and the recognition of that gap promotes dissent. Finally, public school children are exposed to a diversity of perspectives. Such exposure promotes independence, and independence promotes dissent.

Our law reflects this commitment to dissent. Although there is substantial room for improvement, United States law compared with the law of European countries is far more tolerant of speech that criticizes existing customs, habits, traditions, and authorities. Unlike European countries, U.S. law goes so far as to protect the advocacy of illegal action unless it is directed to inciting or producing imminent lawless action and is likely to incite or produce such action. So too, U.S. law protects even grossly negligent defamation of public figures.[75] One might worry that a freewheeling approach to the protection of freedom of speech could produce problems of national instability, particularly in a country as diverse as the

United States. Yet the United States is widely respected for the degree of national stability it has consistently shown in the past century and more.

It is not so everywhere. Religious violence, for example, has plagued Northern Ireland for many years, and the spillover of that violence has plagued England as well. Many reasons might account for the relative stability of the United States, but public schools ought to weigh heavily in the stability balance. It probably makes a difference that 90 percent of U.S. children grow up attending school together in the public schools; and presumably long-range stability in Northern Ireland would be promoted if it were not the case that 94 percent of Catholic and Protestant children attend *separate* schools.[76]

Public schools perform the important task of affirming both community and dissent at the same time. The public school commitment to integrated education recognizes that the tension between these values can be accommodated in a productive way. And that is the heart of why I believe the commitments to dissent and a stable and respectful community should lead us to tilt away from enclaves of separation and toward a strengthened and revitalized system of public education.

Concluding Observations about Part II

Pierce v. Society of Sisters held that young children could not constitutionally be compelled to attend public schools. Chapter 6 concedes that *Pierce* was rightly decided, but argues that *Pierce* should not be extended to adolescents unless the relevant public schools are not diverse or are doing an inadequate job of educating children. The point of this discussion was not to argue for compulsory public education, but rather to argue that there are important interests for children and for the democratic system in maintaining a quality public school system. Those interests, I believe, should overcome any claim that vouchers should be afforded as an alternative to the public school system for any parent who wants it. In recent years voucher proponents have adopted the strategy of pressing for vouchers, not generally, but in circumstances where poor children are not getting a good education in the public schools. Their view is that they can attract a broader constituency for their cause in these circumstances, and, of course, they generally care about poor children. This approach has led to some success.[77] In this chapter, I argue that it is important to examine the empirical evidence of the educational effects on poor children overall. This is a contentious area, but I find the evidence mixed. I also argue that the Court once again wrongly privileged formal equality at the expense of the multiplicity of Establishment Clause values that I outlined in chapter 3. Nonetheless, I believe that the advantages to poor children need to be *weighed* against the Establishment Clause values in coming to a conclusion. Religious liberals bear a strong moral obligation to help the poor. Everyone does. Religious liberals also believe in the multiplicity of values underlying the Establishment Clause. If the empirical evidence suggests that poor children would in fact benefit from vouchers, then I might well sacrifice Establishment Clause values at least as an experiment. But I am not sure the evidence shows it, and it certainly was not shown in *Zelman*.

But *Zelman* illustrates an important point. Although there are some judicial questions left to be decided, for the most part, the church-state questions involving vouchers and many other issues will be fought out in democratic politics, *not* in the court system. We are ready, therefore, to confront a central theme of the book. Religious liberalism is more politically attractive than secular liberalism in confronting and engaging the religious Right in American politics. We turn now from the constitutional framework of the religion clauses to the politics of church-state relations. As we will see, however, the law and politics of church-state relations are not sealed off from each other. To a large degree they interpenetrate.

Part Three _____

RELIGION AND PROGRESSIVE POLITICS

Chapter 7 _____

Religion and Progressive Politics

PARTS I AND II OF THIS BOOK have largely focused on the constitutional aspects of church-state relations. But issues regarding church-state relations are not confined to courts. All levels of government regularly make decisions about how they should interact with religion and religious institutions. Whether government should put up a religious symbol in the town square, whether it should provide financial aid to a religious institution, and how it should deal with religion in the schools are questions asked and decided thousands of times each year in state and municipalities across the country. Some of the same questions are confronted in federal agencies and the Congress itself. To some extent, decisions of the courts limit what governments can do, but considerable room is left for discretion. Even if government need not provide a religious exception to a generally applicable law or regulation, it is permitted to do so. Even if government is permitted to have a display that includes religious symbols, it is not required to do so. Even if government is permitted to aid religious institutions in some way, it is ordinarily not constitutionally required to do so. What government decides to do on matters such as these is in the domain of politics, not of law.

Nonetheless, the arguments made in courts also have power in the political process. All of the arguments made in Parts I and II are admissible in the political process. It may be that the arguments for religious liberty made in *Employment Division v. Smith* did not impress the Supreme Court, but they did impress the State of Oregon, and an exception was crafted. The Court has accepted some displays including religious symbols, but it is still possible, for example, to argue in the political process that such displays violate principles of religious equality and are bad for religion.

Although all of the arguments made in Parts I and II can be made in the political process (though binding court decisions cannot be contradicted), the political process is not confined to arguments that can be made in a court of law. Theological arguments have no traction in a court of law, but religious conservatives have regularly and too often effectively introduced theological arguments into the political process. By *religious conservatives*, whom I use interchangeably with the *religious Right*, I refer to those who belong to theologically conservative religious traditions *and* entertain politically conservative views.[1] It would be a mistake to equate conservative politics with theologically conservative religious traditions. As Andrew Greeley and Michael Hout explain, "The political dissimilarity of religiously conservative black and white Americans calls into question the equation of biblical Christianity and conservative politics."[2] Indeed, slightly less than a majority of those in theologically conservative religious traditions describe themselves as politically conservative.[3] Nonetheless, the religious Right maintains a disturbing presence in the legislative, executive, and judicial branches of the federal government and in local and state governments across the country.

This rise in power of the religious Right over the past quarter century has both frightened and energized the Left. Indeed, in recent years the dominant media picture of the relationship between religion and the Left has been one of hostility, estrangement, and suspicion. In fact, the hostility of a significant part of the Left to religion is of long standing. It includes Voltaire's view that the "church was the implacable enemy of progress, decency, humanity, and rationality"[4] and Marx's dismissal of religion as the opium of the people.[5] This tradition continued in Richard Rorty's hope that institutionalized religion would eventually disappear.[6] And it persists in more muffled tones with many of those who argue that religious arguments do not belong in public life.[7]

I maintain that the commitment to such views, however, is politically naive. There are no signs that religion is about to disappear in the United States or that religious believers are going to withdraw from politics. Indeed, the overwhelming majority of citizens *are* religious believers[8] whose politics range across the political spectrum.[9] It is obviously a mistake to *equate* religion with conservative politics. As I observed in the introduction, the religious Left is almost the same size as the religious Right.

In this part of the book, I aim to make good on the claim that the religious Left is better equipped to engage with or to combat religious conservatism than is the secular Left. I particularly take issue with those secular liberals who argue that religious arguments do not belong in public life. The problem with religious conservatives in my view is not that they participate in the political process. The problem is their politics and their theology. Indeed the two run together. If religious Americans are politically motivated by theology, then it is important to talk about theology in politics. It is important to combat bad theology with good theology. Moreover, it is important to identify the circumstances in which the Left and the religious Right can forge common ground. The secular Left is for the most part poorly equipped to talk about theology or to address religious sensibilities. Instead of participating in dreams of a country without religion, the secular Left needs to join with the religious Left in addressing the world that exists now and will exist in the foreseeable future. Although segments of the secular Left may believe that religion is nothing more than superstition, they need to understand that those beliefs need to be tucked away in private, or, at least, they need to understand that public expressions of religious hostility are politically counterproductive. Instead of dismissing the role of religion in American politics, the secular Left needs to understand that it has much to learn from religious liberalism.

Although I think this is true across a wide range of subjects, I will argue in particular that religious liberalism has a more politically convincing stance on what the relationships should be between religion and the state than does the secular Left. In my view, religious liberalism can give a stronger defense of religious liberty and church-state separation precisely because it does not limit itself to talking about liberty or equality or equal liberty. As was developed in Part I, religious liberalism endorses the pluralistic foundations of the religion clauses. Appealing to a broader range of values than those typically endorsed by secular liberals has greater political traction. As we will see, it is particularly important to argue that tight church-state relations are bad for religion. But in many contexts that argument requires assumptions about what the mission of religious people might be and what does and does not fit within the mission. This requires a theological discussion. Religious liberals welcome that discussion; even if some secular liberals think such discussion is appropriate, they are generally less equipped to engage in it.

In this chapter I first explore the attitudes of significant segments of the secular Left toward religion. For these purposes, I have no interest in those segments of the Left that do not believe in rights, or, more narrowly, do not believe in religious freedom. For my purposes, I use the term *left* to include those liberals, progressives, and radicals who believe in religious freedom and separation of church and state. Although differences among liberals or progressives and radicals are often crucially important on issues like capitalism, the nature of democracy, and how to bring about social change, those differences are unimportant for my topic. I am left free to use the terms *left*, *liberal*, *progressives*, and *radicals* interchangeably.

In my view, the relationship between liberalism and religion has received insufficient attention. To be sure, much literature has explored the role that liberalism would afford religion in democratic life.[10] But it has been too often assumed that there is only one liberalism and that liberalism and religion are inevitable adversaries.[11] Actually, as I show in the next section, there are many liberalisms with many different attitudes toward religion. In the section following that, I explore how these liberalisms approach issues of religious freedom and the relationship between church and state. I am interested in the divisions between secular liberals over

the extent to which religious freedom should be supported and the justifications available to secular liberals for supporting religious freedom. In
exploring these issues, I discuss (1) the government's use of religious symbols; (2) the issue of aid to faith-based organizations; and (3) the issue of
burdens placed on religion by generally applicable regulations. In the section titled "Religious Liberalism," I take a closer look at that outlook,
compare and contrast it with the other forms of secular liberalism, and
explain its understanding of religious freedom and the relationship between church and state, particularly with respect to the same three issues.
After comparing secular and religious liberalism in this way, we will be
prepared to discuss the politics of liberalism in chapter 8.

Secular Liberalism

Secular Liberalism and Attitudes toward Religion

Although secular liberalism stands for freedom of religion and separation
of church and state, it is not monolithic, and it is not necessarily hostile
to religion. Indeed, as I have thought about the relationship between liberalism and religion, I have identified what I will call four families of secular
liberalism. These families are distinguished by their attitudes toward religion. More specifically, they are distinguished by the role that religion
plays or does not play in the *grounding* of their *public* approach to defending liberalism. I do not propose to trace the views of individual liberals. The families I describe are more like ideal types, and they are not
exhaustive. With respect to religion, secular liberalism might be hostile,
indifferent, mixed, or cooperative.

Hostile or antireligious liberalism is sometimes hostile to religion generally or to supernaturalism; it is generally hostile to organized religion.
Indeed, it tends to define itself against religion. It proceeds from the view
that institutional religion has a disreputable record of oppression, persecution, and violence. Hostile liberalism most readily finds a home in
themes that found vigorous expression in the French Enlightenment.[12]
The Enlightenment arose from an antipathy to what it perceived to be
blind adherence to authority, tradition, custom, habit, and faith.[13] It valo-
rized reason, independent thought, autonomy, and scientific method.[14]
Representatives of this strand of liberalism are Voltaire,[15] John Dewey,[16]
and Richard Rorty.[17]

Indifferent liberalism also highlights the importance of reason, independent thought, and autonomy, but defends liberalism without resort to
antireligious premises. In other words, if religion did not exist, indifferent
liberalism's methods of justification would largely be unaffected. Ronald
Dworkin[18] and Joseph Raz[19] belong in this category.

Cooperative liberalism in part stems from a concern about the deep divisions flowing from religion.[20] It regards the pluralism of society as a challenge and an opportunity. It argues that liberalism might be grounded in a variety of possible comprehensive positions, including those that are Kantian, Millian, or religious. The point of cooperative liberalism is that those of secular and religious views would engage in a system of fair cooperation that respected the different views that others hold. At least with respect to constitutional essentials and issues of basic justice, cooperative liberals would argue from *secular* premises[21] that could appeal to those who fit into an overlapping consensus of reasonable comprehensive views. John Rawls in *Political Liberalism* is the leader of this liberal family.[22] Stephen Macedo[23] and Martha Nussbaum[24] also seem to qualify as members. That Rawls designates some religions as "unreasonable"[25] and that Macedo would actively discourage some religions[26] should not blur the fact that their form of liberalism is designed to encourage cooperation between religions and nonreligious perspectives that can commit to arriving at fair terms for a just society.

Mixed liberalism includes a number of attitudes toward religion that do not fit into the other secular families. In other words, different stories could be told about the role of religion in history before leading to some form of secular liberalism, for example, it had and has oppressive and liberating humane aspects; for example, it was useful, but it has outlived its usefulness; for example, it continues to be useful in terms of having influenced modern humane values, but it is unrealistic. John Stuart Mill probably best fits into this category.[27]

A note of emphasis: Although I have designated the hostile, indifferent, mixed, and cooperative families as secular, a religious person could belong to any of these families. To take the most obvious case, by definition a religious person could be a cooperative liberal.[28] Second, a religious person could be an indifferent liberal who believes that liberalism should be justified on secular grounds. One's religion might embrace the view that religious premises should not directly provide a justification for actions that would coerce nonreligious citizens. The concept of a religious neo-Kantian is not oxymoronic.[29] Third, a religious person could be a hostile liberal who believes that institutional religion is harmful and that liberalism should be justified on secular grounds; finally, a mixed liberal might have positive or even mixed views about his or her own religion, and mixed views about other religions. That liberal too might believe that citizens should offer only secular arguments for political conclusions.

The hostile, indifferent, mixed, and cooperative families are *secular* not because you must be an atheist or an agnostic to belong, but because the public justification for liberalism is secular.

Secular Liberals and Government's Relationship with Religion

How do secular liberals approach the questions of government use of
religious symbols, government aid to religious or "faith based" organizations, and freedom of religion? Typically, secular liberals make the same
kinds of arguments in the democratic political forum that they would
make in courts. Indeed, in the democratic political forum, they will typically argue that a proposed government action is itself unconstitutional.
Law and argument in the public forum become inextricably intertwined.
Sometimes a court decision will have foreclosed a claim of illegality, but
they can always argue that the court is wrong about the Constitution.
And they can argue that even if the Constitution permits the government
action, it is bad policy nonetheless.

GOVERNMENT DISPLAY OF RELIGIOUS SYMBOLS

Government display of religious symbols would draw opposition from
each of the four secular families, and they would agree on at least a part
of the rationale. It is no part of the business of the state to take positions
on religious questions. Thus, they would argue that the religion of citizens
or the lack of it should have no bearing on their relationship to the state.[30]
They should not be marked as insiders or outsiders.[31] To place a crèche
in a building that is supposed to stand for the impartial state[32] or to erect
a Ten Commandments monument on state capital grounds[33] is to accord
a privileged status to Christianity in the case of the crèche and to Jews,
Christians, and Muslims in the case of the Ten Commandments.[34] As we
shall see, the case against displays such as these need not be confined to
respect for equality, but religious liberals share that respect.

GOVERNMENT AID TO RELIGIOUS ORGANIZATIONS

The question of government aid to religious organizations is somewhat
more complicated. I want to distinguish here between aid to charitable
religious organizations and aid to religious schools either directly or in the
form of vouchers. Liberals have historically not opposed aid to religious
charities so long as the organizations refrained from discrimination on
the basis of religion with respect to their clients or their employees and
so long as they did not use the funds to present a religious message. Thus,
Catholic, Jewish, and Lutheran organizations have received billions of
dollars of government money in support of services to the poor.[35] These
organizations do not proselytize or discriminate on the basis of religion
regarding their clients or employees, nor do they use government or private funds to promote a religious message. The poor would be significantly damaged if government sources of funding were taken away. Most

secular liberals are not about to harm the poor with such cuts. The high wall separating church and state supported by secular liberals in and out of court is not so high as to block aid of that sort.[36]

On the other hand, there are other legitimate concerns. In many, perhaps most, circumstances, there may be a substantive equality concern that one religion in particular is benefiting from a subsidy program[37] or a concern that some charities are not doing a good job.[38] But neither of these objections, however well founded, is a theoretical objection to funding in general. They depend upon the facts on the ground, though the interpretation of those facts may be influenced by one's attitudes toward religion.[39]

By contrast, secular liberals argue that neither the Constitution nor the citizenry should tolerate the use of government funds to promote a religious message. Thus most secular liberals are not opposed to aid for soup kitchens managed by religious organizations or to religious hospitals, but they firmly oppose aid to religious organizations that dispense family-planning advice. The idea is that food and medical care are not religious, but family-planning advice by a religious organization is inescapably imbued with religious content. This opposition to government aid promoting religion also underwrites the opposition of secular liberals to direct aid or educational vouchers for religious schools as well. As John DiIulio helpfully puts it, there is a distinction to be made between faith-*based* organizations and faith-*saturated* organizations. Aid to the former should be permissible; aid to the latter should not.[40]

Liberals who support aid in some circumstances to faith-saturated organizations might do so for either or both of two considerations.[41] First, the state offers secular education for free, but insists that religious education should be paid with private funds; an egalitarian could argue that this stacks the deck in favor of one perspective over another. Second, secular liberals have historic commitments to combating poverty. They might in a nonideal world weigh the benefits to the poor of voucher funding or direct funding to faith-saturated organizations and conclude that those benefits outweigh the concrete harm flowing from the infringement on the principle of separating church from state. Most secular liberals, however, would not engage in such a weighing process. They believe that the principle of separation of church and state should not be subject to utilitarian balancing and that faith-saturated organizations should not receive a dime of federal or state funds.

Religious Freedom

Secular liberals generally favor more religious freedom than is guaranteed under current law. In chapter 2 we discussed the most important modern case denying the free exercise of religion. *Employment Division v. Smith*[42] held that generally applicable statutes that burden religion are constitutional unless they were intended to burden religion or burdened other constitutional rights as well. Although the overwhelming majority of secular liberals would protect religious liberty in *Smith*,[43] some might not.[44]

Secular liberals generally favor free exercise of religion without thinking religion is special. Secular liberals generally believe that the state should be neutral toward most conceptions of the good life.[45] Religion would be protected under this view, not because it was in any way special, but because it was a conception of the good life.[46] This has implications regarding the question of legislatively enacted religious exemptions from nondiscriminatory laws or accommodations with respect to burdens on the exercise of religion not otherwise required under the Constitution.[47] Such exemptions or accommodations from this perspective would generally be problematic on equality grounds.[48] One can imagine a hostile liberal contending that religion deserves no special treatment, that the burden on religion occurred as the result of a generally applicable law, and that if a religious person violates the law, he or she should accept the consequences.[49] Indeed, John Locke, who clearly was not hostile to religion,[50] maintained that the magistrates acted within their authority when they enacted generally applicable laws burdening religious practice.[51]

Nonetheless, secular liberals are largely opposed to the *Smith* decision, and the grounds are various. One possibility is to recognize that in some cases the affording of religious exemptions might be necessary in order to ensure stability. This, of course, would depend upon the context, but it is an argument that would appeal even to those who are hostile to religion. For many of them, a primary purpose of religious protection is to prevent the instability that follows in the wake of passionately held views.[52] On the other hand, one might wonder in *Smith* whether Native Americans were a significant threat to stability.[53] Perhaps, however, this is the wrong level of abstraction. Perhaps it is wrong to look at the particular threat of any individual group and right to be generally concerned in a post-9/11 era that restrictions on religion can lead to violent reaction.

A secular liberal might also argue that the formalism of the *Smith* decision did not appropriately implement the value of equality. It could be argued that the actors who put the state action into place in *Smith* did so without proper regard for the concerns of the religion involved even if they had no hostile purpose. A test for this type of discrimination might be to ask whether the law in question would have passed if it burdened a religious majority in the same way. This is the approach taken by Christopher Eisgruber and Lawrence Sager.[54] It does not value religion over other forms of the good life,[55] but it can lead to robust protection for the free exercise of religion.

Finally, it might be thought especially cruel to require someone to act or not to act when her conscience or sense of moral obligation demands otherwise.[56] The argument could be that such an approach does not assume that one form of the good life is better than another. Rather it assumes that some impingements on lives are worse than others. Indeed, one could think that a particular religion was preposterous while thinking that a burden imposed by law was especially harsh in individual cases. To be sure, from a secular perspective, one could not distinguish religious invocations of conscience from nonreligious invocations of conscience, but religious freedom would be protected nonetheless.[57]

Some secular liberals, especially hostile liberals, however, might reject this whole line of argument. They might believe that the religious objector is simply another example of a person with expensive tastes who need not be catered to.[58] Or they might think that the privileging of claims of conscience over other preferences in fact unfairly favors one version of the good life over another.[59] In one sense this would be an odd position for most secular liberalisms to take. Secular liberalisms are typically and unmistakably moral theories with moral premises. But they balk at permitting the state to promote particular moral theories. Despite all this, secular liberalisms frequently find room to recognize the particular force of claims of conscience.[60] Indeed, typically because of respect for freedom of conscience, many secular liberals regard freedom of religion as an important basic liberty.[61]

That said, secular liberalism's treatment of religion does not entirely add up. It is reasonable to maintain that impositions on conscience are particularly burdensome, so that religious freedom needs protection. But it is important to notice that protection from that perspective does not mean that religion is valuable. Secular liberalism (whatever the private views of its adherents) ordinarily does not regard religion as especially valuable. Religion is simply one form of the good life or bad life, one form of autonomous choice, one exercise of liberty, basic or otherwise, that deserves to be respected. But this leads to the question why religion would be singled out for special treatment in the Establishment Clause. From the perspective of secular liberals the state should be barred from expressing a position on the good life generally, not just expressing views on religion. Of course, it is important to avoid the marking of outsiders and insiders on the basis of religion, but secular liberals have little basis in principle to worry more about religious outsider status than about outsider status based on other commitments to particular forms of the good life.[62] This criticism naturally flows from the secular liberal idea that freedom of religion is encased in a larger freedom of liberty, not a special right.[63]

On the other hand, the secular liberal might argue that religion, like race and gender, for example, has been a long-standing source of indefensible discrimination. If government cannot endorse white superiority without violating our constitutional conceptions of equality, so too, it cannot endorse a particular religious denomination without violating the Establishment Clause. On this understanding, however, the Establishment Clause is simply an instance of implementing our constitutional commitment to equality. If religion is to be treated equally, however, one might regard aid to religious churches and schools that is used to promote religious messages to be unproblematic (so long as it is part of a program that does not discriminate against nonreligious organizations). Yet most secular liberals balk against any such aid. They want religion to be treated equally in some respects, but not others.[64]

Secular liberals often fear violent struggles over capture of the state by one religion over another. But the fear that the use of religious symbols by the state such as the crèche in Allegheny County or numerous other uses of religious symbols by the state could trigger violence seems excessively fearful. Secular liberals might claim that the Establishment Clause protects the autonomy of the state against religious control. Hostile liberals would be comfortable in making this claim, but most secular liberals are not committed in political theory to a hostile stance toward religion. Cooperative liberals might fear that the autonomy of the state would be compromised if controlled by a comprehensive vision, at least on some issues, but from this perspective the Establishment Clause is underinclusive. By the lights of the cooperative liberal, it should be concerned about the capture of the state by any comprehensive vision.[65]

In the absence of legitimate stability concerns, secular liberalism has a hard time explaining why religion alone is subject to an Establishment Clause. If equality is the only basis for the Establishment Clause, if free exercise is guaranteed, and if religion is simply one of many forms of equal liberty, what is the justification for singling out religion as one of the rare types of speech or activity in which government cannot engage? I do not think secular liberalism has a simple answer to this question.[66] Of course, the secular liberal could maintain that values like liberty, equality, and stability coincide in religion in a special way. I think there might be something to this response, but there is more to the Establishment Clause story.

Religious Liberalism

Religious Liberalism Described

Although the four other families of liberalism justify conclusions from *secular* premises,[67] religious liberalism, simply put, reaches liberal conclusions from *religious* premises. In this respect, it is obviously distinguishable from hostile, indifferent, or mixed liberalism. The relationship between religious liberalism and cooperative liberalism is somewhat more complicated. Like cooperative liberals, religious liberals are comfortable with the understanding that many who endorse free exercise of religion and who reject tight relations between religion and the state might arrive at their conclusions from perspectives differing from their own. And like some cooperative liberals, religious liberals arrive at their conclusions from religious premises. But cooperative liberals who are religious do not *justify* public policies on the basis of religious premises. Rather, in a search for "public reason," cooperative liberals look for premises that are deeply rooted in the culture and widely shared. Religious liberals share this vision in a limited way. Religious liberalism does not believe that *government* can properly give religious arguments to justify public policy. It does not believe that courts can give religious arguments. And it does not believe that the Constitution should be interpreted by judges to be rooted in religious doctrine. Religious liberalism respects other comprehensive visions, and it thinks in the interest of equality that the Constitution should be understood as leaving its foundations open. Religious and nonreligious citizens should be free to trace their constitutional beliefs to a variety of comprehensive views. Nothing would be gained by a constitutional ruling that the Constitution presupposes a Supreme Being. Religious liberals are free to think that rights are best understood as proceeding from a Supreme Being, but those who do not believe in a Supreme Being should be free to trace their assessment of the best justification of constitutional rights to a different comprehensive view. In this respect, religious liberals and cooperative liberals share common ground.

Nonetheless, as I have argued, the Constitution favors religion. Voltaire favored religion among the masses for pragmatic reasons. Religious liberals favor religion for religious reasons. The Constitution protects religion because it is valuable. Many cooperative liberals could not go along that route. In addition, religious liberalism has a more expansive conception of the role of religion in democratic life than is entertained by cooperative liberals. To be sure, as I have just said, religious liberals do not believe that *government* may give religious arguments to justify public policy. But they also do not believe it follows from this that *citizens* must refrain from giving religious arguments in the public square. All that follows is that such religious arguments must be translated by someone into secular arguments if they are to officially ground public policy. Recall that I argued that the best constitutional interpretation of the religion clauses was for the most part the framework that religious liberals could endorse. Although I have argued that theological arguments do not belong in courts, unlike secular liberals, religious liberals make theological arguments in democratic life that they would not make in courts. I will soon discuss aspects of that theology in relationship to church-state issues.

Although religious liberalism can be distinguished from the families of secular liberalism, I should stress that it is not monolithic. Religious liberalism might be represented by John Locke[68] or, in more modern times, Michael Lerner,[69] Joan Chittister,[70] Dorothy Day,[71] Richard Rohr,[72] Barry Linn,[73] Charles Taylor,[74] and in many respects Jim Wallis[75] and Ronald J. Sider.[76] It might also include Martin Luther King,[77] liberation theology,[78] and much of African American religious thought.[79] It could include much of Catholic social thought,[80] and dissenting Catholic moral theologians like Charles Curran.[81] This is a heterogeneous group, but religious premises ground the thinking of millions of citizens regarding liberal attitudes on civil rights, distributive justice, moral limits regarding war, and duties owed to the natural environment. They also ground the case for religious liberty and separation of church and state.

Religious Liberalism and Government's Relationship with Religion

Religious liberalism's approach to religious liberty issues overlaps those of the secular liberals. It too can be concerned about instability and discrimination. But it does not view religious practice to be simply one of many forms of the good life. It regards religious liberty to be particularly valuable, although it need not endorse particular practices that it believes should be protected.[82] This does not mean that religious liberals believe that all religious practices should be protected. Rather the claim would be that freedom of religion should be interpreted broadly: that religious burdens imposed even by nondiscriminatory laws be scrutinized with special care and that the state should intervene to require religious accommodations for those burdened by nongovernmental action.

With respect to the connections between religion and the state, religious liberalism goes beyond the concerns of liberty, equality and stability. Religious liberalism agrees that separation of church and state furthers liberty and equality and promotes stability. Unlike secular liberalism, religious liberalism believes that religious liberty is particularly important, and it would protect and separate religion from associations with government on the ground that *tight connections with government are bad for religion.* In this regard, religious liberalism has an explanation for why the Establishment Clause uniquely protects religion and a powerful argument to make in the democratic forum. Religion from the perspective of religious liberalism is not just another lifestyle, and tight connections between church and state get in the way of religion. Secular liberalism either has limited resources to make this contention or, worse, it suggests that the argument should not be made. Thus, the dominant strain of secular liberalism maintains that robust religion in the public square would create a legitimacy deficit.[83] So, against religious conservatives, the dominant strain maintains that it is wrong for them to introduce their theological views in the public sphere. By contrast, religious liberals argue that religious conservatives do no wrong in introducing their views in the public sphere. What is wrong with religious conservatives is the content of their politics and their theology. My view is the politics of religious liberalism are more promising than those of secular liberalism.

Chapter 8

The Politics of Liberalism

WE HAVE JUST DISCUSSED THE various types of secular liberalism and their perspectives on religious liberty and the relationship between church and state as well as the corresponding perspectives of religious liberalism. We are now prepared to discuss the politics of liberalism. In discussing the politics of liberalism, I maintain in the next section that secular liberalism is understandably on the defensive in American politics with respect to questions involving religion. In the section following that, "Public Reason," I contend that the dominant secular liberal understanding of the role of religion in politics is misconceived and politically counterproductive. In the next section, "Religious Liberalism," I develop the argument that religious liberalism has a politically more convincing account of religious freedom and church-state issues than do secular liberals. In the section "Religion and American Party Politics" I apply the arguments I have made to the role of religion in American party politics. In the final section I turn to the importance of religion in grassroots politics and the need for a coalition between the secular and religious Left, and I combat the excessive religious hostility that might interfere with that coalition.

The Relative Political Attractiveness of Secular and Religious Liberalism

Secular Liberalism

Secular liberals are on the defensive in American politics, and the rhetoric involved in cases involving governmental displays of religious symbols are helpful in seeing why that would be the case. In *Van Orden v. Perry*,[1] Justice Breyer maintained that ordering the removal of a government display of the Ten Commandments in the name of the Establishment Clause would show hostility toward religion.[2] In *County of Allegheny v. ACLU*,[3] where the Court ruled that the display of a nativity scene in a county courthouse violated the Establishment Clause, Justice Kennedy insisted that the Court's view of the Establishment Clause reflected an "unjustified hostility"[4] toward religion. Claims of that sort have substantial power in American rhetorical and political life. They pose an especially difficult problem for secular liberals. With respect to hostile liberals, the claim of hostility, at least with respect to organized religion, is quite true. Though antireligious rhetoric employed against a corrupt church has often been politically helpful in the European context, it is less effective in the American context. To be sure, criticism of the religious Right is a powerful organizing tool in the Democratic Party, and many independents are not allies of the religious Right. But there is a substantial political difference between attacking the religious Right and being hostile to organized religion generally. An American politician who announces her hostility to religion, organized or not, is an officeholder forging a quick path to the private sector.

Most hostile liberals, of course, will not put forth their hostility to religion as the basis for removal of a religious display. Like other secular liberals, they will argue that the state should be neutral about the good life. In the American political context, this too will fall on deaf ears. Governmental neutrality toward the good life has never been practiced in the United States. Subsidies for the arts favor one view of the good life over another. Ronald Dworkin offered a hairsplitting set of arguments to the effect that this was not so,[5] but few voters would have been impressed. In addition, public education has consistently disfavored some views of the good life over others.[6] The autonomous choice to make selfish hedonism and masochism the center of one's life may be respected by some forms of secular liberalism, but it would be discouraged in any public school. The idea that government should be neutral toward the good life is not only a political nonstarter, but also would arouse suspicions of religious hostility. Tearing down religious displays in the name of neutrality is likely to be experienced as an act of hostility covered up in neutrality dress. If Martin Luther King's I Have a Dream speech can be placed on a monument, but the Ten Commandments cannot, what is the neutrality explanation? Hostile and indifferent liberals might argue that these remarks do not refute either form of liberalism; indeed they would suggest that the lack of political appeal of either form of liberalism in the United States only shows how far the United States is from being a just society. I do not claim to have refuted either form of liberalism here. I have only tried to maintain that they are not yet politically attractive options in the American context.

By contrast, as I have suggested, religious liberals can effectively argue that religious displays are politically and theologically unsound. Before exploring this, we should consider the objections of secular liberals, particularly those of John Rawls, to this argumentative path.

Public Reason

The doctrine of public reason put forth by cooperative liberals[7] is that those citizens who participate in the public political forum,[8] at least with respect to constitutional essentials and questions of basic justice,[9] should not argue on the basis of comprehensive views,[10] but should instead employ premises that can be shared by all reasonable citizens seeking to establish fair terms of cooperation.[11] Rawls maintained that "[c]entral to the idea of public reason is that it neither criticizes nor attacks any comprehensive doctrine, religious or nonreligious, except insofar as that doctrine is incompatible with the essentials of public reason and a democratic polity."[12] Thus, religious conservatives could be criticized in the public political forum to the extent their doctrine was "incompatible with the essentials of public reason and a democratic polity," but not on the grounds that they employed bad theology.

Rawls never maintained that these restrictions applied with the force of law. They were understood to be a "duty of civility,"[13] a part of our understanding of what it means to be a good and reasonable citizen. In *Political Liberalism*, he said that "the ideal of public reason does hold for citizens when they engage in political advocacy in the public forum."[14]

According to Rawls, the doctrine of public reason implements a form of civic friendship,[15] an ideal of citizenship in which citizens justify fundamental arrangements in ways that others as free and equal can acknowledge as reasonable and rational.[16] Public reason is needed, argues Rawls, to secure legal legitimacy[17] and a stable society.[18] In my view, however, the doctrine of public reason unnecessarily flees from politics.

The heart of the public reason perspective is the claim that a constitution not based on shared premises is illegitimate.[19] To use force against another based on premises that are not shared is thought to violate the respect owed to another fellow citizen. It is not clear why, however. People may disagree about political decisions and operate from different premises while holding enormous respect for those who would have made a different decision. The fact that some persons hold a different comprehensive doctrine than those who have prevailed in politics need not mean that the winners regard the losing comprehensive doctrines as unworthy of respect. Even if they regarded the losing doctrines as unworthy of intellectual respect, this need not mean that they regard the persons who hold such doctrines without respect.[20] Alternatively, it might be argued that the state may not legitimately use force on the basis of premises that a citizen could reasonably reject. It is, however, unclear why citizens should feel more aggrieved about being compelled on the basis of premises they reasonably reject than being compelled on what they might regard as the utterly unreasonable application of reasonable premises.[21] Indeed, setting aside the case of religious premises, it is especially unclear why citizens would feel particularly aggrieved if Kantian or utilitarian premises were employed.[22]

Beyond illegitimacy, cooperative liberals support the public reason doctrine on the ground that it is necessary to assure stability.[23] But is that so? Suppose that a constitutional essential with respect to freedom of speech is decided with explicit resort to Kantian premises or a significant freedom of press issue by explicit reasoning from comprehensive utilitarian premises. Surely such decisions would not risk instability in a country like the United States. Assuming I am correct that the case for ruling out resort to secular comprehensive visions is weak (either on legitimacy or stability grounds), I suspect that what is really driving the doctrine of public reason is fear about the instability effects of religion[24] and that the entire apparatus has been set up with that concern lurking in the background. At the risk of euphemism, it is fair to say that much European history supports such a concern.[25] American history from the abolitionist movement to the Progressive movement to the civil rights movement to the modern religious Right and left, however, is a different story. The exclusion of comprehensive views has never been a part of American history.[26] As I mentioned previously, American free speech doctrine expresses what the Supreme Court has called "our profound national commitment to the principle that debate on public issues should be uninhibited, robust, and wide-open."[27] There is no exception for religious speech either in law or in culture. This history does not reveal the instability that supposedly warrants the exclusion of religion from public reason.[28]

The same point applies to that part of the doctrine of public reason which limits criticism of opposing comprehensive doctrines.[29] Strictly applied, the doctrine would limit the ability of religious liberals to criticize the comprehensive vision of religious conservatives in the public sphere. In part, the point appears to be that such criticism would not show proper respect. But, as I suggested before, any argument from respect would conflate the need to respect persons with a supposed need to respect positions.[30] A Millian can respect a Kantian while disagreeing with his comprehensive views. Moreover, the argument fails to recognize that a Kantian might learn from a Millian who advances her comprehensive views in the public sphere. So too Millians and Kantians might learn from Christians or Jews.[31] Similarly, it would be hard to show that criticism of comprehensive views has been historically excluded from the public forum.

If comprehensive views have routinely been a part of the political public forum, the public reason doctrine certainly does not describe American politics. It certainly does not describe, for example, our public disagreements over abortion, capital punishment, poverty, the environment, or euthanasia.[32] If the point of public reason theory is to design a utopia for an imaginary pluralistic society without any hope of political implementation, then claims of political infeasibility would miss the mark. But the public reason doctrine has been developed with more ambition than that. Can it be held up as a regulative ideal? The problem with this suggestion is that movement toward the ideal would be counterproductive. This conclusion follows from the fact that arguments from comprehensive views have always been part of the public dialogue, and there is no reason to believe that will ever change.[33] To try to take a step toward the utopian public forum by self-censorship of your own comprehensive views will not produce followers from your adversaries; it will simply leave the field open to them.[34] If the religious Right is in the public forum, it needs to be attacked not because it violates the strictures of public reason, but because of its message.[35]

In an attempt to respond to some of these criticisms, Rawls modified his position by expanding the extent to which comprehensive visions might be introduced in the public forum and narrowing the circumstances in which the doctrine of public reason applied. Although comprehensive views could be mentioned only in rare cases in his early writing, Rawls in later writing moved to the broader view that we could "introduce into political discussion at any time our comprehensive doctrine, religious or nonreligious, provided that, in due course, we give properly public reasons to support the principles and public policies our comprehensive doctrine is said to support."[36]

Allowing comprehensive visions to be freely introduced into the public forum certainly responds to the criticism that citizens cannot really understand their fellow citizens without knowing where they are coming from, not to mention that secular citizens may learn something from religious citizens.[37] It also brings the doctrine closer to the realities of American politics.[38] But it does not get close enough. On the Rawls revision, the doctrines are introduced not for persuasive purposes, but merely for informative purposes. But this too is utopian and also cannot serve as a regulatory ideal for the same reasons rehearsed earlier. Religious conservatives are introducing their comprehensive visions into public life for persuasive purposes, not just to tell us where they are coming from. The same is true of religious progressives.[39]

Appraising the modifications Rawls made to the circumstances in which the public reason doctrine should apply is somewhat more complicated. In his later writing, Rawls significantly modified the application of public reason to the citizenry at large. He argued that the public reason doctrine restricted discourse on constitutional essentials and basic questions of justice by judges, government officials, candidates for public office, and their campaign managers "especially in their public oratory, party platforms, and political statements."[40] But citizens on Rawls's later account "fulfill their duty of civility and support the idea of public reason by doing what they can to hold public officials to it."[41] Finally, political discussions on issues of basic justice and constitutional essentials in the background culture, including the media and universities, were not subject to the restrictions of public reason[42] whether or not they were addressed to the public at large.[43]

I would put on the utopian side the insistence that citizens enforce the doctrine of public reason in their voting. This does not happen and will not happen. Also, I very much doubt that a Kantian legislator or a utilitarian legislator would be remotely deterred from saying so in public utterances unless particular political circumstances happened to dictate otherwise. On the other hand, the Establishment Clause may well put limits on what a government legislator can say about religious purposes in some circumstances.[44] Certainly a legislature could not say that it had religious purposes in passing an act (though it could have Kantian purposes), nor could a court responsibly live up to its oath in supporting the Constitution and give religious reasons for a decision.

On the other hand, Rawls's revised views permit opinion formation to take place in civil society. That formation may well be influenced by religion. If Rawls supposed that legislators are going to ignore public opinion because it has been formed by the introduction of religious comprehensive views, he was supposing ideal legislators who for the most part do not exist.

More significant, Rawls's revision permits criticism of comprehensive views in civil society from the print, broadcast, and blog media to the universities, but apparently prohibits such criticism by political leaders and judges. One could quibble over aspects of this, but the main point is that the retreat of Rawls here opens the field to effective criticism of comprehensive views in most aspects of the public forum. For those who think that "[c]entral to the idea of public reason is that it neither criticizes nor attacks any comprehensive doctrine, religious or nonreligious,"[45] it seems that Rawls's revision took the fangs out of this central aspect. In truth, the choice for Rawls was bleak. Argue either for an unrealistic utopia or for a more realistic doctrine with a scope so limited that the vision of a cooperative citizenry was seriously compromised.

It bears emphasizing, however, that religious liberals agree with Rawls that *government* may *not* use religious reasons in justifying legislation (for example, in "whereas" clauses or legislative reports) or judicial decisions even though citizens and legislators may have been influenced by religious reasons.[46] Government must supply fully adequate secular reasons for its actions in order to avoid violating the Establishment Clause.[47] This puts considerable pressure on legislators not to give religious reasons for legislation,[48] though it need not do so for citizens and it puts no special obligation upon citizens to enforce public reason regarding legislators. As Habermas argues, to the extent religious arguments are to have a policy impact in public life, they must ultimately be translated into secular terms.[49] Religious citizens need to be aware of the necessity for this, but they need not themselves engage in the translation.[50]

Despite agreement on the point that government must give secular reasons for its policies, cooperative liberals will balk at giving up on the idea of public reason. It seems for them to assure illegitimacy. But this form of illegitimacy is dwarfed by far more serious forms of injustice. Indeed, injustice is a permanent feature of any large society. Large societies need hierarchies, and those with power are often corrupt or see things in a biased way that operates to their advantage. In addition, power in one hierarchy spills over to another. Money buys political favors. Distributive injustice is rampant. Environmental exploitation to the detriment of future generations is dangerously persistent. Elites have greater access to the media, and have substantial ability to paper over substantial injustice. In very complex ways, the media's financial interest and various aspects of the American election system and its financing restrict the public agenda.

In my view, the doctrine of public reason with its precious conception of respect, its inflated worries of instability, and its narrow emphasis on a particular aspect of legitimacy is a theory at war with the needs of progressive politics. Let me put it in a less inflammatory way. In Rawlsian terms, at least two conditions must be satisfied in order to achieve legitimacy. The limits of public reason must be respected. The principles of justice must be complied with. In my view, neither condition will ever be satisfied, but progress in satisfying the principles of justice is far more important than respecting the limits of public reason. John Rawls came close to acknowledging this in *Political Liberalism* when he observed that it was appropriate for the abolitionists[51] and Martin Luther King[52] to depart from the limits of public reason. Generously read, I think he might be understood to maintain that it was appropriate for the abolitionists and Martin Luther King not only to argue from their comprehensive position, but also against the comprehensive position of their opponents. This concession of Rawls, however, was too limited. By using the examples of slavery and segregation, he encouraged the view that one might depart from public reason only in rare instances. But the extent of injustice and the pervasive departures from public reason in the public realm should make departures from the limits of public reason appropriate whenever it would advance other principles of justice to do so.[53] Second, Rawls argued that the arguments of abolitionists and Martin Luther King were acceptable because they would strengthen adherence to the limits of public reason in the long run.[54] This strikes me as whistling in the dark. Departures from the limits of public reason legitimize further departures from the limits of public reason. If the notion is that limits on public reason will be more understandable when we reach an otherwise just society, I adhere to my view that we will never achieve a just society.

We can do better. But the doctrine of public reason just gets in the way.

A somewhat different argument for restricting religious arguments in religious life appeals to a particular conception of reason rather than to a need for an overlapping consensus arrived at by those with divergent premises. The argument has taken its sharpest focus in relation to traditional Catholics who are said to have surrendered their reason for allegiance to a foreign power, namely the pope.[55] Or, the religious have surrendered their reason to their minister, or the Bible, the Koran, or what have you.[56] Good citizens do not follow orders. They reason for themselves. So the argument goes.

I am not a traditional Catholic, but it seems to me traditional Catholics could respond in a number of ways. First, characterizing the pope as a "foreign power" seems unfair. The pope is a spiritual leader. Yes, he is the head of the Vatican, but American-Vatican foreign relations are not on the radar screen of significant foreign policy concerns. Second, although the pope speaks on moral issues, the pope does not endorse candidates. Indeed, all of the popes taken together have spoken infallibly only on two occasions and neither involved a matter of morals.[57] On the other hand, the Vatican has taken the position that Catholics are obligated to conform their consciences to the *non*infallible moral teachings of the church.[58] So, for example, it would follow that Catholics are obliged to believe (at least as far as possible) the teachings of the church on homosexuality and contraception. To the argument that Catholics have abandoned their reason, traditional Catholics say that they have made the reasoned choice to follow the teachings of the church. From the perspective of citizenship, they might not see the judgment to follow the moral leadership of church leaders to be much different than the choice of citizens to follow the leadership of the Democratic Party or from the choice of some to follow the teachings of the American Medical Association. Citizens follow the teachings of "experts" everyday; moreover, they never were a *tabula rasa*. Their views are profoundly influenced by their socialization, their family, their social interactions, custom, habit, and tradition, not to mention fifteen-second commercials. I am inclined to say that that those Catholics who follow the teachings of the church are not engaged in civic bad manners, though on some issues their politics and theology are open to serious question.

A final objection to the introduction of religious arguments in the public square is that it is futile: Religion is a "conversation stopper."[59] But this claim is also politically inept. It imagines a conversation between an atheist and a religious fundamentalist who invokes the Bible. Unwittingly, it partly plays on the stereotype of an ignorant and stupid atheist who has not read the Bible and would not understand it if he did (somehow it would be "inaccessible").[60] Moreover, it assumes that the fundamentalist stubbornly adheres to a particular interpretation and cannot be moved by argument. I do not wish to deny that there are atheists who have not read the Bible. I would deny that they have some special inability to comprehend what they read. I do not deny that stubborn, close-minded fundamentalists exist in substantial numbers. But the notion that fundamentalists or evangelicals (they are not the same) cannot be persuaded on theological issues is untenable. Indeed, one of the most important changes in American politics involved persuading religious conservatives to abandon a fundamental aspect of religious doctrine.

For most of the last century, millions of conservative Protestants adhered to a strict interpretation of the doctrine of two kingdoms.[61] Believing that the kingdom of God was not of this world, these Protestants stayed out of American politics.[62] But Jerry Falwell and other conservative Christians argued on theological and political grounds that, properly interpreted, the Bible demanded political participation, not political quietism.[63] The face of American politics changed significantly.[64] Indeed, evangelicals have shifted on the very subject of church-state separation. As E. J. Dionne writes, "There was once a time when the separation of church and state was a central commandment of Southern Baptists and nearly all evangelical Protestants. For most of these Protestants, spending even a dime of public money on religious schools or church programs was to assail the founders, destroy religious freedom, and turn God into a servant of the state."[65]

Approximately 90 percent of Americans believe in God.[66] I would guess that the overwhelming majority of them are not theologically sophisticated.[67] Moreover, I would argue that millions of religious people are open-minded on a broad range of subjects. Between 1963 and 1974, for example, the majority position of American Catholics shifted away from that of the Vatican on issues such as whether sex before marriage was always wrong (from 74 percent to 35 percent), whether divorce after marriage is always wrong (from 52 percent to 17 percent), and whether contraception is always wrong (from 56 percent to 16 percent).[68] A large majority of American Catholics reject some Vatican teachings,[69] and by implication, the Vatican's move to the doublespeak position that freedom of conscience means Catholics must submit to Vatican teachings.[70] Indeed, American priests do not slavishly follow Vatican pronouncements. The Vatican, for example, maintains that homosexual relations, masturbation, and artificial birth control are always wrong, but only 56 percent of priests agree with the Vatican's teachings on homosexuality, 28 percent on masturbation, and 25 percent on birth control.[71]

This does not mean that Christians can be easily persuaded to become Jews or vice versa. Even so, there has been a surprising amount of movement toward and away from religious sects in American history. For example Methodists climbed from ninth place among religious groups in 1776 to first place in 1850.[72] But the goal here is far more modest than religious conversion. A wide variety of political issues fit in indeterminate ways in most religious frameworks. They can and do provoke productive dialogue between and among religious traditions. Although Richard Rorty might be conversationally stopped by religious dialogue,[73] religious debate with political implications is a standard feature of American political life. It seems vastly counterintuitive that liberals should refuse to join that dialogue.

Religious Liberalism

Parts of that dialogue are easy. Christian conservatives would have to get up very early in the morning to suggest that wars, let alone unilateral wars, one-quarter of American children living in poverty, corporate materialism and power, the destruction of the environment, and the torture of human beings are consistent with biblical teachings. It is hard to get a message of war, torture, and ignoring the poor out of the Sermon on the Mount. Increasingly, theologically conservative Christians are moving to more progressive positions on peace, poverty, and the environment.[74] What about religion and the state?

On the question of free exercise, religious liberals and religious conservatives share common ground. Indeed, religious liberals are closer to religious conservatives on this issue than to many on the left. *Smith*, after all was an easy case that was wrongly decided. It involved Native Americans ingesting peyote as a part of a religious ceremony. And the Supreme Court held that no religious issue was even implicated. The Left with its historical concern for the plight of minorities has an easy time in opposing *Smith*. But the world of free exercise does not stop with *Smith*, and religious conservatives are more likely to weigh religion heavily than many on the secular Left. In any event, religious liberals and religious conservatives are unlikely to divide over issues of free exercise on a systematic basis.

When confronting the use of religious symbols by government, however, religious liberals share common ground with secular liberals. Outside museums and the like, they believe that liberal principles condemn government's use of religious symbols. They share the view that government sponsorship of religious views unfairly discriminate.[75] In the case of the Ten Commandments, as previously mentioned, such sponsorship violates equality. It does not show appropriate respect[76] for agnostics, atheists, Buddhists,[77] and Hindus.[78] But much of the public is not moved by concern for agnostics, Buddhists, Hindus, and certainly not atheists. Religious liberals advance arguments that are more challenging in a religious society dominated by Christians.

First and foremost, religious liberals believe that government should not be a theologian. It must not tell us what God has to say about any subject.[79] It should not be able to make religion a tool for its own instrumental purposes even if the purposes are noble. Of course, nobility is not guaranteed. To allow religion to be used by government would permit cynical and corrupt politicians to use religion for their own partisan ends while frequently favoring some religions over others. From a Christian theological perspective, religious liberals argue that an evangelical mission is not assisted by the government's use of religious symbols. One might ask: Is there any reason to believe that Christ thought that God should be worshiped *through* the government?[80] One would look hard to find support for that view. In fact, Christ lived as a part of an oppressed minority in the Roman Empire. It would be hard to miss the anti-imperial thrust of the gospel.[81]

The texts ordinarily cited by the religious Right do not make a case for the government's use of religious symbols. It is true that man is given dominion over the earth in Genesis. But that does not speak to the question how that dominion should be exercised. It in no wise requires a reading that "every institution and organ of civil society [be brought] into conformity with God's will."[82] It is true that the gospel instructs Christian followers "to make disciples of all nations, baptizing them in the name of the Father, and of the Son, and of the Holy Spirit," but this hardly means that a *government* is to be baptized as a disciple. These passages do not contradict and cannot be isolated from the anti-imperial thrust of the Christian gospel. It is hard to believe that the gospel stands for the view that Christians should look to government to promulgate a religious message.

Indeed, when government has promoted religious messages in the United States, it has often cheapened religion. Consider again the placing of *In God We Trust* on coins and currency. When constitutional arguments have been made against this placement, the response is that the motto has been drained of religious meaning. I previously argued that *In God We Trust* asserts a religious proposition, but there is no evidence that it has done anything to help religion; and it appears to have turned a meaningful phrase into an empty slogan. Consider again, the nativity scene in the Allegheny County Courthouse. The Court struck it down, but the Court has also ruled that if a nativity scene is accompanied by Santa Claus and the reindeer along with candy canes, it is constitutional. In other words, if it is tacky, it is constitutional. After the *Allegheny County* case, Pittsburgh Steel, whose headquarters are down the street from the county government buildings, put up a crèche on its grounds during the Christmas season. The city put up "crèche parking" signs; the ACLU complained; and the city took the signs down.[83] But there is no constitutional claim to be made against Pittsburgh Steel. Government may not establish religion, but Pittsburgh Steel is not the government.

Nonetheless, religious citizens of all stripes should find it deeply problematic when market actors use religion to sell their products or to gain a more favorable image for their company. And when government gets together with merchants in late November to string Christmas lights all over town transforming a religious holiday into a guilt-ridden consumer fest, when they use Christmas to encourage an already excessively hedonistic, materialist culture, it ought to seem obvious that this is not good for religion.

The same kinds of abuses have been involved in government displays of the Ten Commandment all over the country. In displaying a version of the Ten Commandments the government necessarily plays theologian. For example, in some translations, the Ten Commandments state, "You shall not covet your neighbor's . . . male or female slave . . . , nor anything else that belongs to him."[84] The language is disturbing. It seems to approve property rights in human beings. Governments that post the Ten Commandments typically leave this language out. For example, in the two cases involving the Ten Commandments that reached the Supreme Court, *McCreary County v. American Civil Liberties Union of Kentucky*,[85] and *Van Orden v. Perry*,[86] the displays left this language out.[87] But it seems deeply problematic for the state to decide what religious doctrines to endorse or not or even to engage in a joint enterprise with a private party that has made the doctrinal choice.

Equally serious, when the state displays the Ten Commandments, it must decide which *version* to post. Christians, Jews, and Muslims do not agree on the proper translation, and the different translations can make a difference.[88] For example, the Catholic and most Protestant Bibles say, "Thou [or you] shall not kill."[89] The Torah and the Lutheran Bible say, "You shall not murder."[90] The former version is an inspiration for Christian pacifists. In addition, the very choice of which biblical translation to pick represents a choice between religions. The different translations order the commandments differently, number the commandments differently, and, as we have seen, word the commandments differently. In *McCreary* and *Van Orden* the displays said, "Thou shalt not kill," siding with most Protestants and Catholics against Jews and Lutherans. In *McCreary* and *Van Orden* the wording of the Ten Commandments prohibited the making of graven images, a matter of dispute between Catholics and most Protestants that lay near the heart of the Reformation.[91] Other governments may make different choices, but religious liberalism would argue that governments should not be making these choices in the first place: not just because the choices deny equality, but because politicians are poor candidates to be good theologians or to help religion.

Moreover, under the current law of religious displays, government may not have a religious purpose. But the purpose of putting up the Ten Commandments is typically religious. This leads government lawyers to try to conceal the true purpose of their clients.[92] But religion is not served by association with lawyers' sleights of hand. Moreover, it is not clear how a government-scripted abridged version of the Ten Commandments serves a religious purpose that a group need care about. In addition, it is hard to believe that the posting of an abridged version of the Ten Commandments in a courthouse actually influences moral behavior. What it can do is trigger resentment in those groups excluded by the language. This too is not a religious advance.

The record in the *Van Orden* case also shows the kinds of behavior that should worry religious citizens when government puts up a religious display such as the Ten Commandments. The monument in that case had been donated to the state more than forty years earlier by the Fraternal Order of Eagles. It contained the text of the Ten Commandments with two Stars of David below it and the superimposed Greek letters chi and rho, which represent Christ, together with a statement indicating that the monument had been donated to the state by the Eagles.

Judge E. J. Ruegemer, a Minnesota juvenile court judge and chairman of the Eagles National Commission on Youth Guidance, initially came up with the idea of distributing paper copies of the Ten Commandments after encountering a juvenile offender who had never heard of them. The Eagles themselves required a belief in God as a condition of membership. Cecil B. DeMille, who at the time was filming the movie called the Ten Commandments, heard of this and joined with the Eagles to produce the granite monolith in front of the Texas capital and others elsewhere.

Van Orden seems to present an unsatisfactory mix of religious and secular motives. The Eagles wished to combat juvenile delinquency not only by using religion for secular ends, but also by using the state to participate in their program of religious evangelism.[93] Cecil B. DeMille's motives may have been exactly the same, but it surely occurred to this astute businessman and showman, if it were not his primary motivation, that promoting memorials to the Ten Commandments promoted his film. It must have also occurred to the politicians who approved the memorial that the use of religious symbols might improve their political appeal. It cannot be good for religion for its symbols to be used instrumentally for commercial and political gain.[94] Even if crass motivation were not present, however, religions that employ the state for evangelistic purposes risk dependency and backlash.[95]

These are among the concerns that give religious liberals pause about financial aid to religious organizations. Those concerns are embedded in liberal theology. One of the recurring theological disputes in the Christian tradition (the tradition that dominates in the United States) concerns the relationship between God's kingdom and this world. One approach is to regard the world as evil, as something from which to withdraw. This approach emphasizes God's kingdom as something to come in the next life. From this perspective evangelizing and proselytizing are of primary importance. The liberal Christian approach affirms the coming kingdom, but emphasizes the importance of establishing God's kingdom "on earth as it is in heaven." Like the tradition of the Jewish prophets, this approach emphasizes the plight of the oppressed and the poor. It maintains that all are to be treated with the respect owed to those made in the image of God. Moreover, leaving aside the question of whether there could ever be a just war, the liberal approach is to bring about God's kingdom on earth through peaceful means, not by force. On this account a major mission of the church is to offer a prophetic voice against injustice.[96]

From the perspective of the Left, there is much injustice to be found. The United States is a superpower. It exercises extraordinary military and financial dominion.[97] It has supported dictatorships and overthrown democratically elected regimes. It has used torture and killed civilians in order to achieve its ends. It has exploited poor countries to support vast inequalities of wealth.[98] To be sure, state and local governments are not tainted with this foreign policy. But, with the federal government, they collectively preside over a country where the poor get poorer, where millions are denied health care, and where perilous ecological damage is tolerated to the detriment of the country and the world. In the midst of this, wealthy business corporations exercise political power in ways that threaten the legitimacy of the democratic process.

Of course, many would disagree with my characterization of the American government. It would hardly appeal to moderates. But few would deny that those in power often abuse it and that they often believe that the common good is their own good. Moreover, it should be recognized that the conservatives have their own story to tell about the injustices associated with American society, a story quite different from that of the Left. Whether the story of injustice comes from the Left or the Right, however, in the absence of an exclusive focus on the next world, it is easy to maintain that the prophetic tradition is a religious responsibility.

The worry for religious liberals is that financial aid to religious organizations will compromise the prophetic voice of the church. There is certainly no reason to believe that Christ could accept the compromise of spiritual integrity in order to receive funding for evangelical purposes or for charitable works. To the extent that vouchers or other forms of financial aid encourage or require churches to trim their prophetic sails, the biblical message seems clear. Christ stood for integrity, not feeding at the trough. The Reformation is a sober reminder of what happens when a church moves from authenticity to corruption. From a biblical perspective and our historical experience, the prospect of maintaining a prophetic stance while maintaining cozy connections between religion and the state is not promising.[99]

As was discussed in chapter 3, years of European experience are disturbing in this regard. The Catholic Church worked hard to secure privileges and funding in southern European countries. But it is hard to believe that the Catholic Church, for example, was helped by its ties with corrupt kings, with Vichy France, Franco, Salazar, and Mussolini. This not only interfered with the kind of witnessing that was called for.[100] It among other things put the church on the wrong side of history in the eyes of millions of Europeans. From the perspective of religious liberals, the church wrongly privileged its evangelical mission over its social justice mission. Instead of trying to bring the kingdom of God to earth, the church sacrificed its integrity in order to secure state funding and privileges for evangelical purposes. Those lessons should be respected. The risks of compromising religious organizations are unlikely to respect geographic boundaries.

It might be argued that the concern that religious organizations will be compromised by receiving financial aid is paternalistic. Thomas Berg, for example, forcefully argues that churches—not a court—should make the decision whether to compromise and accept government regulation as the cost of getting government funding.[101] My view is that this argument assumes the churches will make good decisions, whereas history indicates that Roger Williams and James Madison were on to something in thinking otherwise. It ignores the civic values associated with the checking function of religion and the goal of nurturing civic virtue, and reads an important goal of the Establishment Clause out of the Constitution. Indeed, the concern about compromising religious witness is best understood as a structural concern of the Constitution.[102] It is a constitutional wrong for government to gain control of religious opinion whether or not religious organizations would volunteer for the control in exchange for the bribe of aid.[103]

Ironically, conservatives, including the religious Right, have ordinarily been the first in line to decry the influence of politicians in the private sphere, yet many are enthusiastic about government support for religious education and social welfare activities. The Left, which ordinarily is prepared to support extensive governmental involvement in the private sphere, is quick to see the dangers when government becomes involved with religion. The left position might be recast this way: government involvement in the market is full of dangers, but the failure to intervene is even more dangerous because the market threatens to exploit labor, ruin the environment, and the like. On the other hand, the progressive might believe that the dangers of government involvement in the religious market are not outweighed by a need for intervention. It is unclear, however, why the conservative sees the dangers of intervention in the business market to be greater than the dangers of intervention in the religious market. Conservatives have long been concerned about the impact of autonomy on groups that receive aid from the government. They have traditionally feared the impact of government "strings." More generally, conservatives have been quick to argue that government aid will make problems worse rather than help in their solution.[104] Thus, an important strand of much conservative ideology has been to argue for freedom and to be suspicious of government in a broad swath of areas. This is consistent with their Augustinian distrust of human beings.[105] But somehow they seem comfortable with government promoting religion. If conservatives cannot trust government to handle welfare checks or education or housing, why would they trust government with the promotion of religion? It is doubtful that conservatives can justify being so distrustful of government in one set of cases, but not the other.

Religion and American Party Politics

John Rawls argued that the Supreme Court was the exemplar of public reason. In my view he was only partially right. Rawls to the contrary, any government official, including judges, might argue from Millian or Kantian premises. But it is true that judges cannot explicitly proceed from religious premises in making decisions. That would violate the Establishment Clause. On the other hand, they should be free to recognize that one purpose of the Establishment Clause is to protect religion and that the best understanding of the Constitution is that tight relations between religion and the state are bad for religion. By contrast, citizens appropriately make religious arguments in discussing the proper relationship between religion and the state. So, in my judgment, do candidates for office. On the other hand, I will argue that it is unreasonable to rely on candidates or public officials to generate the kind of change that religious liberals would like to see in this country.

All too frequently, candidates of the Democratic Party have not only avoided religious arguments in discussing the relationship between church and state, but they also have proceeded from an overly rigid view of the relationship and made it appear that religious beliefs were the monopoly of the Republican Party.[106] The impression was created, I believe, because Democratic candidates balked at introducing their religious views in the public square.[107] Part of this failure might be traced to religious liberalism. Religious liberals often believe that the best way to witness one's faith is not to proselytize, but to lead a good life. Yet there is more. Many candidates apparently feared that introducing religious views would violate appropriate principles of church-state relations. In short, they were affected with public reason disease, an affliction not shared by Republican candidates who had a different understanding of the relationship between church and state.

Public reason disease can be fatal in American politics. Christian evangelicals for a significant period of time enjoyed substantial success in American politics. In part, this success can be attributed to the fact that they responded to feelings of alienation and vulnerability. Millions need to feel that there is something more important than money and pleasure.[108] They yearn to be part of something larger than themselves. Christian evangelicalism satisfies needs of security, community, and destiny. Ironically, most of the Christian evangelical community has been allied with the Republican Party and through it with the very corporate forces that contribute to the hedonistic, materialistic culture that most evangelicals oppose.[109] As Thomas Frank writes, Republican conservatives "may talk Christ, but they walk corporate. Values may 'matter most' to voters, but they always take a backseat to money once the elections are won."[110] Corporations spend $265 billion advertising per year in the United States, and the message is that Americans need to buy products to meet their deepest desires. That message together with the exploitative conduct of corporations toward their workers and the environment helps fuel the vulnerability and alienation that fills evangelical churches. Although some evangelical leaders have looked away from corporate exploitation in order to maintain their own political power in the Republican Party, I would not suggest that any of them have supported corporate power in order to fill the ranks of their churches.

I do suggest that the success of Christian evangelicals is not simply a product of astute marketing. They address genuine spiritual needs, and the Republican Party understands the importance of empathizing with those needs.[111] Indeed, as Damon Linker writes, in 2004 it seems undeniable that the "Republicans managed to solidify the impression among large numbers of Americans that they are the country's party of religion— and, conversely, that the Democrats are the party of secularism."[112]

In the aftermath of the 2004 presidential election,[113] many Democrats seriously addressed the concern that the language of secular liberalism was ill designed to meet the religious sensibilities of the nation.[114] Many more Democratic candidates began to make their religious commitments evident.[115] It is not clear what impact, if any, this had in the 2006 midterm elections. The midterm elections may simply have showed that the Democrats are not incapable of winning elections, at least when their opposition has stumbled badly.[116] The midterm elections were a start, or should I say the beginning of a return to the party of, for example, Roosevelt, Carter, and Bill Clinton—all flawed to one degree or another—but each comfortable with his religious identity without suggesting that he had a monopoly on religious wisdom.[117] On the other hand, even as late as August 2008 citizens believed that the Republican party was more favorable to religion than the Democrats by a margin of 52 percent to 38 percent.[118]

By contrast, then presidential candidate Barack Obama was regarded as more religion friendly than John McCain (by a margin of 49 percent to 45 percent)[119] despite attempts to portray Obama's form of Christianity as un-American, accompanied with appeals to anti-Islamic prejudice with suggestions that this committed Christian was really a Muslim.

Obviously, the Democratic Party now understands that addressing material needs in insufficient. Its leaders recognize that they need to understand and respond to the spiritual sensibilities of most Americans while avoiding tight connections between church and state. Democratic Party leaders and candidates need to make clear—when it is true—that their positions on peace and justice are connected to a religious vision. Only if citizens understand that Democratic leaders empathize with their spiritual needs can religion be protected from those who want to "help" it by forging stronger connections between church and state. That is, Democratic leaders can successfully argue that separation of church and state helps religion only if people believe that such leaders genuinely think it is good to help religion.

Nonetheless, it is not at all clear that the Democratic Party has a political soul. Although the last election was marked by an outpouring of small contributions, the groveling for corporate campaign funds did not go away, and the dependence of the party on corporate contributions may well undermine the party's capacity to deliver on a progressive agenda.[120] The long-term political solution is not simply for candidates to appear religious to voters[121] or even to emphasize issues that appeal to religious voters. The political impact of the religious Left depends upon building at the grass roots if the Democratic Party is to nourish a political soul and if tight connections between church and state are to be avoided.

Grassroots Democracy, Liberal Politics, and Excessive Religious Hostility

Although it is good politics for political candidates to make clear that they have religious commitments, it is not good politics for political candidates to use extensive theological arguments. American politics is far too pluralistic for this to be a successful strategy.[122] Not even George W. Bush went that far.[123]

To be sure, government takes positions that have apparent theological implications. As I mentioned in chapter 4, without violating the Constitution government engages in actions that are forbidden by religions. Spending money on national defense and operating hospitals does not violate the Establishment Clause despite the views of pacifists and Christian scientists. But it would violate the Establishment Clause for government explicitly to declare that Christian pacifists are wrong or that Christian Scientists are wrong. Moreover, it is consistent with the Constitution to believe that tight connections between government and religion are bad for religion even though some religious leaders believe the contrary as a matter of doctrine, and even though some secular liberals think that a favorable attitude toward religion should not be part of the Constitution. Government is empowered to make decisions without considering theological positions one way or another.

On the other hand, it does not violate the Constitution for government to directly make some theological assertions: "In God We Trust," "God Save This Honorable Court," this country is "under God." Without withdrawing from the view that our nation wrongly discriminates against Buddhists, Hindus, atheists, and agnostics with its use of religious symbols, prayers, and pledges, I would suggest that the explicit theology permitted by government or that we might expect from candidates will always be relatively thin. It would be an unqualified outrage if the judiciary entertained views about establishing God's kingdom on earth or that the gospel has an anti-imperial stance, or anything of the kind.

On the other hand, I am maintaining that the democratic dialogue about church-state relations rightly involves a thicker theological dialogue—one that I have only gestured at here[124]—than would ever appear in the sound bites of election campaigns or the considered reports of legislative bodies or judicial opinions. Although the media have finally begun to recognize that there is a religious Left in this country, the crucial battle for the future of progressive politics will take place out of the spotlight of the mass media. It will be based on the grassroots communicative interactions of civil society.

Make no mistake. Religious conservatives may not have had a powerful presidential candidate in 2008. But they are not going away. As religious conservatives continue to press for power and for tighter connections between religion and government, the question of what the right relation between religion and that state is will continue to be an important part of our daily local political debates. In opposing these pressures, it is simply more effective politically to argue that conservative victories are bad for religion than to argue that they are bad for atheists, agnostics, or nontheistic religions. Of course, secular liberals can argue that government involvement with the state is bad for religion (indeed, John Rawls made this argument),[125] but the question of what is good or bad for religion ultimately drives one toward theology, which is what secular liberals hope to avoid. With respect to church-state relations, religious liberalism needs to play a comparatively large role in the grassroots struggle. To the extent it is necessary to argue that tight connections between church and state harm religion, religious liberals are more likely to have the theological resources, the motivation, and the credibility, to make such the argument.

Of course, I am not saying that secular arguments or secular liberals should play no role in this struggle. The religious Left and the secular Left both use secular arguments; both have similar aims; and both have powerful advocates within their midst. It would be a shame if they could not participate in a coalition despite their differences. Secular liberals, particularly hostile liberals, might well recognize that religious liberals have a political advantage in arguing about church-state relations in the American polity. Nonetheless, many secular liberals (I would not say most) might balk at forming a coalition. These secular liberals might wish to stand on principle rather than join with (what they regard as) destructive elements in the society. From the perspective of many secular liberals: (1) the march of science and reason will ultimately vanquish religion; (2) religion is a form of cowardly superstition; (3) religion has been a reactionary and destructive element in society.

I want to argue that these contentions are exaggerated and should not support a reluctance to forge a coalition. First, will the march of reason and science ultimately vanquish religion? The sociological prediction of the demise of religious belief was widely held during most of the twentieth century.[126] It pointed to the decline of religion in Europe and saw Europe as the wave of the future. But the United States (with the exception of its universities) is a glaring counterexample to what has come to be known as the secularization thesis. Indeed, the secularization of Europe stands alone when compared with the world's other continents.[127] Even in Europe, the rebellion against religion has been against religious institutions. The majority of Europeans are still believers.[128] Still secular liberals typically believe that religion is contrary to science and reason.[129] They cling to the Enlightenment view that reason will ultimately prevail, that history is a story of reason unfolding in progress.

The world wars and the Holocaust, and the environmental threat to the planet, among many other obscenities, speak loudly against the assumption that reason will prevail or launch history on an upward spiral of human progress.[130] Moreover, secular liberals who view themselves as following science and reason fail to appreciate the limits of both. Science, as science, cannot tell us how to live our lives. At best, it can provide information that can help us form normative judgments. But science is not itself normative.[131] Similarly, science does its best to explain the way the material world works; by definition, it cannot affirm or deny the existence of a supernatural, nonmaterial world. The denial of the supernatural is not a scientific claim.[132]

Reason, combined with experience and scientific information (broadly defined), in my view, is indispensable to the formation of normative judgments. But reason cannot prove or disprove the existence of the supernatural (though attempts have been made). If this is correct, if the existence of God can neither be proved nor disproved, secular and religious liberals share common epistemological ground.[133]

As William James,[134] Hans Kung,[135] and Charles Taylor[136] have emphasized, liberals (and all others) have a *choice* to affirm or deny the existence of the supernatural. For those who take the religious path, the choice need not be based on the hope of an afterlife (as secular liberals often claim).[137] Even if it were, for most of the religious, the charge of cowardice seems way off the mark. True cowards would reject the doctrine of hell out of hand.[138] For someone like Hans Kung, the choice amounts to whether you want to believe that there is something other than a meaningless universe. For Kung, the questions are these: Do you want to believe that there is an order in the universe, that you fit into something larger than yourself, and that you have a role to play as a disciple of God?[139] For many secular liberals, the choice is to believe that there is no meaning in the universe, that we are on our own, and that we must make judgments of value for ourselves.

I do not maintain that believers and nonbelievers necessarily experience their views as the product of choice. Many believers cling to the views they were taught in childhood. They have not seriously considered alternatives. Many nonbelievers find the views of believers to be utterly ridiculous. They do not experience themselves as making a choice. Nonetheless, as Charles Taylor emphasizes in *A Secular Age*, beliefs in God (or not) may be grounded in the attractiveness of a corresponding psychological identity.[140] Secular liberals are right in charging that believers are psychologically attracted to religious views. There is a comfort in believing that lives have genuine meaning, that meaning is not just made up. But the position of secular liberals also has psychological attractions. It is attractive to believe that you have the courage to stare a tragic universe in the face, that you are realistic, scientific, and rational—not sentimental.[141] As I have suggested, however, I agree with Taylor that a part of the identity of secular liberals lacks a sure foundation. The denial of the supernatural is not a scientific judgment; it is not the only conclusion that reasonable persons can make; it is realistic only if it is correct.

This is not to claim that secular liberals are wrong about the existence of God; it is to say that the denial or affirmation of the existence of God both depend upon acts of faith. Secular and religious liberals share more than a limited epistemology. I would guess that most religious liberals entertain doubts about their deepest religious beliefs. For Christians, the idea that God became man is a truly remarkable claim. Any open-minded Christian would sometimes have doubts about the thesis. The same holds true for a God that no one directly sees. Many believers who maintain they are certain are in fact self-deceived. My view is that faith and doubt are companions; genuine certainty is rare.

By the same token the secular liberal who denies the existence of God will often yearn for meaning in life. "Is that all there is," is a haunting question for everyone.[142] It haunts enough people that the secularization thesis seems clearly off the mark.[143] Religion is not going to disappear anywhere, not even in Europe.

Religion is not going anywhere; it is politically important; is it reactionary and destructive? What is the political tilt of religion in public life? No one would argue that it is uniformly conservative, and I do not contend that it has been straightforwardly progressive. Nonetheless, I would initially observe that progressives have been far more active throughout our history than religious conservatives.[144] Although churches were divided on the slavery issue,[145] the antislavery forces dominated. The direct action tactics of the abolitionists have probably influenced progressive movements throughout our history and encouraged those movements to be involved in politics while the Christian Right was sleeping in the private sphere.[146] Churches also took a leadership role in the fight against racial discrimination in the years leading up to the Civil Rights Act of 1964. Of course, the record of churches on women's rights is far less positive. Indeed, many of them are now on the defensive because of their continued failure to recognize the equality of women (others seem to wear their misogyny as a badge of honor).[147] But the story is not uniformly reactionary even on the gender front. The struggle for women's rights in this country was started and led by religious women who argued at the Seneca Falls conference that the equality of women "was intended to be so by the Creator."[148]

Similarly, the progressive reform movement's support of economic reforms had strong religious backing. For example, the 1912 Progressive Party convention, which called for many democratic reforms (including direct primaries, women's suffrage, and the initiative) and economic reforms (including antitrust, prohibition of child labor, and occupational health and safety protections), used "Onward Christian Soldiers" as its theme song.[149] But it must be conceded that religion has played a role in the rise of the greedier aspects of capitalism,[150] and the doctrines of many American churches has contributed to the United States' poor record on welfare in comparison with other industrialized countries.[151] At the same time, however, many churches have been prepared to criticize capitalistic excess. In that connection, religious beliefs have played a significant role in the environmental movement,[152] and many churches have argued that government has a responsibility to assist the poor both here and abroad. Indeed, churches themselves have taken a leading role in helping the poor.

If the United States government has been irresponsible in its policies toward the poor, it has been comparatively strong in affording educational opportunities for all in a system of public education. And religion deserves credit here because public education owes its existence to religiously motivated movements (despite their contamination with anti-Catholic bias). Beyond public education, many of the nation's most distinguished institutions of higher learning were founded by churches.[153]

There is no good way to measure the relative impact of conservative religious argument in the political sphere and that of progressive religious argument.[154] And political self-interest often predominates over contrary religious inclinations. I would expect, though, that arguments to support the status quo (although not in all its aspects) prevail most of the time. The impulse to conform is strong. Moreover, the impulse to conform politically has been reinforced in many denominations. Some denominations have stressed the importance of faith as opposed to good works, concern about a good life in the next world at the neglect of this one,[155] and the virtue of accepting business and governmental institutions as they are, thus encouraging a predominantly secular economy where business is business, and entrenching political institutions where naked self-interest dwarfs ethical considerations.[156]

For the most part, however, religious perspectives bring a moral outlook to a public square dominated by instrumental and egoistic perspectives. In my view, religious perspectives are a necessary counterpoint to the corporate state. I do not suggest that they have been especially effective. But the counterweight to corporate dominance in this country needs all the weight it can muster.

Secular liberals look at history and see intolerance and religious violence; they look at the last twenty-five years, and they see reactionary religious politics in the United States. I have some doubts about the extent to which religion has been the cause of wars rather than a cover for imperialism and the desire for territorial expansion. In addition, in the absence of religion, the legacy of Hitler and Stalin makes one wonder how much violence would recede. Nonetheless, whether or not the role of religion is triggering violence has been exaggerated, I think it clear that religion has played a significant role.[157] Moreover, the rise of the religious Right in American politics has to be regretted by liberals of all stripes. But the notion that religion overall has been politically counterproductive in American life is not at all obvious. Indeed, it seems to lack historical perspective and constructive imagination for the future.

Realistic secular liberals, who know that religion will play a role in American politics, cannot afford to resist alliances with other liberals just because they are religious. I have argued that secular liberals should be upstaged in church-state debates in American politics. I have not made the contention with respect to other issues. To be sure, there are issues where religious liberals have something distinctive to say. Religious liberals in general are in a better position to engage in the theological debate over the Bible's teachings about homosexuality. But on most political issues, secular and religious liberals alike look at political issues through the same humanistic lens. From the secular perspective, there is no alternative. From the perspective of religious liberals, God has not spoken clearly on most political issues, and, although they are aware that they might be quite wrong, the religious liberals' bet is that the humanistic perspective *is* God's perspective.

In the end, secular and religious liberals share common attitudes about politics and how to live their lives. Of course, they have different attitudes about the meaning of life; they have different attitudes toward religious ritual; they both fall short of their ideals; but their differences should not get in the way of their common struggle for justice.

Conclusion _____

IN THIS BOOK, I HAVE ARGUED for a form of religious liberalism. As a matter of constitutional law, religious liberalism maintains that the religion clauses have pluralistic foundations. Religious liberalism places great value on religious liberty and equality, but I have maintained that the most underappreciated insight of the Establishment Clause is that tight connections between church and state are bad for religion. Thus, religious liberalism insists that the use of religious symbols by government violates equality interests, does not help religion, and can harm religion in subtle and not so subtle ways. Nonetheless, from a constitutional perspective, it is futile to argue that *In God We Trust* on the coins and currency is unconstitutional. The Constitution is embedded in a religiously saturated culture with a long history in which many millions have found it necessary for government to engage in monotheistic expressions. This is regrettable, but constitutional accommodation to this form of governmental expression with its accompanying lack of concern for inequality is not accompanied by any broader support of governmental sectarianism. Indeed, the Constitution has generally been interpreted outside the area of governmental monotheistic prayers and pledges to prohibit governmental employment of religious symbols in ways that could be reasonably interpreted to be endorsements of the symbol.

In the near future (in the absence of an unexpected replacement of a conservative justice on the Court with a liberal replacement), I expect the Supreme Court to retreat from this conception of equality. Justice Kennedy has argued that government should be able to use religious symbols so long as they are not used to proselytize or to be relatively permanent in character. I think he probably has the votes to overturn decades of established law in this area. I further expect the Supreme Court to continue to display a deaf ear to Establishment Clause values in the area of vouchers. I do not expect the majority of justices to appreciate the extent to which the financial ties between church and state make churches unduly dependent and undermine their prophetic function. Indeed, I expect the justices to hold that direct financial aid to religious schools is constitutional. No longer will the money need to be laundered in the form of vouchers.

The result of these constitutional shifts will be that even more major battles over the relationship between church and state will be fought out in political channels instead of courtrooms. I have argued that religious liberalism has a distinctive role to play in the democratic process, one that is different from its role in the constitutional process. In the constitutional process, it is inappropriate to make theological arguments to a court. Both secular and religious liberals can argue that the Constitution is supported by pluralistic values, and both can be committed to the constitutional view that government efforts to help religion too often harm religion. Both can point to statements of Madison, Jefferson, and Baptist leaders around the time of the founding—all expressing this concern. Both can point to the continued saliency of this concern in the constitutional culture.

I have argued, however, that the presentation of theological arguments is appropriate whether in or out of the public forum (however it may be defined) in the process of opinion formation. Religious liberals in general have a distinctive advantage over secular liberals in making such arguments. To the extent it is necessary to argue that tight connections between church and state are theologically problematic, religious liberals are more likely to have the theological resources, the motivation (many secular liberals do not think such arguments should be made in the first place), and the credibility, to make the argument. The claim that tight connections between church and state damage religion can force one into a theological discussion of the religious mission: either of the clash between the evangelical mission of the church and its social justice mission or a discussion of the ways in which an evangelical mission should proceed.

I do not operate with any optimism that hard-core members of the religious Right are likely to be persuaded by these arguments. But most religious Americans have not thought hard about these issues and are open to be persuaded. In addition, the long-term religious demographics of the country suggest that the power of the religious Right (currently most significantly reflected on the Supreme Court) is likely to fade.

We are in the midst of a powerful transition. Until recently, the United States has been dominated by a Protestant establishment. By the time John Kennedy took office, the nation had moved from a Protestant establishment to a place where there was room at the table for Catholics and Jews. This was not a seamless transition, and, as the years went on, at least for conservative Protestants, the transition was aggravated by many important social changes: The constitutional decision to remove prayer from the schools; the recognition of increased ethnic and racial pluralism combined with the press toward multiculturalism; the many ways in which conceptions of male hierarchy were challenged; the general easing of limits on the display of sexuality on television, in films, and the Internet, and the sense that chastity was becoming a lost virtue; the rise in divorce rates; the movement to protect the rights of gays and lesbians; and, of course, the rise in the number of abortions and the protection of abortions by the Supreme Court.

Conservative white Protestants began to develop the sense that they were losing "their" country.[1] A backlash was inevitable. It is not surprising that they were attracted by the view that constitutional interpretation should be based exclusively on what the Christian Framers intended[2] in a less pluralistic time (even there the historical reading of the Framers' intent was indefensible). But the hope of reestablishing a "Christian country" was far-fetched from the start, and it will become increasingly unlikely. We are witnessing a transition in which increased pluralism will be difficult to ignore. Already the Buddhist and Hindu population has grown significantly. By the year 2050, the Muslim population is expected to be the second largest denomination in the country.[3] Increased religious pluralism cannot be expected to pass without political consequences. Surely we can expect more religious tension and division. Even conservative Christians might become opposed to government using religious symbols if they realize that many localities might be sporting Muslim symbols. So it is with vouchers. Conservative Christians might balk at government vouchers if they are going to go to be distributed on a nondiscriminatory basis to religious groups that include Muslims, Buddhists, Hindus, and Wiccans.

Conservative Christians now control the Court, and they still have a powerful political voice in large pockets of the country. But time is not on their side. We are looking to a future in which it will become increasingly clear that government needs to respect religious diversity. Tight connections between church and state will someday be a relic of the past. But we have a while to wait.

Notes

INTRODUCTION

1. Robert P. Jones, *Progressive and Religious* (Lanham, Md.: Rowman and Littlefield, 2008); Amy Sullivan, *The Party Faithful: How and Why the Democrats Are Closing the God Gap* 45 (New York: Scribner, 2008); E. J. Dionne Jr., *Souled Out: Reclaiming Faith and Politics after the Religious Right* 4 (Princeton: Princeton University Press, 2008); Frank Lambert, *Religion in American Politics* 218–50 (Princeton: Princeton University Press, 2008).

2. MediaMatters for America, *Left Behind: The Skewed Representation of Religion in Major News Media* 3 (May 2007) (http://mediamatters.org/leftbehind) (last visited June 15, 2007).

3. Dionne, *Souled Out*, 33.

4. John Green and Steven Wildman, "The Twelve Tribes of American Politics," http://www.beliefnet.com/story/153/story_15355_3.html (last visited June 15, 2007). For a brief survey of the religious Left, see John A. Coleman, "Left Behind: Who and Where Is the Religious Left in the United States," 194 *America* 11 (April 24–May 1, 2006).

5. Sam Harris, *The End of Faith: Religion, Terror, and the Future of Reason* 14 (New York: Norton, 2004).

6. Christopher Hitchens, *God Is Not Great: How Religion Poisons Everything* (New York: Twelve, 2007). I do not mean to suggest that either Harris or Hitchens is on the left. Their bellicose foreign policy views are some distance from those associated with the Left, but their hostility toward religion is consonant with that of a part of the secular Left.

7. Christopher L. Eisgruber and Lawrence G. Sager, *Religious Freedom and the Constitution* (Cambridge: Harvard University Press, 2007). For critical commentary, see Thomas C. Berg, "Can Religious Liberty Be Protected as Equality," 85 *Texas Law Review* 1185 (2007); Kent Greenawalt, "How Does 'Equal Liberty' Fare in Relation to Other Approaches to the Religion Clauses," 85 *Texas Law Review* 1217 (2007); Ira C. Lupu and Robert W. Tuttle, "The Limits of Equal Liberty as a Theory of Religious Freedom," 85 *Texas Law Review* 1247 (2007). In response, see Christopher L. Eisgruber and Lawrence G. Sager, "Chips Off Our Block? A Reply to Berg, Greenawalt, Lupu and Tuttle," 85 *Texas Law Review* 1273 (2007).

Martha Nussbaum, in *Liberty of Conscience: In Defense of America's Tradition of Religious Equality* 12, 22 (New York: Basic Books, 2008), recognizes that some arguments other than equality have merit, but concludes that equality and respect are the key concepts. The other arguments do not seem to do any work in her book. This book is in no sense a response to Eisgruber and Sager or to Nussbaum. They barely discuss the underappreciated value of protecting churches. This book advances the position of religious liberalism. I primarily confine my arguments against the position of commentators such as Eisgruber and Sager and Nussbaum to the notes.

8. Vincent Blasi, "School Vouchers and Religious Liberty: Seven Questions from Madison's Memorial and Remonstrance," 87 *Cornell Law Review* 783, 785 (2002).

9. *Zelman v. Simmons-Harris*, 536 U.S. 639 (2002) (upholding vouchers against a constitutional challenge). The issue of vouchers, of course, is still vigorously contested in American politics.

CHAPTER 1
OVERVIEW OF PART I

1. Without approving of the trend, Daniel Conkle has suggested that "formal neutrality has become the dominant theme under both the Free Exercise and Establishment Clauses." Daniel O. Conkle, "The Path of American Religious Liberty: From the Original Theology to Formal Neutrality and an Uncertain Future," 75 *Indiana Law Journal* 1, 10 (2000); see also Thomas C. Berg, "Slouching toward Secularism: A Comment on *Kiryas Joel School District v. Grumet*," 44 *Emory Law Journal* 433, 446–47 (1995) (finding Court decisions "increasingly driven by the equal treatment theme"); Ira C. Lupu and Robert W. Tuttle, "Zelman's Future: Vouchers, Sectarian Providers, and the Next Round of Constitutional Battles," 78 *Notre Dame Law Review* 917, 918 (2003) (movement of cases toward neutrality and away from separation of church and state). The emphasis on equality is closely associated with, but not identical to, a "neutrality" approach to the Establishment Clause. See *Zelman*, 536 U.S. 676 (Thomas, J., concurring); *Mitchell v. Helms*, 530 U.S. 793, 809–10 (2000) (Thomas, J., plurality opinion). Formal—not substantive—equality is the principal—but not exclusive—value of that approach. Neutrality is a doctrinal approach, then; formal equality is the primary value that it serves.

2. *Employment Div. v. Smith*, 494 U.S. 872, 878 (1990). For criticism of *Smith*, see Jesse H. Choper, "The Rise and Decline of the Constitutional Protection of Religious Liberty," 70 *Nebraska Law Review* 651, 670–80 (1991); Michael W. McConnell, "Free Exercise Revisionism and the Smith Decision," 57 *University of Chicago Law Review* 1109, 1152–53 (1990). In support of *Smith*, see William P. Marshall, "In Defense of *Smith* and Free Exercise Revisionism," 58 *University of Chicago Law Review* 308, 308–28 (1991). For debate about the original meaning of the Free Exercise Clause, compare Philip A. Hamburger, "A Constitutional Right of Religious Exemption: An Historical Perspective," 60 *George Washington Law Review* 915, 936–46 (1992), arguing that history does not support religious exemption from laws, with Michael W. McConnell, "The Origins and Historical Understanding of Free Exercise of Religion," 103 *Harvard Law Review* 1409, 1415, 1513–17 (1990), arguing that history supports religious exemptions from laws, and that these exemptions were "consonant with the popular American understanding of the interrelation between the claims of a limited government and a sovereign God." For John Locke's position, see John Locke, *A Letter Concerning Toleration* 41–42 (James Tully ed., Indianapolis: Hackett,

1983). For analysis of the effect of incorporating the clause into the Fourteenth Amendment, see Kurt T. Lash, "The Second Adoption of the Free Exercise Clause: Religious Exemptions under the Fourteenth Amendment," 88 *Northwestern University Law Review* 1106, 1149–56 (1994).

3. See Thomas C. Berg, "Religious Liberty in America at the End of the Century," 16 *Journal of Law and Religion* 187, 189 (2001) (referring to the Court's "shift in emphasis from separation to equality"); Berg, "Slouching toward Secularism," 446–47; Conkle, "Path of Religious Liberty," 6–8; Noah Feldman, "From Liberty to Equality: The Transformation of the Establishment Clause," 90 *California Law Review* 673, 694–700 (2002).

4. See, e.g., Berg, "Religious Liberty," 198 (remarking that there is currently no Supreme Court justice consistently willing to depart from an equal treatment approach in favor of embracing the value of liberty or substantive neutrality); Choper, "Rise and Decline," 680–84 (discussing the limited scope of protection offered by the Free Exercise Clause after *Smith*); McConnell, "Free Exercise Revisionism," 1137–39 (supporting religious exemptions under the Free Exercise Clause).

5. Ira C. Lupu, "Reconstructing the Establishment Clause: The Case against Discretionary Accommodation of Religion," 140 *University of Pennsylvania Law Review* 555, 567–70 (1991) (arguing that the religion clauses protect the values of liberty and equality or a regime of equal religious liberty).

6. Some scholars have somewhat broader views of the scope of religion clause values than most others in the field. See Kent Greenawalt, *Religion and the Constitution*, vol. 1, *Free Exercise and Fairness* 1–10 (Princeton: Princeton University Press, 2006); Laurence H. Tribe, *American Constitutional Law* 1154–1301 (2d. ed., Mineola, N.Y.: Foundation Press, 1988); Timothy L. Hall, "Religion and Civic Virtue: A Justification of Free Exercise," 67 *Tulane Law Review* 87, 112–17 (1992); Timothy L. Hall, "Religion, Equality, and Difference," 65 *Temple Law Review* 1, 77–89 (1992). Daniel Conkle also displays eclectic views of Establishment Clause values. See generally Daniel O. Conkle, *Constitutional Law: The Religion Clauses* (2d ed., St. Paul: Foundation Press, 2009) (maintaining that multiple values underlie the religion clauses); Daniel O. Conkle, "Toward a General Theory of the Establishment Clause," 82 *Northwestern University Law Review* 1113 (1988) (same). Although I share their commitment to a broad understanding of the values underlying the religion clauses, and I greatly respect their work, I typically part company with them concerning the character of the religion clause values, the relative importance of the values, the way in which they should be defended, and the manner in which they should be applied. Moreover, I think it important to focus upon the complicated ways in which equality relates to the religion clauses.

7. For example, many courts and legislatures have not yet addressed whether states should interpret their own constitutions to provide more generous protection for religious liberty than is afforded by the United States Supreme Court. See, e.g., *Catholic Charities of Sacramento v. Superior Court*, 85 P.3d 67, 89–91 (2004) (leaving open the scope of religious liberties covered by the Free Exercise Clause of the California constitution).

8. See, e.g., Berg, "Religious Liberty," 232–47 (describing cases involving government assistance to religious institutions and activities that do not consider the risks of government involvement).

9. See, e.g., Jesse H. Choper, *Securing Religious Liberty* 174–78 (Chicago: University of Chicago Press, 1995) (approving financial aid to religious institutions in some circumstances without considering the issue); in accord are Douglas Laycock, "The Underlying Unity of Separation and Neutrality," 46 *Emory Law Journal* 43, 70–71 (1997); and Michael W. McConnell, "Coercion: The Lost Element of Establishment," 27 *William and Mary Law Review* 933 (1986).

10. H. Jefferson Powell, "The Original Understanding of Original Intent," 98 *Harvard Law Review* 885, 902–48 (1985).

11. Conkle, *Constitutional Law*, 19. For an excellent account of the different paths taken in analyzing the religion clauses and their historical antecedents, see John Witte Jr., *Religion and the American Constitutional Experiment: Essential Rights and Liberties* 7–36 (Boulder, Colo.: Westview Press, 1999). See also Steven Waldman, *Founding Faith: Providence, Politics, and the Birth of Religious Freedom in America* (New York: Random House, 2008).

12. See Gordon S. Wood, "Slaves in the Family," *New York Times Book Review*, December 14, 2003, 10 ("Seeing Washington and Jefferson as slaveholders, men who bought, sold, and flogged slaves, has to change our conception of them. They don't belong to us today; they belong to the eighteenth century, to that coarse and brutal world that is so remote from our own"). Although we might wish that the eighteenth century's coarseness and brutality was more remote from our own, Wood's point about contextualizing the founders is on the mark.

13. Cf. Cass R. Sunstein, *The Partial Constitution* 97 (Cambridge: Harvard University Press, 1993) (suggesting that an originalist view would yield an "understanding of the Constitution [that is] dramatically different from the understanding that prevails today").

14. I am not alone. Stephen G. Gey, "Vestiges of the Establishment Clause," 5 *First Amendment Law Review* 1, 1–4 (2006).

15. Gregory S. Alexander, "Interpreting Legal Constructivism," 71 *Cornell Law Review* 249, 249 (1985) (book review) ("In the deconstructed legal culture lawyers must be intellectual scavengers, raiding other disciplines for helpful vocabularies, using as much of the discourse as seems helpful, and discarding the rest").

16. Although I do not share Henry Monaghan's views of the Due Process Clause, I think it unassailable that there can be a gap between what is constitutional and what is just. See Henry P. Monaghan, "Our Perfect Constitution," 56 *New York University Law Review* 353, 354–60 (1981).

17. Ronald Dworkin, *Law's Empire* 176–275 (Cambridge: Belknap Press of Harvard University Press, 1986).

18. Steven H. Shiffrin, *The First Amendment, Democracy, and Romance* 9–45 (Cambridge: Harvard University Press, 1990) (defending a balancing methodology); Steven H. Shiffrin, "Defamatory Non-media Speech and First Amendment Methodology," 25 *UCLA Law Review* 915, 942–63 (1978) (same).

19. Thomas Berg recognizes that different tests may be appropriate in different Establishment Clause contexts. Thomas C. Berg, "Religious Clause Anti-

Theories," 72 *Notre Dame Law Review* 693, 696–97 (1997). I agree with this methodological perspective, but part company with Professor Berg regarding the scope of values underlying the Establishment Clause.

20. In so arguing, I support the view that interpretation of the Constitution involves mixed normative and descriptive judgments.

CHAPTER 2
THE FREE EXERCISE CLAUSE

1. Timothy L. Hall, *Separating Church and State: Roger Williams and Religious Liberty* 48–49 (Urbana: University of Illinois Press, 1998); James A. Morone, *Hellfire Nation: The Politics of Sin in American History* 70 (New Haven: Yale University Press, 2003). See Gary Wills, *Head and Heart: American Christianities* 5 (New York: Penguin, 2007): "The Puritans hanged Quakers, exiled Dissenters, silenced heretics, and burnt their books." See generally chaps. 1–3 in Wills.

2. Hall, "Religion, Equality, and Difference," 29–30. The colonists thought they were following the will of God. For the more influential argument that most religious persecutors misunderstood the will of God, see Locke, *A Letter Concerning Toleration*, 23–26. Augustine, on the other hand, thought that religious persecution was theologically justified. See Hans Küng, *Great Christian Thinkers* 81–82 (New York: Continuum, 1994). And Locke's toleration did not extend to Catholics, Muslims, and atheists. Locke, *A Letter Concerning Toleration*, at 50–51. For a critical evaluation of Locke's argument for religious liberty, see Stanley Fish, "Mission Impossible: Settling the Just Bounds between Church and State," 97 *Columbia Law Review* 2255, 2255–69 (1997). On the Christian theory of persecution, see generally Perez Zagorin, *How the Idea of Religious Toleration Came to the West* 14–45 (Princeton: Princeton University Press, 2003) (defining "heresy" and addressing how the church treated heretics from the earliest times of Christianity until the end of the Protestant Reformation); John T. Noonan Jr., "Development in Moral Doctrine," in *Change in Official Catholic Moral Teachings* 287, 292 (Charles E. Curran ed., New York: Paulist Press, 2003) (describing how both the church and state "regularly and unanimously denied the religious liberty of heretics" for more than 1,200 years).

3. Sometimes government can interfere with religion without interfering with religious action, for example, by desecrating sacred places. See generally David C. Williams and Susan H. Williams, "Volitionalism and Religious Liberty," 76 *Cornell Law Review* 769, 824–31 (1991) (criticizing the view that "government action desecrating a site would present no cognizable effect, but government action denying access to the site would, because the religious harm would arise . . . from the inability of Indians to perform ceremonies there").

4. See *Church of the Lukumi Babalu Aye, Inc. v. City of Hialeah*, 508 U.S. 520 (1993).

5. As will become clear, some communitarian approaches are secular and some are not.

6. *Employment Division v. Smith*, 494 U.S. 872 (1990).

7. The *Smith* case actually dealt with state denial of unemployment compensation benefits to individuals who had been fired from their jobs at a private drug rehabilitation center for ingesting peyote as a part of a Native American religious service. The Court had to determine whether the law prohibiting peyote ingestion could constitutionally have been applied to the drug use at the religious ceremony to decide whether the applicants were appropriately denied their unemployment benefits. For criticism of Scalia's handling of the unemployment compensation aspects of the case, see Catharine Cookson, *Regulating Religion: The Courts and the Free Exercise Clause* 118–21 (New York: Oxford University Press, 2001).

8. Justice Scalia maintained that a successful religious claim could be maintained only if religion were singled out for special treatment, or when the religious interest was accompanied by another constitutional interest, giving rise to a "hybrid" claim. On the fate of *Smith* in the lower courts, see Carol M. Kaplan, "The Devil Is in the Details: Neutral, Generally Applicable Laws and Exceptions from *Smith*," 75 *New York University Law Review* 1045, 1060–73 (2000) (describing "distortions and inconsistencies" in the lower courts' post-*Smith* jurisprudence).

9. *Smith*, 494 U.S. 890. The sweep of the opinion led Michael McConnell to say that the decision was "undoubtedly the most important development in the law of religious freedom in decades." McConnell, "Free Exercise Revisionism," 1111. In reaction to *Smith* many states passed laws affording greater protection to religious liberty than that assured by *Smith*. Moreover, the federal government did the same. 42 U.S.C. section 2000bb-2(1). But a federal attempt to insure greater religious liberties than *Smith* in every state was declared unconstitutional in *City of Boerne v. Flores*, 521 U.S. 507 (1997) (invalidating a portion of the Religious Freedom Restoration Act). On the other hand, the Supreme Court upheld congressional legislation affording greater religious liberty than *Smith* to those incarcerated in state and local institutions. *Cutter v. Wilkinson*, 544 U.S. 709 (2005) (rebuffing a challenge to a section of the Religious Land Use and Institutionalized Persons Act, 42 U.S.C. 2000cc-1).

10. Laws of general application with an incidental impact on freedom of speech are required to meet what has in practice been a relatively undemanding test. The leading case is *United States v. O'Brien*, 391 U.S. 367, 376 (1968), which upheld a law prohibiting on draft card burning, stating that "when 'speech' and 'nonspeech' elements are combined in the same course of conduct, a sufficiently important governmental interest in regulating the nonspeech element can justify incidental limitations on First Amendment freedoms." See also *City of Erie v. Pap's A.M.*, 529 U.S. 277 (2000) (ban on public nudity upheld as applied to nude dancing); *Clark v. Community for Creative Non-Violence*, 468 U.S. 288 (1984) (ban on sleeping in the park upheld as applied to demonstration against government policy regarding the homeless).

11. On the irony of this, see Kent Greenawalt, *Fighting Words: Individuals, Communities, and Liberties of Speech* 22–24 (Princeton: Princeton University Press, 1995).

12. Immanuel Kant, *The Metaphysical Elements of Justice* 35, 43–44 (John Ladd trans., Indianapolis: Bobbs-Merrill, 1965) (explaining that one individual does an injustice to another when he interferes with the freedom of another); John Rawls, *A Theory of Justice* 204 (Cambridge: Belknap Press of Harvard University

Press, 1971) ("[A] basic liberty covered by the first principle can be limited only for the sake of liberty itself, that is, only to insure that the same liberty or a different basic liberty is properly protected and to adjust the one system of liberties in the best way"); Ronald Dworkin, *Taking Rights Seriously* 199–200 (Cambridge: Harvard University Press, 1977) (maintaining that except in extreme cases, rights may be limited only when another right is abridged).

13. See generally Immanuel Kant, *Foundations of the Metaphysics of Morals* (Lewis White Beck trans., Indianapolis: Bobbs-Merrill, 1959) (explaining concepts of reason, autonomy, and human dignity).

14. See Immanuel Kant, *The Metaphysical Principles of Virtue* 105 (James Ellington trans., Indianapolis: Bobbs-Merrill, 1964) (1888).

15. Friedrich Nietzsche, *The Twilight of the Idols or, How One Philosophizes with a Hammer*, in *The Portable Nietzsche* 463, 470 (Walter Kaufmann ed., trans., New York: Viking Press, 1968).

16. Even better, some scholars who otherwise sympathize with Kant have abandoned Kant's narrow understanding of what makes human beings important or how much the differences between human beings and animals matter. For example, Tom Regan's articulate defense of animal rights rejects the Kantian understanding of autonomy. Tom Regan, *The Case for Animal Rights* 84 (Berkeley and Los Angeles: University of California Press, 1983); see also Christine M. Korsgaard, *The Sources of Normativity* 152–53 (Onora O'Neill ed., New York: Cambridge University Press, 1996) (focusing on the extent to which an animal nature is a part of human nature worth valuing and that both animals and humans have a "way of being" someone that they share). I do not know if Korsgaard is suggesting that we would have to share a way of being with animals to justify obligation. She does make it clear that one may owe obligations to creatures whether or not they are moral agents.

17. Kant, *Metaphysical Principles of Virtue*, 106 (suggesting that cruelty to animals violates a duty to oneself because it reduces compassion, which, in turn, will harm relations with other human beings).

18. Martha Craven Nussbaum, *Frontiers of Justice: Disability, Nationality, Species Membership* (Cambridge: Belknap Press of Harvard University Press, 2006); Steven Shiffrin, "Liberalism, Radicalism, and Legal Scholarship," 30 *UCLA Law Review* 1103, 1138–40 (1983).

19. Cf. Rainer Forst, *Contexts of Justice: Political Philosophy beyond Liberalism and Communitarianism* 69 (John M. Farrell trans., Berkeley and Los Angeles: University of California Press, 1994) ("A person's religious conviction is worthy of protection because it is identity-determining, and not because it is religious").

20. See, e.g., Mary Ann Glendon, *Rights Talk: The Impoverishment of Political Discourse* 109–44 (New York: Free Press, 1991) (discussing how the current focus on individual liberty makes it difficult to cultivate the "values and practices that sustain our republic" through the political process).

21. See, e.g., Alasdair MacIntyre, *After Virtue: A Study in Moral Theory* 252, 257–59 (2nd ed., Notre Dame: University of Notre Dame Press, 1984) (preferring an Aristotelian emphasis on virtues over a liberal emphasis on rational rules); see also Gertrude Himmelfarb, *The De-moralization of Society: From Victorian Virtues to Modern Values* 9, 246–57 (New York: Alfred A. Knopf, 1995) (con-

trasting differences in content and observance of virtues in Victorian and contemporary times, and lauding Victorian ethos requiring respect for others). Many of those associated with communitarianism, including McIntyre, Michael Sandel, and Michael Walzer, do not accept the label for one reason or another. Daniel Bell, *Communitarianism and Its Critics* 1 (Oxford: Clarendon Press, 1993). For the argument that liberalism also seeks to support virtues appropriate for the maintenance of a regime of personal freedom, see Peter Berkowitz, *Virtue and the Making of Modern Liberalism* 189–92 (Princeton: Princeton University Press, 1999).

22. Glendon, *Rights Talk*, 76–108.

23. Self-government does not refer to individual autonomy, but to democratic rule of the polity. At best, of course, it is a metaphor. It would be hard to know who the "self" is that rules in our "democratic" society. On the difficulties associated with the metaphor, see Steven H. Shiffrin, "Liberal Theory and the 'Loyal Opposition' in Democratic Justice," 11 *Good Society* 78, 79 (2002) (book review).

24. Michael J. Sandel, *Democracy's Discontent: America in Search of a Public Philosophy* 321–28 (Cambridge: Belknap Press of Harvard University Press, 1996) (arguing that cultivating religion and morality is necessary for appropriate discourse in a self-governing society). Compare Sunstein, *The Partial Constitution*, 347–54, with John Hart Ely, *Democracy and Distrust: A Theory of Judicial Review* (Cambridge: Harvard University Press, 1980) (providing a liberal pluralist defense of rights grounded in processes of representative democracy).

25. On the problem, see Robert A. Dahl, *Democracy and Its Critics* 180–92 (New Haven: Yale University Press, 1989).

26. See Michael J. Perry, *Religion in Politics: Constitutional and Moral Perspectives* 59, 64–65 (New York: Oxford University Press, 1997); Michael J. Sandel, "Political Liberalism," 107 *Harvard Law Review* 1765, 1794 (1994) (book review).

27. Sunstein, *The Partial Constitution*, 133–41, 307.

28. John H. Garvey, *What Are Freedoms For?* 48–49 (Cambridge: Harvard University Press, 1996).

29. For a description of traditional communitarianism, see Ian Shapiro, *The Moral Foundations of Politics* 171 (New Haven: Yale University Press, 2003): "The communitarian outlook is distinctive, and distinctively at odds with the Enlightenment, in that its proponents see the good as collectively given, embedded in the evolving traditions and practices of political communities."

30. See Will Herberg, *Protestant—Catholic—Jew: An Essay in American Religious Sociology* 231–34 (rev. ed., Garden City, N.Y.: Doubleday, 1960); John C. Jeffries Jr. and James E. Ryan, "A Political History of the Establishment Clause," 100 *Michigan Law Review* 279, 299–305 (2001).

31. Stephen M. Feldman, *Please Don't Wish Me a Merry Christmas: A Critical History of the Separation of Church and State* (New York: New York University Press, 1997) (describing the history of anti-Semitism, with an emphasis on American culture).

32. On the Mormons, see Sarah Barringer Gordon, "A War of Words: Revelation and Storytelling in the Campaign against Mormon Polygamy," 78 *Chicago-*

Kent Law Review 739 (2003); on the Jehovah's Witnesses, see Vincent Blasi and Seana V. Shiffrin, "The Story of *West Virginia State Board of Education v. Barnette*: The Pledge of Allegiance and the Freedom of Thought," in *Constitutional Law Stories* 433–75 (Michael C. Dorf ed., New York: Foundation Press, 2004).

33. Rowan Williams, *Writing in the Dust: After September 11*, 67–68 (Grand Rapids, Mich.: Eerdmans, 2002); R. Laurence Moore, *Touchdown Jesus: The Mixing of Sacred and Secular in American Culture* 111–12 (Louisville, Ky.: John Knox Press, 2003).

34. See Will Kymlicka, *Contemporary Political Philosophy: An Introduction* 227 (Oxford: Clarendon Press, 1990) ("[T]he problem of the exclusion of historically marginalized groups is endemic to the communitarian project").

35. Shapiro, *Moral Foundations of Politics*, 175 ("In most, if not all, communities, there is considerable disagreement about how the collectively given norms and practices that have been inherited should be interpreted and what they require in practice").

36. " '[R]eligion was especially important to the development of a republican culture,' with religious (including especially Christian) values and insights playing prominent and substantial roles." Daniel O. Conkle, "Secular Fundamentalism, Religious Fundamentalism, and the Search for Truth in Contemporary America," 12 *Journal of Law and Religion* 337, 356 (1995–96) (quoting Richard Vetterli and Gary C. Bryner, "Religion, Public Virtue and the Founding of the American Republic," in *Toward a More Perfect Union: Six Essays on the Constitution* 92 [Neil L. York, ed., Provo, Utah: Brigham Young University Press, 1988]); see also Lash, "Second Adoption," 1118–22 (discussing the view that commitment to a republican culture involved the promotion of Christian values). As will become clear, stress on cultural values does not exhaust the richness of the case for religious freedom.

37. On the perils of religious communitarianism, see Frederick Mark Gedicks, *The Rhetoric of Church and State: A Critical Analysis of Religion Clause Jurisprudence* 122–25 (Durham, N.C.: Duke University Press, 1995) ("Religious communitarian discourse is not a viable alternative to secular individualism"); Hall, "Religion and Civic Virtue," 119 ("Historically, republican principles were a poor ally for religious liberty. They could as easily justify jailing a dissenting preacher who threatened republican solidarity as giving him free room to propagate minority religious tenets, and they were the joists over which the platform of religious establishment was most frequently laid").

38. See Stephen L. Carter, *The Culture of Disbelief: How American Law and Politics Trivialize Religious Devotion* 17 (New York: Basic Books, 1993) (defining religion in terms of group worship).

39. Cf. *Torcaso v. Watkins*, 367 U.S. 488, 495–96 (1961) (holding unconstitutional a state requirement that a notary swear a belief in God because it invaded freedom of belief and religion).

40. Resisting the free exercise claim of obligation, Professor Marshall argues that religion might be best understood as a "product of man's freedom rather than his external obligation." Marshall, "In Defense of Smith," 327. He suggests that his conception of religion is more consistent with the commitment to freedom in the First Amendment than is Judge McConnell's argument that "religion should

be treated as the product of an externally imposed obligation." Marshall, 327. Marshall's conception of religion is underdeveloped, and seems to be beside the point. Certainly it is not inconsistent with the Constitution to interpret free exercise of religion to embrace individuals' duties to follow obligations when they are freely accepted. To the extent obligations are deemed to be imposed without the possibility of rejection (presumably under some deterministic reasoning), the case for protection seems even stronger. On the importance of obligation to religion and the role of subjectivity in accepting the obligation, see Karl Rahner, *Foundations of Christian Faith: An Introduction to the Idea of Christianity* 343–44 (William V. Dych trans., New York: Seabury Press, 1978).

41. One might argue that the problem is not cruelty, but rather that the state has no jurisdiction to interfere in the religious sphere. See Michael W. McConnell, "Religious Freedom at a Crossroads," 59 *University of Chicago Law Review* 115, 173 (1992) (discussing the "view that the relations between God and Man are outside the authority of the state"). To be sure, the Framers had a widespread view that some things belonged to God and others to the state, see Hall, "Religion, Equality, and Difference," 32–36, but it is not clear from the historical evidence that exemptions of this type fell on God's side of the ledger. See Hamburger, "Constitutional Right," 932–33, 936–46. Treating state interference with religion as "jurisdictional overreaching" is difficult to reconcile with a balancing approach that seems inevitable once exemptions are recognized. See text accompanying notes 67–94 *infra*. Moreover, the "jurisdiction" view of free exercise would afford no protection for those who acted on the basis of moral conscience, not based on belief in God. Cf. *United States v. Seeger*, 380 U.S. 163, 176 (construing "religious training and belief" to include "[a] sincere and meaningful belief which occupies in the life of its possessor a place parallel to that filled by . . . God"). One might still argue that the jurisdiction view is a part of the values underlying the Free Exercise Clause. Given the originalist pedigree for the argument, this argument makes some sense. See Hall, "Religion, Equality, and Difference," 32–33 (discussing conceptions of religious liberty from the colonial period to the adoption of the First Amendment).

42. See McConnell, "Religious Freedom at a Crossroads," 173 ("The Free Exercise Clause does not protect autonomy; it protects obligation"); Geoffrey R. Stone, "Constitutionally Compelled Exemptions and the Free Exercise Clause," 27 *William and Mary Law Review* 985, 993 (1986) (contending that requiring conduct that is at odds with religious duty is more serious than overriding speech preferences). As Professor McConnell observed elsewhere, an analogy to discrimination against the handicapped appropriately illustrates the importance of accommodating religious duty. Failing to accommodate the handicapped treats them as if they are the same when they are differently situated than other people. By contrast, racial discrimination ordinarily treats people who are the same as if they are different. See McConnell, "Free Exercise Revisionism," 1109, 1140.

43. It is enough that the obligation is morally based. See *Welsh v. United States*, 398 U.S. 333, 343–44 (1970) (interpreting the University Military Training and Service Act to protect conscientious objection on "deeply held" moral grounds without belief in God); *United States v. Seeger*, 380 U.S. 176 (interpreting the University Military Training and Service Act to protect conscientious objection

not based upon belief in a traditional God); Amy Gutmann, *Identity in Democracy* 168–78 (Princeton: Princeton University Press, 2003) (discussing the extent to which ethical obligations should be accommodated whether or not based on religious premises); see also William Herbrechtsmeier, "Buddhism and the Definition of Religion: One More Time," 32 *Journal for the Scientific Study of Religion* 1, 15–17 (1993) (arguing that theistic definitions of religion are too narrow and cannot account for religions such as Buddhism). For an outstanding discussion of military service exemptions, see Greenawalt, *Free Exercise and Fairness*, 49–67, 124–56.

44. An alternative would be to protect moral obligations under the Equal Protection Clause. See Greenawalt, *Free Exercise and Fairness*, 146–56.

45. Joshua Cohen, pointing to the special nature of believers' moral and religious obligations, argues that deliberative democrats should support religious liberty because rejecting it would deny the principles of equal citizenship undergirding deliberative democracy. See Joshua Cohen, "Democracy and Liberty," in *Deliberative Democracy* 202–7 (Jon Elster ed., Cambridge: Cambridge University Press, 1998). This claim accents the liberal character of liberal communitarianism: liberal communitarianism derives from rights theory what is owed to citizens for them to participate in a community, rather than focusing upon rights they have that flow from the nature of a community. Michael Sandel argues that the unencumbered self of individualism wrongly emphasizes choice and that it cannot explain freedom of religion. See Sandel, *Democracy's Discontent*, 64–66. He suggests that observers have no choice but to follow conscience, and that treating religion as a mere choice "may thus fail to respect persons bound by duties derived from sources other than themselves" (67). This characterization ignores the extent to which conscience can be cultivated or desensitized through voluntary action, and it further ignores what the Christian tradition would call sin, which in many cases involves succumbing to temptation despite conscience. See also *supra* note 40 (discussing the relationship between freedom and obligation).

46. For the claim that free exercise claims of this stripe should be limited to those claimants who fear extratemporal consequences, see Choper, "Rise and Decline," 679. For a vigorous critique, see Gary J. Simson, "Endangering Religious Liberty," 84 *California Law Review* 441, 446–51 (1996) (arguing that limiting protection to those who face extratemporal consequences is underinclusive, ignoring religions and tenets that encourage compliance out of reverence and love of God and duty to others).

47. The existence of obligation need not necessarily be a prerequisite for a Free Exercise claim. See *infra* note 58.

48. Locke, *A Letter Concerning Toleration*, at 27; see also James Madison, "Memorial and Remonstrance" (1785), reprinted in *The Mind of the Founder: Sources of the Political Thought of James Madison* 12 (Marvin Meyers ed., Indianapolis: Bobbs-Merrill, 1973) ("Religion both existed and flourished . . . in spite of every opposition from [laws]").

49. See Madison, "Memorial and Remonstrance," 15.

50. See Locke, *A Letter Concerning Toleration*, at 33; Madison, "Memorial and Remonstrance," 14; J. Judd Owen, *Religion and the Demise of Liberal Rationalism: The Foundational Crisis of the Separation of Church and State* 168–70

(Chicago: University of Chicago Press, 2001); Stephen Pepper, "Conflicting
Paradigms of Religious Freedom: Liberty v. Equality," 1993 *BYU Law Review* 7,
17–18. For an argument that the goal of religious peace has moral dimensions
stretching beyond pragmatism, see John Courtney Murray, S.J., *We Hold These
Truths: Catholic Reflections on the American Proposition* 56–78 (New York:
Sheed and Ward, 1960). For doubts about the distinctiveness and cogency of religious peace as a value, see Steven D. Smith, "The Rise and Fall of Religious Freedom in Constitutional Discourse," 140 *University of Pennsylvania Law Review*
149, 207–10 (1991).

51. Christopher L. Eisgruber and Lawrence G. Sager, "The Vulnerability of
Conscience: The Constitutional Basis for Protecting Religious Conduct," 61 *University of Chicago Law Review* 1245, 1248 (1994), developed further in Eisgruber
and Sager, *Religious Freedom*; see also Jesse H. Choper, "Religion and Race under
the Constitution: Similarities and Differences," 79 *Cornell Law Review* 491, 491–
93 (1994) (arguing that a history of hostility and hate toward religious beliefs and
race provides a strong justification for strict scrutiny of government discrimination based upon either); Stephen Pepper, "Taking the Free Exercise Clause Seriously," 1986 *BYU Law Review* 299, 307 (arguing that religion is perceived to be
"subject historically to abuse and persecution and therefore 'inherently suspect'
as a basis for governmental classification"); Michael J. Perry, "Freedom of Religion in the United States: Fin de Siècle Sketches," 75 *Indiana Law Journal* 295,
299 (2000) (contending that at a minimum the free exercise norm is an antidiscrimination norm). For doubts that an antidiscrimination principle would have
yielded substantial protection in the areas where judicial scrutiny has been the
most effective in protecting religion, see Prabha Sipi Bhandari, Note, "The Failure
of Equal Regard to Explain the Sherbert Quartet," 72 *New York University Law
Review* 97 (1997). For a wide-ranging and sensitive exploration of the possibilities
of the equality value regarding the religion clauses, see Hall, "Religion, Equality,
and Difference."

Eisgruber and Sager deny that the value of religion entitles it to constitutional
protection. Eisgruber and Sager, "The Vulnerability of Conscience," 1248. Their
argument in part turns on objections to the subjective character of balancing tests
and views about the proper roles of judges and legislators (1248–59). These familiar objections, however, would seem to apply to vast areas of constitutional adjudication—including freedom of speech—which they regard as a model instance
of constitutional value (1250–51). They also deny that the cruelty of burdening
conscience makes religion special, arguing that it would be equally cruel to burden
the conscience of the nonreligious, or to punish or deny benefits to the disabled
for that which they cannot do (1262–65). Although they are correct in this respect,
they provide no ground for denying a measure of protection to religious believers,
but instead show that those of nonreligious moral conscience and the disabled
should also be protected. To be sure, the cruelty rationale does not show that
religion is itself valuable, but it provides an additional basis for denying that equality is the exclusive rationale for free exercise protection.

Finally, Eisgruber and Sager argue that religion can be a force for good or evil.
"The Vulnerability of Conscience," 1265–67. They suggest that believers who

violate otherwise valid laws do not likely engage in actions that are for the good of the republic, and find government endorsement of one (religious) view about what is valuable in life to be "indefensibly partisan" (1265–66). Even assuming a nonpartisan government on this understanding was workable and desirable (but see Shiffrin, "Liberalism, Radicalism"), this, as I argue below, slides too fast over the question whether our Constitution can best be interpreted in this way. As I argue below, we might have a better Constitution if it did not privilege religion in some contexts, but we have a flawed Constitution.

52. Nussbaum, *Liberty of Conscience.*

53. See also Madison, "Memorial and Remonstrance," 11 (speaking of the "*equal* title to the free exercise of Religion").

54. Jack N. Rakove, "Once More into the Breach: Reflections on Jefferson, Madison, and the Religion Problem," in *Making Good Citizens: Education and Civil Society* 233, 256 (Diane Ravitch and Joseph P. Viteritti eds., New Haven: Yale University Press, 2001).

55. See *supra* notes 30–34 and accompanying text. See also R. Laurence Moore, *Religious Outsiders and the Making of Americans* (New York: Oxford University Press, 1986) (surveying the treatment by historians of different religious groups in America).

56. See Jeffries and Ryan, "Political History."

57. *Church of the Lukumi Babalu Aye, Inc. v. City of Hialeah,* 508 U.S. 520, 546–47 (1993).

58. Suppose a law prohibits gender discrimination and does not provide an exemption for the selection of religious leaders such as priests or ministers. Suppose further that the particular religion bringing the claim does not argue that it is obliged to discriminate on the basis of gender, but chooses to follow tradition or does so in order to avoid schism. Presumably, applying the law to the selection of religious leaders would violate both freedom of association and free exercise. For powerful argumentation in support of equality and dissenting rights within private associations, see Madhavi Sunder, "Piercing the Veil," 112 *Yale Law Journal* 1399 (2003) and Madhavi Sunder, "Cultural Dissent," 54 *Stanford Law Review* 495 (2001).

59. But see Seana Valentine Shiffrin, "What's Wrong with Compelled Association," 99 *Northwestern University Law Review* 839 (2005).

60. Association issues arise in a variety of contexts that will not be discussed here, but the literature is large and growing. See, e.g., *Freedom of Association* (Amy Gutmann ed., Princeton: Princeton University Press, 1998) (analyzing the issue of freedom of association from various perspectives); Nancy Rosenblum, *Membership and Morals* (Princeton: Princeton University Press, 1998) (arguing that associations need not reflect public values to warrant constitutional protection).

61. Cf. Conkle, "Toward a General Theory."

62. John J. DiIulio, *Godly Republic: A Centrist Blueprint for America's Faith-Based Future* 35–46 (Berkeley and Los Angeles: University of California Press, 2007); McConnell, "Origins and Historical Understanding," 1515–16. But see Smith, "Rise and Fall," 204–7 (questioning the pluralism rationale).

63. William P. Marshall, "Religion as Ideas: Religion as Identity," 7 *Journal of Contemporary Legal Issues* 385, 402 (1996) (observing that the interpretation of religion clauses has much to do with how we identify with our country) (citing Shiffrin, *First Amendment*, 5 [making similar argument for the speech clause]).

64. Charles Taylor, "Religion in a Free Society," in *Articles of Faith, Articles of Peace: The Religious Liberty Clauses and the American Public Philosophy* 109–13 (James Davison Hunter and Os Guinness eds., Washington, D.C.: Brookings Institution, 1990).

65. Abner Greene argues that constitutional limitations on the effectiveness of religious groups in the political process justify religious exemptions. See Abner S. Greene, "The Political Balance of the Religion Clauses," 102 *Yale Law Journal* 1611, 1643–44 (1993). Although no legislature could base legislation upon what God's will might be on a subject, religious groups can be enormously powerful in politics. Consider the Mormons in Utah or the Lutherans in Minnesota. The inability to include religious terminology in the preamble to legislation is of little political moment. Argument ultimately based on religious foundations is routinely presented in public life, and—whether the issue be civil rights, the environment, or what have you—it is typically easily translated in secular terms. Finally, as will be discussed in further detail, the Establishment Clause does not generally foreclose legislatively created religious exemptions. Although Greene's argument is elegantly presented, to my mind it does not present a persuasive argument for religious exemptions.

66. To argue that it is crueler to force one to violate one's conscience than to force one to abandon a personally vital artistic project is not to say that religion is more important than art; it is to say that violating conscience punishes more harshly wholly apart from the value of the religion or the value of the artistic project. On the other hand, if religion is independently valuable from a constitutional perspective, theological arguments for freedom of religion might then be recognized as part of the structure underlying the religion clauses. For example, Locke and others made theological arguments about the limited jurisdiction of government with respect to religion and about the un-Christian character of persecution. Locke, *A Letter Concerning Toleration*. To accept Lockean arguments necessarily is to reject arguments based on other theologies with different conceptions of the propriety of persecution or the relationship between church and state. This seems ironic on some readings of the Establishment Clause. See Smith, "Rise and Fall," 149–50, 153–66. In my view, the religion clauses are not neutral. They favor religion over nonreligion and theistic religion over nontheistic religion. If theological grounding of the religion clauses is accepted (see Smith, 160–64), theological partisanship is unavoidable. Although such theological arguments have a historic pedigree and independent theological appeal—for reasons that will become clear—I believe it best to restrict, to the greatest extent possible, the formal grounding of the clauses to a civic perspective, recognizing, however, that any governmental arrangements could in effect favor one religion or another.

67. Indeed, even before *Smith*, courts were not particularly sensitive to religious claimants. See Choper, "Rise and Decline," 684; Ira C. Lupu, "The Trouble with Accommodation," 60 *George Washington Law Review* 743, 756 (1992). See James E. Ryan, Note, "*Smith* and the Religious Freedom Restoration Act: An

Iconoclastic Assessment," 78 *Virginia Law Review* 1407 (1992) (tracing the cases). Aside from inflating the importance of governmental interests, the Court has exhibited a "distressing insensitivity" to what amounts to a burden on the free exercise of religion. See Ira C. Lupu, "Where Rights Begin: The Problem of Burdens on the Free Exercise of Religion," 102 *Harvard Law Review* 933, 945, 960–66 (1989). To some extent, this narrow conception of burden stems from the Court's favoring of the dominant American religious tradition over minority religions. See Williams and Williams, "Volitionalism and Religious Liberty," 797 (arguing that the Court had protected "nonvolitionist religious beliefs" like most Native American religions only from facially discriminatory regulations while protecting volitionist religions from both facially discriminatory and facially neutral regulations). For particularly strong claims in favor of religious liberty, see Kathleen M. Sullivan, "Religion and Liberal Democracy," 59 *University of Chicago Law Review* 195, 219 (1992), suggesting that voluntary crucifixion should perhaps be protected. See also Stephen L. Pepper, "The Case of the Human Sacrifice," 23 *Arizona Law Review* 897 (1981) (using human sacrifice as the vehicle for an innovative discussion of the scope of free exercise). For support of the contention that religious claimants should receive no judicial assistance when their conduct causes harm, see Marci A. Hamilton, *God vs. the Gavel: Religion and the Rule of Law* (Cambridge: Cambridge University Press, 2005). For an extremely critical review, see Douglas Laycock, "A Syllabus of Errors," 105 *Michigan Law Review* 1169 (2007).

68. Donald A. Giannella, "Religious Liberty, Nonestablishment, and Doctrinal Development: Part I. The Religious Liberty Guarantee," 80 *Harvard Law Review* 1381, 1390 (1967). For an outstanding analysis of the factors that should be taken into account in evaluating free exercise claims, see Alan Brownstein, "Taking Free Exercise Rights Seriously," 57 *Case Western Reserve Law Review* 55 (2006).

69. Greenawalt, *Free Exercise and Fairness*, 125.

70. Winnifred Fallers Sullivan, *The Impossibility of Religious Freedom* (Princeton: Princeton University Press, 2005).

71. *Warner v. Boca Raton*, 64 F. Supp.2d 1272 (1999), aff'd 420 F.3d 1308 (8th Cir. 2005).

72. Sullivan, *Impossibility of Religious Freedom*, 116.

73. I wish I could say this was uncommon. We have already discussed *Smith* in the religion area (though technically it should not apply, given the presence of speech *and* religion interests in the *Warner* case). Perhaps the leading case elevating bureaucratic over speech interests is *Clark v. Community for Creative Non-Violence*, 468 U.S. 288 (1984) (outlawing sleeping in a park across the street from the White House as a part of a demonstration to dramatize the plight of the homeless).

74. The desire for statues would clearly be impaired by this, as would, for example, monuments that could keep people from walking on the grave.

75. *Warner*, 1290–92.

76. 887 So.2d 1023, 1033 (Fla. S.Ct. 2004). The protection in question was granted by a Florida statute that purported to afford a level of freedom greater than that guaranteed in the Federal Constitution. The Eighth Circuit Court of

Appeals had asked the Florida Supreme Court to clarify the meaning of the statute.

77. On the dynamic interaction between the lived religious experience of the people and the doctrines of the elite, see Charles H. Lippy, *Being Religious, American Style* (Westport, Conn.: Praeger, 1994).

78. Sullivan, *Impossibility of Religious Freedom*, 105.

79. But see 64 F.Supp.2d at 1284–85.

80. See note 43 *supra*.

81. Sullivan, *Impossibility of Religious Freedom*, 149–50, 159.

82. Kent Greenawalt, "Moral and Religious Convictions as Categories for Special Treatment: The Exemption Strategy," 48 *William and Mary Law Review* 1605, 1640 (2007).

83. Even during Prohibition, mainstream religious services whose rituals required alcohol were exempt from prosecution. National Prohibition Act, Pub. L. No. 66–66, 41 Stat. 305, 308 (1919) ("Liquor for nonbeverage purposes and wine for sacramental purposes may be manufactured, purchased, sold, bartered, transported, imported, exported, delivered, furnished, and possessed, but only as herein provided").

84. It might be argued that ingesting peyote is more dangerous than drinking wine, but the record in the *Smith* case showed that peyote ingestion in the Native American Church led members to resist drug abuse, particularly alcoholism. Moreover, the church forbade nonreligious use of peyote. See *Smith*, 494 U.S. 913–16 (Blackmun, J., dissenting); see also McConnell, "Free Exercise Revisionism,"1135 (noting that evidence showed peyote use in the church was not dangerous and did not lead to substance abuse).

85. I am assuming that the state does not single out penalties for only those animal sacrifices performed by religious groups or in the exercise of any particular religion. Any such law would plainly be unconstitutional. See *Church of the Lukumi Babalu Aye, Inc. v. City of Hialeah*, 508 U.S. 520, 546–47 (1993).

86. On ethical issues concerning the relationships between humans and other animals, see *Animal Rights and Human Obligations* (Tom Regan and Peter Singer eds., 2nd ed., Englewood Cliffs, N.J.: Prentice Hall, 1989); Tom Regan, *Defending Animal Rights* 1–27 (Urbana: University of Illinois Press, 2001); Peter Singer, *Animal Liberation* 1–23 (2d ed., New York: Random House, 1990).

87. Singer, *Animal Liberation*, 95–157.

88. Cf. Pepper, "Taking Free Exercise Clause Seriously," 313 ("If Catholic or Jewish beliefs prohibited photos on drivers' licenses, would they be required?").

89. To be sure, some religions may do otherwise objectionable things to animals as a sign of spiritual respect to God. The ascription of "inhumanity" in the interest of animal protection is taken from a civic perspective.

90. See Sidney Gendin, "The Use of Animals in Science," *in Animal Sacrifices: Religious Perspectives on the Use of Animals in Science* 15–60 (Tom Regan ed., Philadelphia: Temple University Press, 1986).

91. Compare Justice O'Connor's concurrence in *Smith*, 494 U.S. 891, 904–7, with Justice Blackmun's dissent, joined by Justices Brennan and Marshall, *Smith*, 907–17.

92. See *Prince v. President of the Law Soc'y of the Cape of Good Hope*, Case CCT 36/00, 2, 134–36 (2000) (freedom of religion guarantee in South African constitution did not preclude denial of admission to the bar by applicant who previously used and continued to use cannabis as a religious practice).

93. Robert H. Bork, *The Tempting of America: The Political Seduction of the Law* 129–32 (New York: Free Press, 1990); Antonin Scalia, *A Matter of Interpretation: Federal Courts and the Law* (Princeton: Princeton University Press, 1997).

94. Philip B. Kurland, "Of Church and State and the Supreme Court," 29 *University of Chicago Law Review* 1, 5 (1961). For the claim that discrimination in favor of religious claimants violates the freedom of speech clause, see Marshall, "Religion as Ideas," 393–97.

CHAPTER 3
ESTABLISHMENT CLAUSE VALUES

1. In a sense there is no good starting point, because it could be argued that the line of cases involving government appropriation of religious symbols is quite different, for example, from cases involving financial aid to religious organizations. One attempt to unify the multifaceted factual contexts is to analyze them using the *Lemon* test, which scrutinizes government actions for a primary religious purpose or effect, or excessive governmental entanglement. See *Lemon v. Kurtzman*, 403 U.S. 602 (1971). Many, including a fair number of justices, have attacked the test in ways that would weaken Establishment Clause protection. See, e.g., *Santa Fe Indep. Sch. Dist. v. Doe*, 530 U.S. 290, 319–20 (2000) (Rehnquist, C.J., dissenting) (describing *Lemon*'s career as "checkered" and collecting cases questioning it). Gary Simson has argued that the test should be strengthened in ways that so far as I can tell mark him out along with Kathleen Sullivan as the two strongest defenders of free exercise and separation of church and state (taken together) among academics. Gary J. Simson, "The Establishment Clause in the Supreme Court: Rethinking the Court's Approach," 72 *Cornell Law Review* 905, 935 (1987); Sullivan, "Religion and Liberal Democracy," 219, suggesting that voluntary crucifixion should perhaps be protected. See also Pepper, "Case of Human Sacrifice."

2. *County of Allegheny v. ACLU*, 492 U.S. 573 (1989).

3. The justices also considered a display of a Chanukah menorah with a Christmas tree and a "sign saluting liberty" in front of a city-county building, but the simpler issue of the nativity scene suffices to expose the larger issues.

4. Chief Justice Rehnquist and Justices White and Scalia joined Justice Kennedy. Although Justice White is deceased, Justice Thomas has since joined this voting bloc.

5. William Van Alstyne, "Trends in the Supreme Court: Mr. Jefferson's Crumbling Wall—a Comment on *Lynch v. Donnelly*," 1984 *Duke Law Journal* 770, 771 (referring to the shift from walls to bridges in a similar case).

6. Here, of course, the religious Right parts company with Justice Kennedy, who favors strong free exercise interpretation, but weak Establishment Clause interpretation.

7. An alternative view would be that these justices are simply statist, that they are replacing "an inordinate distrust of religion" with "an inordinate faith in government." McConnell, "Religious Freedom at Crossroads," 116. Certainly these justices ordinarily opt for a limited judicial role with respect to the state except, for example, with respect to affirmative action, attempts to increase black representation, the 2000 election, and some First Amendment cases, See, e.g., *Gratz v. Bollinger*, 539 U.S. 244, 387 (2003) (striking down the undergraduate admissions program at the University of Michigan); *Bush v. Gore*, 531 U.S. 98, 111 (2000) (employing an innovative equal protection analysis in a way that effectively decided the 2000 presidential election); *Miller v. Johnson*, 515 U.S. 900, 927 (1995) (striking down Georgia's attempt to increase black representation after Justice Department refused to preclear other plan); *McConnell v. FEC*, 124 S.Ct. 619 (2004) (Rehnquist, C.J., Kennedy, Scalia, and Thomas, JJ., dissenting, vote to invalidate loophole closing sections of the Bipartisan Campaign Reform Act of 2002 on First Amendment grounds). Why the activity in some spheres and not in others? My suspicion and suggestion is that these justices' capacity to empathize with some groups more than others plays a role in their willingness to engage in searching judicial review of a state decision.

8. *Lynch v. Donnelly*, 465 U.S. 668, 687–88 (1984) (O'Connor, J., concurring).

9. *County of Allegheny*, 492 U.S. 592–94 (Blackmun, J., joined by Brennan, Marshall, Stevens, and O'Connor, JJ).

10. *Lynch*, 465 U.S. 688 (O'Connor, J., concurring); see also William W. Van Alstyne, "What Is 'An Establishment of Religion' ? " 65 *North Carolina Law Review* 909, 914 (1987) (arguing that a mingling of church and state denies equal respect owed to citizens); cf. Eisgruber and Sager, "The Vulnerability of Conscience," 1283 (advocating an "equal regard" analysis for free exercise issues). It is possible to read this test as simply protecting the feelings of citizens. So understood, the test is vulnerable to substantial objections. See William P. Marshall, "The Concept of Offensiveness in Establishment and Free Exercise Jurisprudence," 66 *Indiana Law Journal* 351, 373 (1991) (arguing that "the concern with offense contained in the current religion clause doctrine should be abandoned" as inconsistent with speech clause theory and law). A better understanding of the current endorsement approach is that the feelings of a reasonable person are a proxy for whether the government has deviated from religious equality. The *deviation*, not the reaction to it, is itself the violation. The endorsement test is vulnerable to other serious objections, though most of them have bite only if applied to cases other than those involving the use of religious symbols by government. See McConnell, "Religious Freedom at Crossroads," 155–57 (arguing that the endorsement test should be modified to be a "favoritism" or "preference" test even when applied in the context of government symbols).

11. Shiffrin, *First Amendment*, 9–45 (explaining approaches employed by the Court and advocated by constitutional theorists regarding content-based and conduct-based speech restrictions).

12. Most Establishment Clause scholars do not support balancing. Gary Simson, however, explicitly argues for a form of balancing, albeit more restricted than what I recommend. Simson, "Establishment Clause," 923–32 (proposing that if a law has a substantial adverse effect on the Establishment Clause, it must serve

a substantial government interest in order to stand). The debate on whether to balance and, if so, how open-ended the balancing should be is, of course, well developed in the free speech context. See, e.g., Steven H. Shiffrin and Jesse H. Choper, *The First Amendment: Cases—Comments—Questions* 143 n.b (4th ed., St. Paul: West Group, 2006) (citing sources).

13. The liberty aspect of the Establishment Clause is emphasized in Choper, *Securing Religious Liberty*, 174–78; Noah Feldman, *Divided by God: America's Church-State Problem–and What We Should Do About It* (New York: Farrar, Straus and Giroux, 2005); and McConnell, "Coercion," 941. I use the term *liberty* to include the right to make autonomous choices about the particular character of religious exercise to follow.

14. *Lee v. Weisman*, 505 U.S. 577, 598–99 (1992).

15. Berg, "Slouching toward Secularism," 452 (suggesting religious voluntarism is at the heart of both clauses); Donald A. Giannella, "Lemon and Tilton: The Bitter and the Sweet of Church State Entanglement," 1971 *Supreme Court Review* 147, 153 (explaining the "free exercise aspect of neutrality" where religious liberty is seen as the central value of both clauses); Wilber G. Katz, "Freedom of Religion and State Neutrality," 20 *University of Chicago Law Review* 426, 429–33 (1953) (maintaining that protecting religious freedom by passing legislation that would be precluded by a rule of complete church-state separation does not violate the Establishment Clause); cf. Jesse H. Choper, "The Free Exercise Clause: A Structural Overview and an Appraisal of Recent Developments," 27 *William and Mary Law Review* 943, 948 (1986) (suggesting that cases granting religious exemptions are ordinarily constitutional because an Establishment Clause violation requires a purpose to aid religion and significantly endangering "religious liberty in some way by coercing, compromising, or influencing religious beliefs"); McConnell, "Coercion," 939–40 (suggesting that accommodating religion is unproblematic because an Establishment Clause violation requires coercion or interference with religious choice); Michael A. Paulsen, "Religion, Equality, and the Constitution: An Equal Protection Approach to Establishment Clause Adjudication," 61 *Notre Dame Law Review* 311, 313 (1986) (stating that both clauses support religious liberty so no tension between them). I do not mean to suggest that promoting religious liberty can never violate the Establishment Clause. Supporting the religious liberty of some, but not others, might do so. So might supporting religious liberty beyond what is necessary to prevent free exercise violations in some contexts. If equality is respected, however, stopping free exercise violations can never violate the Establishment Clause.

16. Madison argued that the compulsion to pay even three pence was objectionable because it opened the door to "force him to conform to any other establishment." James Madison, "Memorial and Remonstrance," 10. Isaac Backus vigorously complained of the "extortion" involved when taxpayers were forced by the state to support religions. See Isaac Backus, "An Appeal to the Public for Religious Liberty," in *Isaac Backus on Church, State, and Calvinism* 303, 325–43 (William G. McLoughlin ed., Cambridge: Belknap Press of Harvard University Press, 1968). On this aspect of religious liberty, see Leonard W. Levy, *The Establishment Clause* 1–26 (2d ed., Chapel Hill: University of North Carolina Press,

1994) (in colonies), 29–78 (in states); Douglas Laycock, "The Benefits of the Establishment Clause," 42 *DePaul Law Review* 373, 376–77 (1992).

17. Another possibility would be to require that those who have religious objections give a somewhat higher amount (to assure sincerity) to charity. See Kent Greenawalt, "Conflicts of Law and Morality—Institutions of Amelioration," 67 *Virginia Law Review* 177, 208 (1981). I return to discussion of this value in chapter 6.

18. See, e.g., Pierre deVos, "South Africa's Constitutional Court: Starry-Eyed in the Face of History," 26 *Vermont Law Review* 837, 854 (2002) (suggesting that marginalization of non-Christian South Africans could be linked to "social exclusion and political disempowerment").

19. Levy, *The Establishment Clause*, 77; see also 134–37; Douglas Laycock, " 'Nonpreferential' Aid to Religion: A False Claim about Original Intent," 27 *William and Mary Law Review* 875, 878 (1986) (describing disproportionate impact as the source of "bitter religious strife"); cf. Alan E. Brownstein, "Constitutional Questions about Vouchers," 57 *New York University Annual Survey of American Law* 119, 126 (2000) ("Facial neutrality of government action does not guarantee religious equality").

20. See, e.g., Levy, *The Establishment Clause*, 139–42.

21. The law harmed a Native American religion, but had no impact on Christian religions or those of other traditions.

22. The Court's general handling of inequality of effect in constitutional law is perverse. For example, one of the great scandals of constitutional law is its refusal to take seriously the inequalities associated with disproportionate racial impact while studiously policing state regulations that have a disproportionate impact on interstate commerce. Compare *Washington v. Davis*, 426 U.S. 229 (1976) (holding that disproportionate impact on race does not ordinarily trigger elevated scrutiny) with *Pike v. Bruce Church, Inc.*, 397 U.S. 137 (1970) (holding that disproportionate impact on interstate commerce gives rise to elevated scrutiny).

23. I return to this issue in chapter 7.

24. See chapter 8 *infra*.

25. *New York Times Co. v. Sullivan*, 376 U.S. 254, 270 (1964).

26. Jay P. Dolan, *In Search of an American Catholicism: A History of Religion and Culture in Tension* 56–57 (Oxford: Oxford University Press, 2002) (referring to nativist church burnings and Bible riots).

27. Discrimination against Muslims long preceded the attacks on the World Trade Center. Edward McGlynn Gaffney Jr., "Hostility to Religion, American Style," 42 *DePaul Law Review* 263, 274–79 (1992).

28. On the other hand, the potential for instability may differ depending on the issue. I return to this in chapter 6.

29. For a powerful argument against the use of an instability argument in the Establishment Clause context, see Richard W. Garnett, "Religion, Division, and the First Amendment," 94 *Georgetown Law Journal* 1667 (2006); see also Lupu and Tuttle, "Zelman's Future," 953–54.

30. England continues to do so to this day.

31. Conkle, "Toward a General Theory," 1166–69.

32. See *Lemon*, 403 U.S. 623. See generally Marci Hamilton, "The Constitution's Pragmatic Balance of Power between Church and State," SD02 American Law Institute–American Bar Association Continuing Legal Education 501 (1998) (exploring dangers accompanying politically powerful religious interests); Marci A. Hamilton, "Power, the Establishment Clause, and Vouchers," 31 *Connecticut Law Review* 807, 821 (1999) ("Religion is not a passive participant in the political process but rather a potent presence with the capacity to overreach"); Pepper, "Conflicting Paradigms," 18–19 (expressing concern that a church-state alliance would threaten liberty and good government). But cf. Ira C. Lupu, "Threading between the Religion Clauses," 63 *Law and Contemporary Problems* 439, 445–46 (2000) (suggesting that religious groups "deserve[ ] the same political liberty as other" groups).

33. Stephen Macedo, *Diversity and Distrust* 61–63 (Cambridge: Harvard University Press, 2000) (discussing the contribution of pre–Vatican II Catholic attitudes toward liberty and democracy to anti-Catholic hostility); John T. McGreevy, *Catholicism and American Freedom: A History* 170 (New York: Norton, 2003) (referring to the "familiar" arguments about potential Catholic threats to religious liberty).

34. Conkle, "Path of Religious Liberty," 4 ("[T]hroughout most of our country's history, there has been an overt Christian, and primarily Protestant, dominance in American law and public life").

35. Michael J. Perry, *Under God? Religious Faith and Liberal Democracy* 20–21 (Cambridge: Cambridge University Press, 2003); Shiffrin, "Religion and Democracy," 1652–56.

36. Mark De Wolfe Howe, *The Garden and the Wilderness: Religion and Government in American Constitutional History* 5–12 (Chicago: University of Chicago Press, 1965); see also Isaac Kramnick and R. Laurence Moore, *The Godless Constitution: The Case against Religious Correctness* 46–66 (New York: Norton, 1996) (describing Roger Williams as "ahead of his time"); Perry Miller, *Roger Williams: His Contribution to the American Tradition* 254–57 (Indianapolis: Bobbs-Merrill, 1953) (explaining Williams's significance to contemporary conceptions of religious liberty); Edmund S. Morgan, *Roger Williams: The Church and the State* 115–42 (New York: Harcourt, Brace, and World, 1967) (describing Williams's ideas about the state and the church). But Howe emphasizes an aspect of Williams that was not central to his thinking. Nussbaum, *Liberty of Conscience*, chap. 2 (freedom of conscience was the central aspect of Williams thought anticipating Locke). On some of the personal complications of Williams, see Hall, *Separating Church and State*, 17–33, 37–38; Steven D. Smith, "Separation and the Fanatic," 85 *Virginia Law Review* 213, 216–19 (1999) (reviewing Hall, *supra*). For an excellent comparison of the views of Williams with those of Locke, Jefferson, and Madison, see Timothy L. Hall, "Roger Williams and the Foundations of Religious Liberty," 71 *Boston University Law Review* 455 (1991).

37. Howe, *Garden and Wilderness*, 5–6, 12; Conkle, "Toward a General Theory," 1181–82 (endorsing Williams's view that government support of religions may be counterproductive); Van Alstyne, "What Is an Establishment," 914 (arguing that state involvement with religion risks "profaning religion"); see Wills, *Head and Heart*, 75: "America has defied predictions that secularization will dry

up religious devotion. Separation of church and state did not endanger this religiosity but protected it"; see also 548–49.

38. See Hall, "Roger Williams," 27 ("Williams ultimately refused spiritual communion with everyone, including his wife").

39. Wills, *Head and Heart*, 96. Philip Hamburger shows that Williams's theological views were extreme, but Hamburger apparently intends this as a way of discrediting Williams's political views and in that respect is unsuccessful. See Philip Hamburger, *Separation of Church and State* 38–53 (Cambridge: Harvard University Press, 2002).

40. It is necessary to separate Williams's political arguments from their theological underpinnings. It is not necessary to believe that the number of authentic Christians constitutes a small portion of the population in order to believe that there are dangers to religion when government seeks to promote religion, but, for Williams, this was an important truth. Kramnick and Moore, *The Godless Constitution*, 48.

41. James Madison argued in the remonstrance that the notion that the civil magistrate is a competent judge of religious truth "is an arrogant pretension falsified by the contradictory opinions of rulers in all ages and throughout the world." Quoted in Wills, *Head and Heart*, 212. He maintained that religious establishments "instead of maintaining the purity and efficacy of Religion, have had a contrary operation." Madison, "Memorial and Remonstrance," 12; Hall, "Religion and Civic Virtue," 121 ("The revolutionary generation was also repeatedly warned that government sponsorship of religion frustrated the very process of virtue creation"). Madison cautioned that government support of religion "corrupted religion itself, and thus corrupted religious capacity for generating true virtue." Hall, "Religion and Civic Virtue," 121. For religion to flourish, and with it the possibility for citizens to acquire the virtues necessary for self-government, "Roger Williams's wall of separation between the fruit-producing garden and the destructive encroachment of the wilderness had to be vigorously maintained" (121).

42. As Jefferson put it, "I do not believe it is for the interest of religion to invite the civil magistrate to direct its exercises, its discipline, or its doctrines." Van Alstyne, "Trends in the Supreme Court," 775.

43. Waldman, *Founding Faith* argues that separation of church and state "would not exist if not for the efforts of eighteenth-century evangelicals."

44. Donald Skaggs, *Roger Williams' Dream for America* 15–17 (New York: P. Lang, 1993).

45. According to Williams, "Whenever civil rulers had emerged as would-be protectors or champions of religion, they had appropriated religion to profane interests—to their own quest for profit and power." Kramnick and Moore, *The Godless Constitution*, 57; in accord is Morgan, *Roger Williams*, 119–20; cf. *Zorach v. Clauson*, 343 U.S. 306, 320 (1952) (Black, J., dissenting) ("State help to religion injects political and party prejudices into a holy field. . . . Government should not be allowed, under cover of the soft euphemism of 'co-operation,' to steal into the sacred area of religious choice"); McConnell, "Origins and Historical Understanding ," 1438 ("It is anachronistic to assume, based on modern pat-

terns, that governmental aid to religion and suppression of heterodoxy were opposed by the more rationalistic and supported by the more intense religious
believers of that era. The most intense [colonial] religious sects opposed establishment on the ground that it injured religion and subjected it to the control of civil
authorities"); McConnell, "Religious Freedom at Crossroads," 146 ("[G]overn-
ment is unlikely to be a valuable contributor to our understanding of spiritual
truth").

46. See Taylor, "Religion in a Free Society," 103 ("[T]he separation of church
and state did not have to mean bracketing God or religion. It may have for some,
but that is not the way most Americans understood disestablishment. In fact,
many supported the measure in the name of religion, to preserve its strength and
integrity from the enervating and corrupting effect of state interference").

47. See Thomas C. Berg, "Church-State Relations and the Social Ethics of
Reinhold Niebuhr," 73 *North Carolina Law Review* 1567, 1625–27 (1995).

48. Steve Bruce, *Politics and Religion* 4 (Cambridge: Polity, 2003) ("Everyone
claims divine approval. All states mobilize for war by first enlisting God as their
recruiting sergeant"). As Bob Dylan sang, "And that land that I live in—Has God
on its side. . . . The Germans now too have God on their side. . . . If God's on our
side—He'll stop the next war." Bob Dylan, "With God on Our Side," on *The
Times They Are A-Changin'* (Sony 1964).

49. Van Alstyne, "What Is an Establishment," 914 ("[I]t profanes religion for
any secular authority to trade on its practices for its (the state's) civil or secular
ends, *i.e.*, it is a trespass on religion by the state; the state has no right to take
things from the voluntary communities of faith and entangle them as instruments
in the conduct of civil affairs").

50. See Backus, "An Appeal to the Public," 333–34; see also T. B. Maston,
Isaac Backus: Pioneer of Religious Liberty 71–73 (Rochester, N.Y.: American
Baptist Historical Society, 1962) (describing Backus's distrust of evangelical uses
of state power).

51. Nicholas Atkins and Frank Tallett, *Priests, Prelates, and People: A History
of European Catholicism since 1750* 324 (Oxford: Oxford University Press, 2003)
(explaining that, in return for benefits from the state, the church preached submission to the temporal authority, though it practiced extensive charitable work). The
church's commitment to social justice, however, did not include a commitment to
religious freedom. René Rémond, *Religion and Society in Modern Europe* 173–74
(Antonia Nevill trans., Oxford: Blackwell, 1999) (discussing the Catholic church's
resistance to religious liberty prior to 1945); J. Bryan Hehir, "Catholicism and
Democracy: Conflict, Change, and Collaboration," in Curran, *Change in Official
Catholic Moral Teachings*, 20, 22 ("Throughout the nineteenth century, Catholic
teaching resisted the idea of religious freedom in the name of standing against
philosophical relativism and for the interests of the church"). Instead the church's
commitment was to support the truth, thus the burning of heretics at the stake,
the Inquisition, and the like. Although the Protestant commitment to religious
freedom preceded that of the Catholic Church, it too was not easy to come by.
For example, Thomas C. Berg writes:

[As] Niebuhr pointed out, the Puritan faction in seventeenth-century England "pled for liberty of conscience when it was itself in danger of persecution; and threatened all other denominations with suppression when it had the authority to do so." In America, of course, it is a familiar story that the Puritans who came seeking their own religious freedom immediately denied it to others. Even after official disestablishment . . . American authorities put in place a range of preferences for generic Protestantism, despite the supposed Protestant commitment to "soul liberty" and to the exemption of religious concerns from the cognizance of government. It has always proved difficult for religious persons to see the practices familiar to them as anything other than "natural" and necessary to public order.

Berg, "Church-State Relations," 1612 (citations omitted).

52. Speaking of the position of the Catholic Church in many European countries well into the twentieth century, René Rémond writes:

Imbued with the juridical tradition inherited from Rome, the [C]atholic church attached great importance to an explicit recognition of its rights, written into laws, which obviously ruled out any separation [of church and state]. The Pope continued to reaffirm as ideal a Christian state whose leaders made open reference to religion, made its teaching the rule of their actions and imposed on their nationals a respect for the obligations fixed by the church.

Rémond, *Religion and Society*, 160.

53. Cf. Robert P. Kraynak, *Christian Faith and Modern Democracy: God and Politics in the Fallen World* 3 (Notre Dame: Notre Dame University Press, 2001) ("[T]he Roman Catholic Church supported emperors and kings throughout much of its history; and although it resisted them on many occasions to defend the freedom of the church and the needs of the people, it did not really accept liberal democracy until very recently, when the Second Vatican Council [1962–65] endorsed a qualified version of democratic human rights"); Charles R. Morris, *American Catholic: The Saints and Sinners Who Built America's Most Powerful Church* 69 (New York: Vantage, 1997) (noting that Pope Gregory XVI and Pope Pius IX maintained that it was "insanity to believe in liberty of conscience and worship or of the press"). For the claim that the church's move to accept liberal democracy at Vatican II was preceded by other steps beginning in 1945, see Rémond, *Religion and Society*, 174–77. Rémond writes that the church regarded the Enlightenment's emphasis on rationalism and its companion devotion to democracy as the major threat to the evangelical mission of the church, but the administrations of Franco, Mussolini, Hitler, and Vichy France taught the church that there were some things worse than democracy. Accordingly, the church simultaneously embraced liberal democracy and opposed communism (167–77). Although Rémond's analysis is plausible when applied to the church in France—which was in no position to push for control after its collaboration with the Vichy regime—the church in Italy took the position that "Fascism's failing was not due to its authoritarianism, its violence or denial of democracy, but to 'its refusal to found itself on the Church and to profess itself Catholic.' " Carolyn M. Warner, *Confessions of an Interest Group: The Catholic Church and Political Parties in Europe*

80 (Princeton: Princeton University Press, 2000). On the other hand, the American bishops supported freedom of speech and religion long before the Vatican. See Morris, *American Catholic*, 135 (discussing the tendency of the American bishops to ignore Vatican pronouncements when they conflicted with American conceptions of free speech and religion).

54. One exception was that the church would often remain quiet in circumstances where speaking out would risk persecution by the government. This pattern of church behavior persisted in Mexico for much of the twentieth century, despite the courageous actions of many. See Vikram K. Chand, *Mexico's Political Awakening* 153–203 (Notre Dame: Notre Dame University Press, 2001).

55. For the suggestion that Pope Pius XII was relatively silent about Hitler largely because he felt that a strong Germany was necessary as a buffer against communism, see William J. O'Malley, S.J., *Why Be Catholic* 161 (New York: Crossroad, 2001). Compare O'Malley, with Alister E. McGrath, *The Future of Christianity* 10 (Oxford: Blackwell, 2002) ("[The] failure of the German churches to make a significant impact on Hitler's rise to power, and his gradual move toward reaffirmation of German imperial claims, raised serious questions concerning the moral credentials of Christianity"). Fear and anti-Semitism surely played a significant role in the silence. See Rémond, *Religion and Society*, 168–69.

56. Michael Fleet and Brian H. Smith, *The Catholic Church and Democracy in Chile and Peru* 4 (Notre Dame: Notre Dame University Press, 1997) ("During the late 1960s and 1970s, the Church emerged as a critic and antagonist of repressive military regimes in several [Latin American] countries. Catholic bishops became champions of human rights and popular interests. . . . [A decade later,] Church leaders and activists helped to persuade a number of military governments to relinquish power to civilian successors. . . . The Church thus played a generally progressive role in most of Latin America during the last thirty years"). See generally Jeffrey Klaiber, S.J., *The Church, Dictatorships, and Democracy in Latin America* (Maryknoll, N.Y.: Orbis, 1998) (providing a comprehensive overview of the Catholic Church's role in defending human rights and promoting democracy in Central and South America from the 1960s to the 1980s).

57. Brian H. Smith, *Religious Politics in Latin America, Pentecostal vs. Catholic* 51, 67 (Notre Dame: Notre Dame University Press, 1998).

58. Cf. Atkins and Tallett, *Priests, Prelates and People*, 324 (suggesting the "enlightened absolutism" of the eighteenth century defined a symbolic relationship between church and state in which the church "functioned in some measure as a state bureaucracy and mouthpiece"). The church's "political influence has been decidedly conservative for most of its history." Fleet and Smith, *Catholic Church and Democracy*, 13. The church continues to promote its evangelical interests through ties with governments when it is able to do so even in the post–Vatican II context. (The church maintains privileges to teach in many European public schools.) For a nuanced discussion of the power and limits of the church's involvement in politics, see generally Timothy A. Byrnes, *Transnational Catholicism in Postcommunist Europe* (Lanham, Md.: Rowman and Littlefield, 2001); Timothy A. Byrnes, *Catholic Bishops in American Politics* (Princeton: Princeton University Press, 1991).

59. The church moved to regain control in the middle of the nineteenth century, but it took nearly a century to complete the task. See Rémond, *Religion and Society*, 180–83. In Latin American colonies, the church permitted political leaders to censor ecclesiastical communications, including those from the Vatican. See José Casanova, *Public Religions in the Modern World* 114 (Chicago: University of Chicago Press, 1994). This practice was not eliminated in Brazil until 1890. Casanova, 114.

60. McGrath, *The Future of Christianity*, 12; in accord are Michael M. Winter, *Misguided Morality: Catholic Moral Teaching in the Contemporary Church*, xiv, 38, 56–57, 83–87 (Aldershot: Ashgate, 2002); and Damon Linker, *The Theocons: Secular America under Siege* 223 (New York: Doubleday, 2006). Cal Thomas and Ed Dobson, "Blinded by Might: The Problem with Heaven on Earth," in *What's God Got to Do with the American Experiment?* 51, 52 (E. J. Dionne Jr. and John J. DiIulio, Jr. eds., Washington D.C.: Brookings, 2000) (warning that when the clergy participate in political processes, they risk being compromised by the dangerous attraction of political power); Peter Wehner, "A Screwtape Letter for the Twenty-first Century: What a Senior Devil Might Think about Religion and Politics," in Dionne and DiIulio, *What's God Got to Do*, 41, 43 (same).

61. For eloquent discussion of this phenomenon by an evangelical participant, see David Kuo, *Tempting Fate: An Inside Story of Political Seduction* (New York: Free Press, 2006).

62. One might argue that religious participation in democratic life makes churches too dependent on the state. This would seem to depend on the content of the participation. Religious lobbying for church privileges would certainly be troubling, but religious lobbying on moral issues would be less worrisome.

63. *County of Allegheny*, 492 U.S. 655.

64. See Robert Booth Fowler and Allen D. Hertzke, *Religion and Politics in America: Faith, Culture, and Strategic Choices* 10–11 (Boulder, Colo.: Westview Press, 1995); see also Conkle, "Toward a General Theory," 1180 ("[O]ur judicially enforced separation of religion and government may well invigorate religion and work to its long-term benefit"); Hugh Heclo, *Christianity and American Democracy* 14–15 (Cambridge: Harvard University Press, 2007) (discussing Tocqueville's views). For a sustained argument to this effect, see Roger Finke and Rodney Stark, *The Churching of America, 1776–1990: Winners and Losers in Our Religious Economy* 18–21 (New Brunswick, N.J.: Rutgers University Press, 1992) (suggesting that a diversity of faiths untethered from the state is necessary for religion to thrive). It is not clear that the Framers foresaw that separation of church and state would promote religion. See Rakove, "Once More into the Breach," 254 (Jefferson expected religion to fade; Madison did not). But see Moore, *Touchdown Jesus*, 17 (contending that the founders thought religion would prosper if government stopped enforcing religious orthodoxy or appearing to care about it).

65. See Finke and Stark, *Churching of America*, 15–16.

66. One religious leader has remarked, "It would not be unduly dramatic to claim that Western Europe, at least, is suffering from a spiritual and moral crisis of immense proportions." Basil Hüme, *Remaking Europe: The Gospel in a Divided Continent* 59 (London: SPCK, 1994). On the other hand, North American elites

are surely as secular as European elites. Philip Jenkins, *The Next Christendom: The Coming of Global Christianity* 161 (Oxford: Oxford University Press, 2002); see also Peter L. Berger, "The Desecularization of the World: A Global Overview," in *The Desecularization of the World: Resurgent Religion and World Politics* 1, 10–11 (Peter L. Berger ed., Washington, D.C.: W. B. Eerdmans, 1999) (discussing a "globalized *elite* culture"). Indeed, Berger is quoted as saying, "If India is the most religious country on our planet, and Sweden is the least religious, America is a land of Indians ruled by Swedes." Huston Smith, *Why Religion Matters: The Fate of the Human Spirit in an Age of Disbelief* 103 (New York: HarperCollins, 2001). For the argument that religious institutions in the United States may decline in the future, see Robert Wuthnow, *Saving America? Faith-Based Services and the Future of Civil Society* 96–98 (Princeton: Princeton University Press, 2004). For the argument that European religiosity may survive the relative abandonment of religious institutions, see Grace Davie, "Europe: The Exception That Proves the Rule," in Berger, *Desecularization of the World*, 68–71; see generally Grace Davie, *Religion in Britain since 1945: Believing without Belonging* (Oxford: Blackwell, 1994) (using a sociological approach to describe and explain religion in contemporary Britain); Grace Davie, *Religion in Modern Europe: A Memory Mutates* (New York: Oxford University Press, 2000) (using same approach to analyze European religious trends). For research suggesting that religion is more alive in Europe than is generally supposed, see Andrew M. Greeley, *A Sociological Profile: Religion in Europe at the End of the Second Millennium* 1–20 (New Brunswick, N.J.: Transaction, 2003) (providing statistical evidence that belief in God persists in Europe: "Europe is hardly godless"). Part of what Davie and Greeley are arguing is that the glass is half full; part is to question what measures are appropriate to focus upon. Greeley, in particular, argues that Europe is an aggregation that hides too much, that there are obvious transnational categories, e.g., age, gender, class, but the particular national experience is more important than the European experience in explaining religious phenomena. See Greeley, *A Sociological Profile*, xi. For example, those who generalize about Europe need to explain the religiosity of Ireland, north and south, as well as Poland. See Bruce, *Politics and Religion*, 44–46 (discussing interaction of religion and politics in Poland and Ireland). See generally Greeley, *A Sociological Profile* (providing sociological data on religious beliefs in various European countries). They must also account for the substantial difference on most measures between the French and those in countries such as Spain, Portugal, and Italy. In addition, for example, Greeley finds significant attitudinal differences between the Catholics of Northern Ireland and the Catholics of the south. See *A Sociological Profile*, 133–51.

67. Derek H. Davis, "The U.S. Supreme Court as Moral Physician: *Mitchell v. Helms* and the Constitutional Revolution to Reduce Restrictions on Governmental Aid to Religion," 43 *Journal of Church and State* 213, 229 (2001); cf. Stephen M. Feldman, "Critical Questions in Law and Religion: An Introduction," in *Law and Religion: A Critical Anthology* 1, 2 (Stephen M. Feldman ed., New York: New York University Press, 2000) ("A 1997 Gallop Poll found that 90 percent of Americans pray, 96 percent believe in God, 63 percent give grace or give thanks to God aloud, and 42 percent attended organized religious services the previous week"). In fact, 60 percent of people believe that one can only be a

Christian if he believes in the divinity of Christ; 90 percent believe that Christ actually lived; 70 percent believed he was truly God (Feldman, 2) (remarking further that other studies document "consistently high levels of belief in life after death, heaven, and Christ's presence in heaven"). Although belief and attendance rates are generally lower in most European countries than in the United States, it would not be appropriate to describe European countries as secular: "[E]ven in the most apparently 'secular' of contemporary societies there are areas of society or of individual life where religious influences remain important." Hugh McLeod, *Religion and the People of Western Europe: 1789–1989*, at 154 (2nd ed., Oxford: Oxford University Press, 1997). On the European demographics, see Jenkins, *The Next Christendom*, 94–96 (describing the declining Christian and Catholic religious identification in European countries). Modern-day commentators might well have described eighteenth-century American society as secular. Moore, *Touchdown Jesus*, 15 ("Most Americans in 1787 neither belonged to nor regularly attended any house of worship. Church membership varied from place to place but stood somewhere around 10 percent of the total population").

68. See generally Madison, "Memorial and Remonstrance," 12–13 (explaining that a "just government" will not use clergy as auxiliaries, nor curtail the rights of a religion, nor permit one religion to interfere with the rights of another). For the claim that monopoly churches "tend to be lazy and will fail to mobilize high levels of commitment," see Rodney Stark and James C. McCann, "Market Forces and Catholic Commitment: Exploring the New Paradigm," 32 *Journal for the Scientific Study of Religion* 111, 118 (1993).

69. See McLeod, *People of Western Europe*, 16. During some of his reign, Franco nominated half of the bishops in Spain. George Huntston Williams, *The Contours of Church and State in the Thought of John Paul II* 29 (Waco, Tex.: Baylor University Press, 1983). Late in 1953, a new concordat lessened his control and declared Catholicism to be the only religion of the Spanish nation—though citizens were to be free to practice other religions. See Williams, 29. In 1978, however, the Spanish Constitution disentangled church and state, declaring: "There shall be no state religion. The public authorities shall take account of the religious beliefs of Spanish society and shall accordingly maintain relations of cooperation with the Catholic Church and other faiths." C.E. Ch.2 Div.1 § 16(3), quoted in *Freedom of Religion and Belief: A World Report* 383 (Kevin Boyle and Juliet Sheen eds., London: Routledge, 1997). For discussion of the negative impact of the church's embrace of Franco, see Casanova, *Public Religions*, 75–91.

70. Federal Research Division, Library of Congress, Portugal—a Country Study, http://www.memory.loc.gov/frd/cs/pttoc.html (last visited September 6, 2004).

71. Warner, *Confessions*, 71 (arguing that the French church "was undeniably an integral part of the Vichy order," that it made the mistake of condemning De Gaulle, and that in the aftermath of the war it "would no longer be viewed as the guardian of things eternal, and certainly not of France"). Even if the leaders of the French church had wished to distance the church from the Vichy regime— clergy were in fact divided over the desirability of the Resistance—policies of several popes had decentralized the French church to make it less able to offer resistance to Rome, which it was richly inclined to do. See Warner, 68–69. The by-

product of the ecclesiastical struggle was that the French church was unable to offer a strong voice in French politics (Warner, 68). Interestingly, the politics of those bishops who wanted distance from Rome tended to be monarchist and conservative; those who wanted closer political ties with Rome tended to favor Republican politics (62–64).

72. See John G. Francis, "The Evolving Regulatory Structure of European Church-State Relationships," 34 *Journal of Church and State* 775, 786 (1992).

73. Despite courageous exceptions, the complicity of German Protestants was widespread. See John S. Conway, "The Political Role of German Protestantism, 1870–1990," 34 *Journal of Church and State* 819, 828–29 (1992).

74. Hans Küng, *The Catholic Church: A Short History* 176–80 (John Bowden trans., New York: Modern Library, 2001); Warner, *Confessions*, 188, 190 (showing that the church encouraged the Zentrum, a German Catholic political party, to sign the 1933 Enabling Act, which gave Hitler dictatorial powers, turned over birth records to the Nazis (facilitating the identification of Jews), and told Catholics that they were to obey the Nazi regime); Morris, *American Catholic*, 242 (citing John Diggins's suggestion that the Catholic Church was "the last organization in the world" that should have been relying on pragmatic arguments in dealing with Hitler given its claims to moral clarity regarding other political regimes). On the other hand, the church had some distance from the Nazis enabling it to achieve a substantial amount of political damage control. See Warner, *Confessions*, 186–92. The church in Italy was even more successful in the latter regard. In general, "The Pope agreed to accept the Fascists and Mussolini agreed that the Catholic religion would be taught in every Italian school. He also promised to pay the salaries of Catholic priests and set up the Vatican City in Rome." BBC, *Modern World History: Fascism in Italy*, http://www.bbc.co.uk/education/ modern/fascism/fascihtm.htm (last visited September 25, 2004). Despite this agreement, the church and Mussolini had many disagreements over the years that allowed the church to "distance itself from Fascism without also incriminating Catholicism, or appearing to reverse itself." Warner, *Confessions*, 53. The demand that the church "disown certain political and social movements in exchange for limited ecclesiastical freedoms" was a frequent problem in Eastern Europe and Third World countries. Eric O. Hanson, *The Catholic Church in World Politics* 57 (Princeton: Princeton University Press, 1987).

75. Indeed, Roman Catholics now outnumber Anglicans in England. See Michael W. McConnell, "Establishment and Disestablishment at the Founding, Part I: Establishment of Religion," 44 *William and Mary Law Review* 2105, 2115 (2003) ("The main victim of the establishment today, if there is one, may be the established church itself"). On the prospects for an Anglican recovery and reconceptualization, see generally *Beyond Colonial Anglicanism: The Anglican Communion in the Twenty-first Century* (Ian T. Douglas and Kowk Pui-Lan eds., New York: Church Pub., 2001).

76. See Eva M. Hamberg and Thorleif Pettersson, "The Religious Market: Denominational Competition and Religious Participation in Contemporary Sweden," 33 *Journal for the Scientific Study of Religion* 205, 206 (1994) (claiming that individuals' religious choices can be better explained by inertia).

77. At least since Vatican II, the Catholic Church has accepted religious plural-ism as a political fact, has abandoned the view that the state has the responsibility to defend and promote religious truth, and has settled on the view that the state is obliged to embrace the secular value of protecting religious freedom. See John Courtney Murray, S.J., "The Issue of Church and State at Vatican Council II," in *The Church in the World* 35, 41–44 (Charles P. O'Donnell ed., Milwaukee: Bruce, 1967). Pope Pius XI had stated as recently as 1933 that the separation of church and state was "impious and absurd." Morris, *American Catholic*, 236–37.

78. See *supra* notes 55–56.

79. McLeod, *People of Western Europe*, 20–21.

80. Charles Taylor, *Varieties of Religion Today: William James Revisited* 77 (Cambridge: Harvard University Press, 2002) (observing that the French Cana-dian identity is bound up with Catholicism).

81. Fighting against imperialism can be a major source of growth in the church. See George Scialabba, "A Faith That Shaped Today's World," *Boston Sunday Globe*, August 18, 2002, D5 (book review) ("The faith grew astonishingly fast in the second and third centuries, especially among the lower classes. . . . Roman persecution was fitful, but even at its fiercest was unavailing. The blood of martyrs was indeed the seed of the church"). For the claim that the church's activities on behalf of the poor—and particularly poor non-church members—was also a significant factor in its growth, see Anton Wessels, *Europe: Was It Ever Really Christian: The Interaction between Gospel and Culture* 196 (John Bowden trans., London: SCM Press, 1994). The primary thesis of Wessels's monograph is that the evangelical success of Christianity depended upon its ability to adapt its mes-sage to the customs, habits, and rituals of the different cultures it encountered.

82. Casanova, *Public Religions*, 22, 29.

83. Finke and Stark, *Churching of America*, 18–21; see also Rakove, "Once More into the Breach," 254 ("[T]o judge by the results, [the] market-oriented approach offers the best explanation for the remarkable success of the American experiment in religious pluralism"). For a powerful criticism of the Finke and Stark perspective in the context of Great Britain, see Steve Bruce, "The Truth about Religion in Britain," 34 *Journal for the Scientific Study of Religion* 417 (1995). See also Steve Bruce, *God Is Dead: Secularization in the West* 204–28 (Oxford: Blackwell, 2002) (criticizing the Finke and Stark perspective in the con-text of the United States).

84. Küng, *The Catholic Church*, 35–37 (describing Constantine's recognition of Christianity).

85. Nicholas Burns, "A Diplomat's Journey," in *Why I Am Still a Catholic* 66, 75 (Kevin Ryan and Marilyn Ryan eds., New York: Riverhead Books, 1998).

86. The Catholics' forcible conversion of the Donatists yielded unanticipated consequences: "[T]he African churches, even those of Carthage and Hippo, were overwhelmed by Islam in the seventh century without resistance and vanished without a trace into history." Küng, *Great Christian Thinkers*, 81.

87. See Jenkins, *The Next Christendom*, 57–58.

88. See Jenkins, *The Next Christendom*, 56–60, 153.

89. "In all European countries, regardless of religious complexion, the state has sloughed off notions of partnership with the Church, the possible exception

being Ireland." Atkins and Tallett, *Priests, Prelates and People*, 324. For the claim that new religions are flourishing in Europe, see Rodney Stark, "Europe's Receptivity to New Religious Movements: Round Two," 32 *Journal for the Scientific Study of Religion* 389, 396 (1993).

90. The probable complexity of the appropriate analysis is indicated by Jose Casanova. Krishan Kumar and Ekaterina Makarova, "An Interview with Jose Casanova," 4 *Hedgehog Review* 91, 92 (2002) ("The traditional model of secularization offers a plausible account of European developments but not of American ones. The alternative American paradigm linking religious vitality to free religious markets works relatively well for the United States but not for contemporary Europe. Neither can offer a plausible account of the significant internal variations within Europe. Most importantly, neither works very well for other world religions and other parts of the world").

91. McGrath, *The Future of Christianity*, ix. Support for religion in Ireland has wavered in part because of corruption in the clergy (McGrath, x), and presumably because of increased wealth.

92. McLeod, *People of Western Europe*, 15, 26–29, 57, 60–62, 72, 82–83. The split between clericals and anticlericals has long been central to French politics. Küng, *The Catholic Church*, 155. Anticlericism need not signal a rejection of religion. For an interesting account of anticlericism in Spain, see Ruth Behar, "The Struggle for the Church: Popular Anticlericalism and Religiosity in Post-Franco Spain," in *Religious Orthodoxy and Popular Faith in European Society* 76 (Ellen Badone ed., Princeton: Princeton University Press, 1990).

93. According to George Shuster, other factors "could not have decimated Christendom so savagely had it not been for the rise of the conviction that the problem of evil is beyond solution. It was the powerlessness of the individual in the face of tyranny which was so awesome and awful, so shattering and unnerving an experience." George Shuster, "Christian Culture and Education," in O'Donnell, *Church in the World*, 86, 92. For discussion of the problem of evil, see Susan Neiman, *Evil in Modern Thought: An Alternative History of Philosophy* (Princeton: Princeton University Press, 2002).

94. Shuster, "Christian Culture and Education," 75–97. In some cases this phenomenon is better explained by class difference. Moreover, the hopelessness for many of urban life sometimes pushes them toward religion. Taylor, *Varieties of Religion Today*, 38–39. Nonetheless, socioeconomic modernization tends toward secularization. See Peter L. Berger, *The Sacred Canopy: Elements of a Sociological Theory of Religion* 108–9, 130–31 (Garden City, N.Y., Doubleday, 1967).

95. McLeod, *People of Western Europe*, 28–35. One explanation for women's greater religiosity proposes that "religion stresses the 'feminine' values of kindness, empathy, and compassion, and does not value the masculine characteristics of aggression and dominance." Benjamin Beit-Hallahmi and Michael Argyle, *The Psychology of Religious Behaviour, Belief, and Experience* 65 (London: Routledge, 1997). Women tend to see God as supporting, loving, and forgiving; men tend to see God as a planner, supreme power, and controller. Beit-Hallahmi and Argyle, 140. It is ironic that the Catholic Church would insist on limiting important ministerial functions to males, although some steps have been taken to loosen the historic restrictions. See Hüme, *Remaking Europe*, 54. On the political

impact of female religiosity, see Morris, *American Catholic*, 46 ("Avoiding undue clerical influence in public affairs was advanced in the French Parliament as an important reason for denying women suffrage").

96. See Morris, *American Catholic*, 409–11, 423, 430. For a critique of the church's position, see Hans Küng, *Christianity: Essence, History, and Future* 79–83, 53–62, 604–14, 752–61 (2003). For a political defense, see Jenkins, *The Next Christendom*, 196, 198–200, 209.

97. The American experience in this regard presumably mirrors that of Europe. The Catholic Church experienced a significant decline in attendance and a substantial decline in contributions. Andrew Greeley, *The Catholic Myth* 15–16, 23–24, 134–35 (New York: Scribner, 1997). This amounted to nothing less than a historic crisis of church authority. Andrew Greeley, *The Catholic Revolution: New Wine, Old Wineskins, and the Second Vatican Council* 8, 55–57, 73 (Berkeley and Los Angeles: University of California Press, 2004).

98. On the limits of a naturalistic view, see Alan Donagan, "Can Anybody in a Post-Christian Culture Rationally Believe the Nicene Creed?" in *Christian Philosophy* 92 (Thomas P. Flint ed., Notre Dame: Notre Dame University Press, 1990). For a brilliant discussion of the relationship between scientism, religion, and romanticism, see Peter L. Thorslev Jr., *Romantic Contraries: Freedom versus Destiny* (New Haven: Yale University Press, 1984). See also Reinhold Niebuhr, *Does Civilization Need Religion? A Study in the Social Resources and Limitations of Religion in Modern Life* 5 (New York: Macmillan, 1928) ("The sciences have greatly complicated the problem of maintaining the plausibility of the personalization of the universe by which religion guarantees the worth of human personality; and science applied to the world's work has created a type of society in which human personality is easily debased"). On the limits of science, see Smith, *Why Religion Matters*. For the methodological atheism of Habermas, see Jürgen Habermas, *Religion and Rationality: Essays on Reason, God, and Modernity* 78–91 (Eduardo Mendieta ed., Cambridge: MIT Press, 2002). See also Margaret M. Campbell, *Critical Theory and Liberation Theology: A Comparison of the Initial Work of Jürgen Habermas and Gustavio Gutiérrez* (New York: P. Lang, 1999) (exploring and analyzing the work of Jürgen Habermas); Marc P. Lalonde, *Critical Theology and the Challenge of Jürgen Habermas* 33–37 (New York: P. Lang, 1999) (same).

99. On the other hand, an emphasis on reason and science "undermines all the old certainties; uncertainty is a condition that many people find very hard to bear; therefore, any movement (not only a religious one) that promises to provide or to renew certainty has a ready market." Berger, "Desecularization of the World," 7.

100. Finke and Stark argue that the uncompromising character of religious institutions is a strong factor in maintaining their power to attract and maintain membership. Thus they argue that the liberalization of Vatican II in the Catholic Church caused its lay membership and the number of priests to decline. Finke and Stark, *Churching of America*, 255–75.

101. In countries where Catholicism dominates, the potential for schism seems less in this post–Reformation era. Catholics who can no longer live with the church frequently leave organized religion altogether. Perhaps because Protestant denominations emphasize the lack of a central authority, the potential for multiple

schisms has been greater. See Timothy P. Schilling, "When Bishops Disagree: Rome, Hunthausen and the Current Church Crisis," *Commonwealth*, September 12, 2003, 15, 21 (contrasting the propensities of Catholics and Protestant to engage in schism); cf. Fowler and Hertzke, *Religion and Politics*, 33 ("In Europe, if you have become alienated from the established church you likely drift away; in America you are as likely to form or join a new church").

102. George Washington, Farewell Address (September 17, 1796), in *A Compilation of the Messages and Papers of the Presidents, 1789–1897*, 213, 220 (James D. Richardson ed., Washington, D.C.: U.S. Congress, 1900); cf. Alexis de Tocqueville, *Democracy in America* 293 (George Lawrence trans., J. P. Mayer ed., New York: Harper and Row, 1966) ("I do not know if all Americans have faith in their religion—for who can read the secrets of the heart?—but I am sure that they think it necessary to the maintenance of republican institutions. That is not the view of one class or party among the citizens, but of the whole nation; it is found in all ranks"). Moore, *Touchdown Jesus*, 15 ("We ... know that, whether [the Framers] were Deist or Congregational or Episcopalian, or not much of anything, they shared an important assumption: Religion was the foundation of virtue").

103. John Stuart Mill, "Utility of Religion," in *Nature and Utility of Religion* 50–51 (George Nakhanian ed., New York: Liberal Arts Press, 1958).

104. Mill, "Utility of Religion," 68.

105. For the argument that many East Asian countries have been organized—with considerable success—through the aggressive promotion of a form of secular humanism, see T. R. Reid, *Confucius Lives Next Door: What Living in the East Teaches Us about Living in the West* 227–28, 246 (New York: Random House, 1999).

106. Niebuhr, *Does Civilization Need Religion?* 14.

107. For reflections on living without an explanation, see Thomas Nagel, *What Does It All Mean: A Very Short Introduction to Philosophy* 95–101 (New York: Oxford University Press, 1987).

108. Niebuhr, *Does Civilization Need Religion?* 4.

109. See generally Küng, *The Catholic Church*, 57–65 (stressing the idea of being a disciple).

110. Niebuhr, *Does Civilization Need Religion?* 5; see also Michael J. Perry, *Love and Power: The Role of Religion and Morality in American Politics* 69–70 (New York: Oxford University Press, 1991) ("One polar response to the problem of meaning is to conclude that life is, finally and radically meaningless. . . . The other polar response, . . . is 'religious': the trust that life is ultimately meaningful, meaningful in a way hospitable to our deepest yearnings"); Jonathan Sacks, *The Dignity of Difference* 82 (London: Continuum, 2002) (remarking that religions are "a significant space outside of and in counterpoint to a late-modern Western culture that tends systematically to dissolve the values and virtues that give meaning to a life"); Marshall, "Concept of Offensiveness," 387 ("Religion addresses the most important questions at the core of human existence—the existential questions of meaning, morality, and the nature of Truth. It provides many with a sustaining meaning for life—and an explanation for death"). Marshall, however, argues that the psychological need to hold on to these explanations leads to

intolerance, particularly when everlasting life is thought to be at stake (388–90). On the latter point, see William P. Marshall, "The Other Side of Religion," 44 *Hastings Law Journal* 843, 858 (1993) (suggesting religious believers may view forces that assault their religious structure "as threatening evils that must be eliminated"); cf. Berg, "Church-State Relations," 1589–90, 1596–97 (suggesting that believers' recognition that only one God exists can induce humility, but can also lead to false absolutes and arrogance).

111. Thanks to Seana Shiffrin for the points made in this paragraph.

112. The evidence regarding actual congregant behavior is mixed. See Beit-Hallahmi and Argyle, *Psychology of Religious Behaviour*, 200–203. But churches generally work to promote altruism and oppose the notion of "every man for himself." Hüme, *Remaking Europe*, 14; see also Hüme, 48 (arguing that "it is important for the churches to stress the moral imperative to help those in need").

113. Glendon, *Rights Talk*, 107.

114. Bill McGibbon, "The People of the (Unread Book)," in *Getting on Message: Challenging the Christian Right from the Heart of the Gospel* 14 (Peter Laarman ed., Boston: Beacon Press, 2006).

115. Hans Küng, *On Being a Christian* 28–31 (Garden City, N.Y.: Doubleday, 1978).

116. For extensive discussion relevant to this issue, see Davie, *Religion in Modern Europe*, 38–194.

117. Peter Dobkin Hall, "The History of Religious Philanthropy in America," in Robert Wuthnow, Virginia A. Hodginson, and associates, *Faith and Philanthropy in America: Exploring the Role of Religion in America's Voluntary Sector* 38, 38–39 (San Francisco: Jossey-Bass, 1990) (churches and denominationally tied institutions account for close to two-thirds of philanthropic contributions); Wuthnow et al., *Faith and Philanthropy*, xiii ("Millions of Americans regularly attend religious services, and a large proportion give of their time and money to charitable causes and voluntary organizations").

118. Fowler and Hertzke, *Religion and Politics*, 32 ("On the social and civic level, religious people are more likely to give to charity, vote, and be influenced in community activities than the nonreligious"). Obviously other associations promote civic virtue, but the contribution of religion to civic virtue can in combination with other factors serve to justify special constitutional protection. See, e.g., Hall, "Religion and Civic Virtue," 112–17 (arguing that religious liberties should be protected on several grounds, including that religion serves a distinctive role in value inculcation and the production of civic virtue).

119. See Carter, *The Culture of Disbelief*, 112.

120. For arguments that it should be so interpreted, see Garvey, *What Are Freedoms For?* 49–57, which argues that religious freedom is protected because the law views religion as a good thing. Cf. Smith, "Rise and Fall," 157 (contending that a religious justification for religious freedom had substantial force in the founding period). The Framers certainly had no interest in promoting false religions. This was one of the reasons for the notion that persons should not be forced to support religions to which they were opposed. Tribe, *American Constitutional Law*, 1160–61. Moreover, the early American church histories were written to

allay the worry that disestablishment would promote quack religions and undermine the morality of the nation. Moore, *Religious Outsiders*, 5–13.

121. See Conkle, "Toward a General Theory," 1132–35. But cf. Steven D. Smith, *Foreordained Failure: The Quest for a Constitutional Principle of Religious Freedom* 18–19 (1995) (arguing that the exclusive purpose of the Establishment Clause was to assign jurisdiction over religious issues to the states); Akhil Reed Amar, "The Bill of Rights as a Constitution," 100 *Yale Law Journal* 1131, 1157–60 (1991) (applying the Establishment Clause against states eliminates the states' rights to establish religion—a right the clause itself explicitly confirms).

122. Conkle, "Toward a General Theory," 1134 ("The national government was conceived as a government of limited and enumerated powers, and these powers did not extend to matters of religion"); see *supra* note 40.

123. John Locke was influential in this regard. Locke, *A Letter Concerning Toleration*, 26–30; see also Madison, "Memorial and Remonstrance," at 9–10 ("[I]n matters of religion, no man's right is abridged by the institution of Civil Society, and . . . Religion is wholly exempt from its cognizance"); Michael McConnell, " 'God Is Dead and We Have Killed Him!': Freedom of Religion in the Post-modern Age," 1993 *BYU Law Review* 163, 167–70 (discussing the lack of government power over the soul); Michael W. McConnell, "Why Is Religious Liberty the 'First Freedom' ? " 21 *Cardozo Law Review* 1243, 1245–50 (2000) (exploring the relationship of two-kingdoms theology to the First Amendment). This argument has also been used to oppose democracy. See Kraynak, *Christian Faith*, 45–106.

124. See *supra* note 101 and accompanying text.

125. Eugene R. Sheridan, *Jefferson and Religion* 67–68 (Charlottesville: Thomas Jefferson Memorial Foundation, 1998) (describing Jefferson as revering Jesus as a moral reformer, but rejecting the Bible as divine revelation and rejecting Christianity's theological, metaphysical, and ecclesiological doctrines as corruptions of Jesus' message).

126. Sheridan, *Jefferson and Religion*, 19.

127. See Moore, *Touchdown Jesus*, 15 (explaining that Jefferson and other Deists found evidence of God in the "machine-like perfection of the natural order"); Rakove, "Once More into the Breach," 254 (noting that Jefferson hoped religious discussion would produce "rational deists"). Although Jefferson opposed doctrines associating Jesus Christ with the divine, he ultimately came to favor Christian moral teachings. See Sheridan, *Jefferson and Religion*, 68 ("If the acceptance of orthodox Christian doctrines produced virtuous lives, he welcomed the result without approving the cause").

128. William Lee Miller argues that religion cannot be viewed as the sole and necessary foundation of American institutions. See William Lee Miller, "The Moral Project of the American Founders," in Hunter and Guinness, *Articles of Faith*, 17, 35 (the Enlightenment, with its edge of skepticism, was too much present in the Revolution, in the new nation's institutions, in key founders, in the mind of significant segments of the people—and, in effect, in the great silences and protections and negations of the Constitution itself—for that to be persuasive). Instead, Miller maintains that the distinctive feature "of the American beginning was neither the religious underpinnings nor the emancipation from them but

the combination" (37). Nonetheless, the Enlightenment theme in the United States was not as hostile to religion as it was in Europe. In part, this was because those who supported religion also supported republicanism, contrary to the pattern in Europe. See Miller "Moral Project"; cf. Wills, *Head and Heart*, 2, 7, 152 (the main and most numerous followers of the Enlightenment in America were religious, though evangelicals were not prominent in the crucial constitutional period).

129. Although the original intent of the Framers is relevant to constitutional adjudication, multiple sources should guide constitutional interpretation. Shiffrin, "Liberalism, Radicalism," 1197–98. But see McConnell, "God Is Dead," 168–72 (placing stress on original intent).

130. Cf. Berg, "Church-State Relations," at 1581–82 (suggesting there was an overlapping consensus about the purposes of the religion clauses at the founding, but arguing that the rise of the welfare state tears the consensus apart). Of course, in the concrete, no consensus exists as to how to define religious freedom in specific contexts.

131. The same could not be said from this perspective of Roger Williams's concern that the wilderness of the state would compromise the garden of religion. From a religious perspective, protecting religions from the corrosive effects of state interference is of religious importance. From the perspective of the nonreligious, compromising the garden of religion might or might not serve civic purposes.

132. Thomas Berg argues that "the reliance on religious voluntarist beliefs to ground religious freedom is not the sort of reliance that amounts to real favoritism or preference for religion or a particular faith." Berg, "Religious Clause Anti-Theories," 734. Instead, the voluntarist principle is intended to "give equal liberty to all beliefs" (734). Although the government may rely upon one specific belief to ground the general principle, this fact "does not in itself create any favoritism in how government actually treats its citizens—and again, it is how government actually treats citizens, not the grounds on which it relies, that is most important to neutrality" (734).

133. U.S. Const. art. VI, cl. 3 ("[N]o religious Test shall ever be required as a Qualification to any Office or Public Trust under the United States"). On the significance of this provision, see Kramnick and Moore, *The Godless Constitution*, 26–45.

134. See Berg, "Church-State Relations," 1630–31.

CHAPTER 4
APPLYING THE ESTABLISHMENT CLAUSE

1. Compare, for example, the treatment of government prayers such as "God save this honorable Court" with cases such as *Santa Fe Indep. Sch. Dist. v. Doe*, 530 U.S. 290 (2000), striking down school-sponsored prayer at football games, *Lee v. Weisman*, 505 U.S. 577 (1992), striking down school-sponsored prayer at graduation, and *Engel v. Vitale*, 370 U.S. 421 (1962), striking down state-sponsored prayer in classrooms.

2. See *County of Allegheny*, 492 U.S. 655 (Kennedy, J., concurring).

3. See generally Richard John Neuhaus, *The Naked Public Square: Religion and Democracy in America* (Grand Rapids, Mich.: Eerdmans, 1984) (arguing that the idea of America as a secular society is "demonstrably false" and "exceedingly dangerous").

4. On the other hand, the Constitution itself deliberately does not refer to God.

5. *Engel*, 370 U.S. 436.

6. *Sch. Dist. v. Schempp*, 374 U.S. 203, 223–27 (1963).

7. *Newdow v. U.S. Congress*, 292 F.3d 597 (9th Cir. 2002) (judgment stayed on June 27, 2002, pending en banc review). The opinion was ultimately withdrawn in favor of an opinion declaring unconstitutional a school district policy requiring the recitation of the Pledge of Allegiance daily by willing students in each elementary school class, but not invalidating the congressional act adding the words under God to the Pledge. *Newdow v. U.S. Congress*, 328 F.3d 466, 483, 490 (9th Cir. 2003), *cert denied*, 124 S. Ct. 383 (2003), *and cert. granted sub nom*, *Elk Grove Unified Sch. Dist. v. Newdow*, 124 S. Ct. 384 (2003).

8. *Newdow*, 292 F.3d 600.

9. *Everson v. Bd. of Educ.*, 330 U.S. 1, 15–16 (1947).

10. *Newdow*, 292 F.3d 607–8; cf. *Larson v. Valente*, 456 U.S. 228, 244 (1982) ("The clearest command of the Establishment Clause is that one religious denomination cannot be officially preferred over another").

11. *Newdow*, 292 F.3d 609 (quoting 100 Cong. Rec. 8618 (1954)).

12. Of course, many nonreligious products of the Enlightenment would argue that there is a moral order and that the U.S. Constitution is best understood as requiring that the government create and comply with that order. While the writers of the Declaration of Independence looked to God as the source of that order, nonreligious moralists find that the order is grounded in nature alone, or in some concept of civilization, or even in supposedly unchallengeable a priori principles, often inspired by Kant. So some Americans want to rescue the Constitution from God, whereas others, with deeper historical roots, see this desire as doing violence to it. Hence the contemporary American Kulturkampf. Taylor, *Varieties of Religion Today*, 70. For an argument that the existence of a moral order shows the existence of God, see C. S. Lewis, *Mere Christianity* 3–32 (rev. ed., New York: Macmillan, 1953). For additional discussion of that issue, see Alan Ryan, *John Dewey and the High Tide of American Liberalism* 360–62 (New York: Norton, 1995).

13. *Elk Grove United School District v. Newdow*, 542 U.S. 1, 124 S. Ct. 2301 (2004).

14. *Elk Grove*, 124 S. Ct. 2330 (Thomas, J., concurring). Justice Thomas argued that the Establishment Clause did not apply to the states and, if it did, it would only prevent coercion by force of law or penalty, which the pledge policy did not do (2330) (Thomas, J., concurring). As Justice Thomas understands, his rendition of the Establishment Clause would "probably cover little more than the Free Exercise Clause" (2328) (Thomas, J., concurring). From the perspective detailed in this book, this approach would ignore important Establishment Clause values while embracing a shriveled conception of the Free Exercise Clause. I make some remarks on the incorporation of the Establishment Clause issue in Steven H.

Shiffrin, "Liberalism and the Establishment Clause," 78 *Chicago-Kent Law Review* 717 (2003).

15. *Elk Grove*, 124 S. Ct. 2319 (Rehnquist, C.J., concurring) (*quoting* H.R. Rep. No. 83–1693 (1954)).

16. *Elk Grove*, 124 S. Ct. 2317 (Rehnquist, C.J., concurring).

17. *Elk Grove*, 124 S. Ct. 2321–22 (O'Connor, J., concurring).

18. *Elk Grove*, 124 S. Ct. 2322 (O'Connor, J., concurring).

19. *Lynch*, 465 U.S. 688 (O'Connor, J., concurring).

20. *Elk Grove*, 124 S. Ct. 124 S. Ct. 2321 (O'Connor, J., concurring).

21. *Elk Grove*, 124 S. Ct. 2325. (O'Connor, J., concurring).

22. *Lynch*, 465 U.S. 716 (Brennan, J., dissenting). This argument is even less persuasive when used to support the governmentally sponsored ceremonies featuring prayer in the wake of the September 11 tragedy. For the argument that governmentally sponsored prayers should be immune from constitutional objection in exceptional circumstances—such as a national crisis combined with public mourning—so long as the government response occurs within a limited time period from the date of the tragedy, see William P. Marshall, "The Limits of Secularism: Public Religious Expression in Moments of National Crisis and Tragedy," 78 *Notre Dame Law Review* 11, 31–33 (2002).

23. Despite ceremonial deists' claims to the contrary, the brevity of the ceremonies and their likely ineffectiveness do not rob them of their religious character.

24. Harold J. Berman, "Religious Freedom and the Challenge of the Modern State," in Hunter and Guinness, *Articles of Faith*, 45 ("[T]he great apostle of the public school, Horace Mann, . . . continually emphasized that only through public education could a Christian social consciousness and a Christian morality be inculcated in the population as a whole").

25. R. Laurence Moore, "Bible Reading and Nonsectarian Schooling: The Failure of Religious Instruction in Nineteenth-Century Public Education," 86 *Journal of American History* 1581, 1598 (2000). For arguments that the Pledge may have more importance in inculcating religious values than I recognize, see Shiffrin, "What's Wrong with Compelled Association."

26. *Elk Grove*, 124 S. Ct. 2324–25 (O'Connor, J., concurring).

27. *Elk Grove*, 124 S. Ct. 2327 (O'Connor, J., concurring).

28. *Elk Grove*, 124 S. Ct. 2326 (O'Connor, J., concurring).

29. *Elk Grove*, 124 S. Ct. 2325 (O'Connor, J., concurring).

30. *Elk Grove*, 124 S. Ct. 2326 (O'Connor, J., concurring).

31. Steven G. Gey, " 'Under God,' The Pledge of Allegiance, and Other Constitutional Trivia," 81 *North Carolina Law Review* 1865, 1873–80 (2003).

32. See Gey, "Under God," 1914–16. Similar considerations lead me to conclude that "In God We Trust" on coins is not de minimis.

33. James Davison Hunter, "Religious Freedom and the Challenge of Modern Pluralism," in Hunter and Guinness, *Articles of Faith*, 54, 55 ("While no one Protestant denomination enjoyed the patronage of the state, the cause of a 'pan-Protestantism' had a substantial, if unofficial, governmental endorsement. The consequence was the restriction of the full civil liberties of other, non-Protestant communities of belief"); see also Berg "Church-State Relations," 1612 (discussing the American authorities' preferences for "generic Protestantism" even

after disestablishment); cf. Tocqueville, *Democracy in America*, 293 ("For the Americans the ideas of Christianity and liberty are so completely mingled that it is almost impossible to get them to conceive of the one without the other; it is not a question with them of sterile beliefs bequeathed by the past and vegetating rather than living in the depths of the soul").

34. Finke and Stark, *Churching of America*, 139–40 (New Brunswick: Rutgers University Press, 1992); Lash, "Second Adoption,"1120–22; McConnell, "Religious Freedom at Crossroads," 121.

35. See Michael deHaven Newsom, "Common School Religion: Judicial Narratives in a Protestant Empire," 11 *S. California Interdisc. Law Journal* 219, 223–37 (2002).

36. Thomas M. Cooley, *A Treatise on the Constitutional Limitations* 967 (Walter Carrington ed., 8th ed., Boston, Little, Brown and Co.,1927); see Steven K. Green, "Private School Vouchers and the Confusion over 'Direct' Aid," 10 *Geo. Mason U. Civ. Rts. Law Journal* 47, 50–51 (2000) (describing how, from the second half of the nineteenth century into the twentieth, state courts consistently invalidated financial aid to religious schools). Consider Stephen M. Feldman, "The Theory and Politics of First Amendment Protections: Why Does the Supreme Court Favor Free Expression Over Religious Freedom?," 8 *University of Pennsylvania J. Const.L.* 431, 472–73 (2006): "The Justices would occasionally behind closed doors reveal their religious prejudices. For example, Justice William O. Douglas passed a note to Justice Hugo Black during an oral argument complaining that '[i]f the Catholics get public money to finance their schools, we better insist on getting some good prayers in public schools or we Protestants are out of business.' " See generally McGreevy, *Catholicism and American Freedom*.

37. Reading without commentary suggested that it was up to the individual to interpret the scripture, but the Catholic Church taught that its hierarchy was necessary for guidance in the interpretation. See Macedo, *Diversity and Distrust*, 54–59, 64–76.

38. Hamburger, *Separation of Church and State*, 364–65. For the contention, somewhat exaggerated to my mind, that anti-Catholic prejudice remains common, see Philip Jenkins, *The New Anti-Catholicism: The Last Acceptable Prejudice* (Oxford: Oxford University Press, 2003).

39. *Everson v. Board of Education* 330 U.S. 1, 15 (1947).

40. For criticism of the Court's expansion of such practices by resort to analogy, see William Van Alstyne, "Trends in the Supreme Court," 782–87.

41. For arguments that they should be eliminated, see Steven B. Epstein, "Rethinking the Constitutionality of Ceremonial Deism," 96 *Columbia Law Review* 2083, 2173–74 (1996); Douglas Laycock, "Equal Access and Moments of Silence: The Equal Status of Religious Speech by Private Speakers," 81 *Northwestern University Law Review* 1, 8 (1986); Arnold H. Loewy, "Rethinking Government Neutrality Towards Religion under the Establishment Clause: The Untapped Potential of Justice O'Connor's Insight," 64 *North Carolina Law Review* 1049, 1054–60 (1986).

42. For defense of the notion that America has a civil religion that includes God, see Robert N. Bellah, "Civil Religion in America," in *Religion in America* 3, 5 (William G. McLoughlin and Robert N. Bellah eds., Boston: Houghton Mifflin,

1966): "[T]he separation of church and state has not denied the political realm a religious dimension." More generally, the Bill of Rights might be understood to presuppose a Supreme Being. For an argument that the notion of equality among human beings cannot be supported without resort to such a conception, see Jeremy Waldron, *God, Locke, and Equality: Christian Foundations of John Locke's Political Thought* (Cambridge: New York University Press, 2002). Although there is a strong case for the proposition that religion has on balance been a progressive force in American politics, I do not believe it follows that religion has been a progressive force when employed by American politicians. Particularly problematic has been the theme that God has a "special concern for America." Bellah, "Civil Religion in America," 9. The notion that God has sanctioned our colonizing efforts in the name of democracy, let alone in the name of God, is plainly distasteful.

43. Michael Perry suggests that America follows a moderate version of the nonestablishment norm that includes a loving, judging God and that we are all sacred because God created us and loves us. Perry, "Freedom of Religion," 309–10. He states that government may affirm these views, but may not impose them on others. Daniel O. Conkle, "Religious Expression and Symbolism in the American Constitutional Tradition: Governmental Neutrality, But Not Indifference," 13 *Indiana J. Global Legal Stud.* 417, 434 (2006) suggests that a narrow exception to the endorsement test, as applied to government use of symbols, exists when the endorsement is supported by longstanding widely accepted tradition, is general and nonsectarian, and is not coercive.

44. I do not mean to suggest that Muslims suppose that Allah is a different God than that worshiped by Jews and Christians. Even if the equivalence were generally understood, however, the cultural importance of saying "In God We Trust" instead of "In Allah We Trust" would remain formidable.

45. *McCulloch v. Maryland*, 17 U.S. 316, 408 (1819) ("[W]e must never forget, that it is a *constitution* we are expounding").

46. William W. Van Alstyne, *Interpretations of the First Amendment* 6–7 (Durham, Duke University Press, 1984).

47. Similarly, the weight of history suggests that the already-established cities of Los Angeles and St. Paul do not violate the Establishment Clause, though these names should not act as precedent for new names of governmental entities.

48. Judge Goodwin's revised opinion in *Newdow* does not maintain that the Congressional amendment is unconstitutional, but it does invalidate the school district's policy of having the pledge recited in the classroom. *Newdow v. U.S. Congress*, 328 F.3d 466, 489–90 (9th Cir. 2003), *rev'd sub nom.*, *Elk Grove Unified Sch. Dist. V. Newdow*, 124 S. Ct. 2301 (2004).

49. In truth, the worst aspect of the Pledge's content is not the under God phrase—though it is an outrage. The worst aspect is that we place pressure on small children to repeat words saying that we live in a country with liberty and justice for all. This lie is not cured by the assertion that the Pledge really means that we have an *ideal* of liberty and justice for all. Does anybody believe that little third graders make this distinction?

Finally, there is a strong First Amendment case for the proposition that forcing school children to make a pledge is an unconstitutional method of instilling values. See Seana Valentine Shiffrin, "What's Wrong with Compelled Association."

50. *Lee v. Weisman*, 505 U.S. 577, 598–99 (1992).

51. Cf. Gey, "Under God," 1893–97 (suggesting even more coercion in the Pledge atmosphere than at a football game or graduation, because the student who opts out will be tainted not only as unreligious, but also unpatriotic).

52. Cf. Richard H. Fallon, Jr., *Implementing the Constitution* 54 (Cambridge: Harvard University Press, 2001) ("Justices otherwise most committed to strict separation of church and state apprehend that judicial rejection of those entrenched practices [such as 'In God We Trust' on coins and 'Under God' in the Pledge] would engender widespread anger and resentment—and perhaps not unreasonably so (even if not rightly) in light of historical understandings of what the Establishment Clause permits").

53. See Steven D. Smith, "Believing Persons, Personal Believings: The Neglected Center of the First Amendment," 2002 *University of Illinois Law Review* 1233, 1317 (arguing that nonreligious explanations are disingenuous and offensive).

54. For the claim that it would be wrong to deny a constitutional right in order to protect the Court, but that the "under God" practice and the "In God We Trust" practice can be defended as a part of the historical understanding, see Fallon, *Implementing the Constitution*, 55. See generally Dworkin, *Taking Rights Seriously*, 199–200 (opposing strategic conceptions of rights).

55. Such an approach employing the "passive virtues" might be permissible in other contexts.

56. "My position is that it isn't government's job to mandate patriotism. To me mandating a pledge of allegiance to a government is something Saddam Hussein would do." David Wallis, "Questions for Jesse Ventura: Still Wrestling with It," *New York Times Magazine*, August 18, 2002, 11. On the other hand, Michael Dukakis's decision to veto a similar bill in Massachusetts certainly did not help his presidential campaign. Gey, "Under God," 1868.

57. See Berg, "Church-State Relations," 1612 ("[S]ome Americans repeat the pattern of ignoring or underestimating the harm done to dissenters from explicit government advancement of particular religious truths"); Berg, "Religious Liberty," 190 ("The separationist approach . . . relied implicitly on the existence of a general religious and moral consensus that made specific references to God seem less necessary; as that moral consensus has broken down, more citizens feel the need to reassert the religious foundations of morality explicitly"). For example, it is fair to say, as does Douglas Laycock, that many of those who advocate government-initiated displays and rituals, when they could use government outlets for such expression, simply place little or no value on the costs to religious minorities. Laycock, "Benefits of Establishment Clause," 379–80; cf. Van Alstyne, "Trends in the Supreme Court," 787 (stating that the use by government of religious symbols such as the crèche "are disappointing reminders that religious ethnocentrism, as well as religious insensitivity, are still with us. I do not know whether Mr. Jefferson would have been surprised, but I believe he would have been disappointed").

58. See Berg, "Religious Liberty," 190.

59. Numerous justices have lodged constitutional objections, but they have never been able to deliver a knockout blow. Jesse H. Choper et al., *Constitutional Law* 511–37 (9th ed. St. Paul: West, 2001).

60. The question I am posing might be presented by a taxpayer in a school district, even if the objector had no children in the school.

61. Owen, *Religion and the Demise*, 129, 168; cf. Sullivan, "Religion and Liberal Democracy," 198–99 (arguing that the Establishment Clause creates secular governance of public affairs). I think Sullivan leaves too little room for religious speech in democratic life, but whatever secular governance may mean, it must exclude governmental determinations of what God has to say. Consider Laycock, "Equal Access," 7–8 ("'Agnostic' is the label that comes closest to describing the attitude required of the government, but that label is misleading in an important way. An agnostic has no opinion on whether God exists, and neither should the government. But an agnostic also believes that humans are incapable of knowing whether God exists. If the government believed that, it would prefer agnostics over theists and atheists. . . . Agnostics have no opinion for epistemological reasons; the government must have no opinion because it is not the government's role to have an opinion").

62. Tribe, *American Constitutional Law*. As I have suggested, monotheistic affirmations such as those appearing on the coins are limited exceptions to this principle.

63. Shiffrin, "Liberalism and Establishment Clause," 726–27. But cf. Steven D. Smith, "Barnette's Big Blunder," 78 *Chicago-Kent Law Review* 625 (2003) (arguing that there is no meaningful way to draw such distinctions).

64. Some secular humanists might be agnostic or even might believe that God exists, but would argue that a belief in God is not important for the conduct of life. The public schools also do not advocate these variations of secular humanism.

65. See Smith, "Rise and Fall," 174.

66. Cf. Richard A. Baer Jr., "The Epicycles of the Church-State Debate," *Cornell Daily Sun*, April 12, 2004, 5, col. 4 (maintaining, as an "Orthodox Christian, that whenever it [the secular] addresses the 'Big Questions,' such as who we are, how we should live, and the meaning of life, . . . the secular must itself be considered a form of religion").

67. Mark V. Tushnet, "Disaggregating 'Church' and 'Culture,'" 42 *DePaul Law Review* 235, 239 (1992) ("In a religiously pluralist society, *any* particular pattern will constitute an endorsement of the normative stance of some churches and a rejection of the stance of others. Therefore, the only way to devise proper First Amendment jurisprudence is to determine which pattern is normatively desirable").

68. Discussion of the general free exercise issue primarily focuses on the *Mozert* litigation culminating in *Mozert v. Hawkins County Bd. of Educ.*, 827 F.2d 1058 (6th Cir. 1987). For analysis of *Mozert*, see Stephen Bates, *Battleground: One Mother's Crusade, the Religious Right, and the Struggle for Control of Our Classrooms* 233–302 (New York: Poseidon Press, 1993) and Nomi Maya Stolzenberg, "'He Drew a Circle That Shut Me Out': Assimilation, Indoctrination, and the Paradox of a Liberal Education," 106 *Harvard Law Review* 581 (1993).

69. For strong arguments in favor of legislative accommodation, see Berg, "Slouching toward Secularism," 476–83, which examines textual, structural, and normative arguments, as well as views of original understanding and case law precedent, that support accommodating religious conscience, and Michael W. McConnell, "Accommodation of Religion: An Update and a Response to the Critics," 60 *George Washington Law Review* 685 (1992).

70. One might argue that if *Smith* was rightly decided, Establishment Clause problems are more formidable because religious actors are favored over nonreligious actors in circumstances that are not required under the Free Exercise Clause.

71. 50 U.S.C. App. § 456(j) (2000).

72. See *Gillette v. United States*, 401 U.S. 437, 460 (1970).

73. See *Gillette*, 401 U.S. 460.

74. See Jesse H. Choper, "The Religion Clauses of the First Amendment: Reconciling the Conflict," 41 *University of Pittsburgh Law Review* 673, 698–700 (1980); cf. Berg, "Slouching toward Secularism," 463 (arguing that the real issue with regard to religion-specific accommodation is whether "its greater effect [is] to permit religious practice to continue freely, or to induce people to switch to the accommodated religion").

75. My contention, therefore, is that religious exemptions in this context should be constitutionally required. For the suggestion that such exemptions should be permitted, but not required, see McConnell, "Accommodation of Religion," 702. On military service exemptions generally, see Greenawalt, *Free Exercise and Fairness*, 49–67, 124–56.

76. Lupu, "Reconstructing the Establishment Clause," 586.

77. For consideration of a wide range of circumstances, both religious and nonreligious, in which burdens are imposed upon others because of autonomous choices together with a strong argument for the virtue of supporting such choices, see Seana Valentine Shiffrin, "Egalitarianism, Choice-Sensitivity, and Accommodation," in *Reasons and Value: Themes from the Moral Philosophy of Joseph Raz* 270 (R. Jay Wallace, Philip Pettit, Samuel Scheffler, and Michael Smith eds., Oxford: Clarendon Press; New York: Oxford University Press, 2004).

78. *Estate of Thornton v. Caldor*, 472 U.S. 703 (1985).

79. Regrettably, the Supreme Court has interpreted Title VII's "reasonable accommodation" of religion requirement to require very little of employers. See *Ansonia Bd. of Educ. v. Philbrook*, 479 U.S. 60 (1986) (rejecting the proposition that an employer must accept the employee's proposed accommodation unless it would result in undue hardship); *Trans World Airlines, Inc. v. Hardison*, 432 U.S. 63 (1977) (holding that an employer need not accommodate an employee whose religious beliefs prevented Saturday work if doing so would cause it to bear more than a de minimis cost).

80. Justice O'Connor, joined by Justice Marshall, thought that permitting persons to take off work on the Sabbath constituted an endorsement of the Sabbath. See *Estate of Thornton*, 472 U.S. 711 (O'Connor, J., concurring). I do not see why this law endorses religion any more than laws exempting believers from controlled substance laws if they ingest peyote in a religious ceremony. Presumably, the law was passed primarily to support minority religions since the majority of believers would typically have Sunday off. Even if the law helped majority believers exercise

their religious liberty, however, the removal of an obstacle to religious practice should not, without more, be considered an endorsement.

81. Mark Tushnet does an admirable job of showing that there can be many hard cases under the accommodation principle, but this demonstration itself does not imperil the project of protecting religious liberty against the actions of private actors altogether. Mark Tushnet, "The Emerging Principle of Accommodation of Religion (Dubitante)," 76 *Georgetown Law Journal* 1691, 1704–8 (1988). Tushnet also argues that accommodation does not easily follow from a republican or pluralist conception of government (1695–1701). The accommodation strand of religion law seems most closely tied to the liberty value. This presents no problem for actions at the state and local level, where officials enjoy general police powers. It could, however, present problems at the federal level since the religion clauses confer no power upon the federal government (except through section 5 of the Fourteenth Amendment). This could lead to questions of whether Congress can pass legislation under the Commerce Clause for noncommercial reasons. Assuming sufficient commercial reasons were not presented and only a tie to commerce were present, one might wonder why Congress could protect morals under the Mann Act, but not religious practice under acts such as Title VII.

82. McConnell, "Accommodation of Religion," 704. One might argue that permitting the discretionary removal of burdens on free exercise places churches in a position of dependence that could have a chilling effect on their criticism of government. This, for example, has been a historic problem in Mexico. Chand, *Mexico's Political Awakening*, 196–203. In Mexico, however, the government denied basic freedoms to those who wished to practice their religion (see Chand, 156–59), chilling religion more than if the government removed burdens preventing free exercise. But see Chand, 196 (explaining that the Salinas government removed anticlerical articles from the Mexican constitution in an attempt to contain the growing activism of the Mexican clergy). This makes it all the more important that Free Exercise doctrine err on the side of protecting religious freedom to minimize the chilling effects associated with governmental discretion.

83. See, e.g., Mark E. Chopko, "Vouchers Can Be Constitutional," 31 *Connecticut Law Review* 945, 948 (1999) (arguing that broadly based neutral voucher programs meet constitutional requirements); Eugene Volokh, "Equal Treatment Is Not Establishment," 13 *Notre Dame Journal of Law, Ethics and Public Policy* 341, 366–68 (1999) (arguing that nondiscrimination is required).

84. I leave to the side the potentially difficult question of how to determine who can qualify as a religious teacher. For example, "70% of the imams in France are self-proclaimed." "Special Report: Muslims in Western Europe: Dim Drums Throbbing in the Hills Half Heard," *Economist*, August 10, 2002, 21, 23.

85. For a case striking down a school district's program permitting clergy to enter the schools for group counseling about civic values—among other things, on the ground that it favored religion over nonreligion, see *Doe v. Beaumont Indep. Sch. Dist.*, 173 F.3d 274, 287–89, 291–92 (5th Cir. 1999).

86. *McCollum v. Board of Education*, 333 U.S. 203 (1948). The program was applied in grades 4 through 9 with weekly classes of thirty minutes in the lower grades and forty-five minutes in the higher grades. *McCollum*, 207–8. The instructors were employed by an interfaith council and were approved and super-

vised by the superintendent of schools (208). Only Catholics, Protestants, and Jews participated in the program (207). In some years there were no Judaism classes (209).

87. See generally Jay D. Wexler, "Preparing for the Clothed Public Square: Teaching about Religion, Civic Education, and the Constitution," 43 *William and Mary Law Review* 1159 (2002) (arguing, among other things, that schools should teach about religion to prepare students to be citizens of a religious world and nation). The school board might argue that arguments are best evaluated by hearing their presentation by true advocates. Cf. John Stuart Mill, *On Liberty* 45 (David Spitz ed., New York: Norton, 1975).

88. Étienne Balibar, *We the People of Europe: Reflections on Transnational Citizenship* 202 (James Swenson trans., Princeton: Princeton University Press, 2004). Thomas Berg maintains that instruction in public schools would inevitably slight some religions at the expense of others. Berg, "Religious Clause Anti-Theories," 745. My view would be that the disadvantage of the deviation from equality is outweighed by the educational interests at stake.

89. See *Good News Club v. Milford Cent. Sch.*, 533 U.S. 98, 120 (2001) (holding that a school district was required to permit Christian prayer group to use elementary school facilities when the facilities had been open to nonreligious groups); *Lamb's Chapel v. Cent. Moriches Union Free Sch. Dist.*, 508 U.S. 384, 395–97 (1993) (holding that a school district was required to permit a church to use school facilities to show a religious film series when facilities had been open to nonreligious groups). For criticism of permitting religious exercises in the public schools, see Ruti Teitel, "When Separate Is Equal: Why Organized Religious Exercises, Unlike Chess, Do Not Belong in the Public Schools," 81 *Northwestern University Law Review* 174, 187–89 (1986).

90. There would invariably be nonneutrality of effect, but, at least in theory, the program could be open to those who wish to teach, regardless of religious persuasion.

91. Boyle and Sheen, *Freedom of Religion*, 328–29. In Northern Ireland, the religious curriculum must be taught in those private schools that receive public funds. Catholic schools, the main class in this category, use the mandated religious curriculum, but add to it. Boyle and Sheen, 328–29. The state-run Protestant schools simply follow the curriculum without systematic additions (328–29). The Republic of Ireland has no state-operated schools at the primary level, but it funds and regulates private schools, the overwhelming majority of which are Catholic schools (348). A contentious issue in those state-funded schools is not whether religion should be taught, but whether religion can be interwoven in the curriculum (348). The concern is that an integrated religious curriculum discriminates against religious objectors who have a right to be excused from religious instruction (348).

92. Boyle and Sheen, *Freedom of Religion*, 384.

93. U.S. Department of State, International Religious Freedom Report 2002, http://www.state.gov/g/drl/rls/irf/2002/13956.htm (last visited September 20, 2004).

94. U.S. Department of State, International Religious Freedom Report 2002, http://www.state.gov/g/drl/rls/irf/2002/13941 (last visited September 20, 2004).

95. Boyle and Sheen, *Freedom of Religion* 309.

96. According to the United States State Department:

Although the Constitution gives parents the right to bring up their children in compliance with their own religious and philosophical beliefs, religious education classes continue to be taught in the public schools at public expense. While children are supposed to have the choice between religious instruction and ethics, the Ombudsman's office states that in most schools ethics courses are not offered due to financial constraints. Although Catholic Church representatives teach the vast majority of religious classes in the schools, parents can request religious classes in any of the religions legally registered, including Protestant, Orthodox, and Jewish religious instruction. Such non-Catholic religious instruction exists in practice, although it is not common, and the Ministry of Education pays the instructors. Priests and other instructors receive salaries from the State for teaching religion in public schools, and Catholic Church representatives are included on a commission that determines whether books qualify for school use.

Bureau of Democracy, Human Rights, and Labor, U.S. Department of State, Poland: International Religious Freedom Report, http://www.state.gov/g/drl/rls/irf/2001/5727.htm (last visited September 9, 2004).

97. France is a conspicuous exception to this pattern. Religion is absent from the public schools, and the French constitution forbids giving state money to religions for any purpose (though tax benefits are provided to "long-established Christian churches and their Jewish counterparts"). "Special Report: Muslims in Western Europe," 23. For many years, the Christian religion was taught in the Ontario public schools, but the Ontario Court of Appeal struck down the practice on the ground that it violated § 2(a) of the Canadian Charter of Rights and Freedoms, guaranteeing freedom of conscience and religion. *Corp. of the Can. Civil Liberties Ass'n v. Ontario* [1990], 71 O.R. 2d 341. The court argued that the purpose and effect of the practice was to indoctrinate in the Christian faith, and this was not saved by a provision exempting those who did not wish to participate.

98. For discussion of the nature and limits of this right, see Ingrid Brunk Wuerth, "Private Religious Choice in German and American Constitutional Law: Government Funding and Government Religious Speech," 31 *Vanderbilt Journal of Transnational Law* 1127, 1143–58 (1998).

99. See Charles Fried, "Five to Four: Reflections on the School Voucher Case," 116 *Harvard Law Review* 163 (2002). Fried maintains that the widespread support in foreign countries of private religious schools should be an embarrassment to those who oppose vouchers (183–84). But, aside from the differences in culture, whether a foreign government's support for religion in public schools or for private religious schools should be considered embarrassing to those who oppose vouchers depends entirely on how well these other countries' arrangements work in practice. The existence of an arrangement is not a demonstration of its sagacity.

100. Tribe, *American Constitutional Law*, 1174.

101. For reflections about this process, see David Tracy, *The Analogical Imagination: Christian Theology and the Culture of Pluralism* 405–55 (New York: Crossroad, 2002).

102. As we have discussed, fundamentalist Christians in particular think that this is unfair to them. And this is correct in the sense that the system cannot be justified in terms that any reasonable person would be bound to accept. See Fish, "Mission Impossible," 2256–57 n. 4. On the other hand, if Christian fundamentalists achieved what they want, the system would be unfair to others in exactly the same sense. As Fish states, "The only real question is whether the unfairness is the one we want." Cf. Fish, 2256. Our choice is to determine which unfair system is better.

103. Hunter, "Religious Freedom," 68–73.

104. As I have already suggested, it is hard to believe that the absence of school prayer could account for this rise. See *supra* note 25 and accompanying text.

105. The thesis that religions will disappear as a society develops is shattered by the American religious experience. The U.S. experience forces sociologists to recognize that the phenomenon is more complicated.

106. Benjamin Beit-Hallahmi and Michael Argyle's reading of the literature suggests that "[t]he effects of religious education seem to be quite weak, when other variables are taken into account." Beit-Hallahmi and Argyle, *Psychology of Religious Behaviour*, 109. They report greater effects in Catholic schools (109–11) ("[I]t has been found consistently that going to a Catholic school does have a definite effect on religious beliefs, attitudes, and later church attendance"). Others argue that the most important religious education occurs in early childhood, and that adopting modern educational assumptions about when instruction should begin causes these religious groups to "neglect the most formative time in children's lives. In a religious community, five or six years of age is rather late for learning the important attitudes and rituals of a religious life." Gabriel Moran, "Religious Education after Vatican II," in *Open Catholicism: The Tradition at Its Best: Essays in Honor of Gerard S. Sloyan* 151, 154 (David Efroymson and John Raines, eds., Collegeville, Minn.: Liturgical Press, 1997).

107. *Zorach v. Clauson*, 343 U.S. 306 (1952).

108. *Zorach*, 343 U.S. 324 (Jackson, J., dissenting).

109. For commentary, see Lupu, "The Trouble with Accommodation," 743–45.

110. On the other hand, the Court stated that there was no "indication that the public schools enforce attendance at religious schools by punishing absentees from the released time programs for truancy." *Zorach*, 343 U.S. 311 n. 6. It is not clear what the Court thought the attendance reports were to be used for or what effect they had. Justice Jackson opined that "[t]he greater effectiveness of this system over voluntary attendance after school hours is due to the truant officer who, if the youngster fails to go to the Church school, dogs him back to the public schoolroom" (324) (Jackson, J., dissenting). The Court did conclude that the teacher could appropriately make efforts to confirm that the student was not a truant. Justice Black, dissenting, maintained that "the sole question is whether New York can use its compulsory education laws to help religious sects get attendants presumably too unenthusiastic to go unless moved to do so by the pressure of this state machinery. That this is the plan, purpose, design, and consequence of the New York program cannot be denied. The state thus makes religious sects beneficiaries of its power to compel children to attend secular schools. Any use of

such coercive power by the state to help or hinder some religious sects or to prefer all religious sects over nonbelievers or vice versa is just what I think the First Amendment forbids" (317) (Black, J., dissenting).

111. One of the merits of the approach to equality employed by Eisgruber and Sager is that they look beyond the form of equality to its substance.

112. See Christopher L. Eisgruber, *Constitutional Self-Government* 113 (Cambridge: Harvard University Press, 2001) (criticizing the aesthetic fallacy).

113. Cf. John Rawls, *A Theory of Justice* 105 (rev. ed., Cambridge: Belknap Press of Harvard University Press, 1999) ("We should strive for a kind of moral geometry with all the rigor that this name connotes"). Of course, the drive toward proofs satisfying the ideals of geometry is not just aesthetic, see Thomas C. Grey, "Langdell's Orthodoxy," 45 *University of Pittsburgh Law Review* 1, 16–20 (1983), but the aesthetic aspect is not trivial. See Shiffrin, *First Amendment* 121.

114. As Noonan writes, "There is a praiseworthy desire to maintain intellectual consistency. There is a longing in the human mind for repose, for fixed points of reference, for absolute certainty. There is alarm about the future." Noonan, "Development in Moral Doctrine," 300.

115. See Shiffrin, *First Amendment*, 120–28 (discussing the appeal of the Kantian approach).

116. Cf. Roberto Mangabeira Unger, *Knowledge and Politics* 288 (New York: Free Press, 1975).

CHAPTER 5
COMPULSORY PUBLIC EDUCATION

1. For a mid-nineteenth-century defense by one of its most important supporters, see *The Republic and the School: Horace Mann on the Education of Free Men* 79–112 (Lawrence A. Cremin ed., New York: Teachers College, Columbia University, 1957). For a rebuttal of some of the most prominent criticisms, see Kevin B. Smith and Kenneth J. Meier, *The Case against School Choice: Politics, Markets, and Fools* 16–19 (Armonk, N.Y.: M. E. Sharpe, 1995).

2. Despite the increased public criticism, 64 percent of a national sample of parents grades the public schools as A or B. Statistics such as these have not significantly changed in a generation. Robert C. Bulman and David L. Kirp, "The Shifting Politics of School Choice," in *School Choice and Social Controversy: Politics, Policy, and the Law* 38 (Stephen D. Sugarman and Frank R. Kemerer eds., Washington, D.C.: Brookings Institution Press, 1999). In addition, the International Study of Civic Education "found that the United States had the highest score among 28 countries in civic skills and the use of civic-related knowledge. It finished among the top group in civic knowledge and slightly above average in civic content." Henry M. Levin, "A Comprehensive Framework for Evaluating Educational Vouchers," 24 *Educational Evaluation and Policy Analysis*, 159, 172 n. 21 (2002). Although both public and private school students were included in the study, it hardly suggests that American public school students are as ill-educated as is often suggested.

3. For debate about the degree of monopolization of the public schools, compare Paul E. Peterson, "Monopoly and Competition in American Education," in

Choice and Control in American Education, vol. 1, 47 (William H. Clune and John F. Witte eds., London: Falmer, 1990) (emphasizing the monopolistic aspects) with John F. Witte, "Introduction," in Clune and Witte, *Choice and Control*, 1 (emphasizing the diverse aspects of the public schools) and David B. Tyack, "The Public Schools: A Monopoly or a Contested Public Domain," in Clune and Witte, *Choice and Control*, 86 (arguing that monopoly is too murky a concept to be of assistance in analyzing school politics).

4. Even supporters of the public schools express concerns along this line. See Mark Yudof, *When Governments Speak* 229–30 (Berkeley and Los Angeles: University of California Press, 1983); Sanford Levinson, "Some Reflections on Multiculturalism, 'Equal Concern and Respect,' and the Establishment Clause of the First Amendment," 27 *University of Richmond Law Review* 989 (1993).

5. John E. Coons and Stephen D. Sugarman, *Education by Choice: The Case for Family Control* (Berkeley and Los Angeles: University of California Press, 1978).

6. Milton Friedman, *Capitalism and Freedom* 93 (Chicago: University of Chicago Press, 1962); John E. Brandl, "Governance and Educational Quality," in *Learning from School Choice* 55, 65–67 (Paul E. Peterson and Bryan E. Hassel eds., Washington, D.C., Brookings Institution Press, 1998). Ironically, many who argue from microeconomic models to support vouchers rely for support on the quality of private Catholic schools that are themselves nonmarket actors. See Jeffrey R. Henig, "School Choice Outcomes," in Sugarman and Kemerer, *School Choice*, 81.

7. Michael W. McConnell, "Governments, Families, and Power: A Defense of Educational Choice," 31 *Connecticut Law Review* 847, 849 (1999).

8. See Coons and Sugarman, *Education by Choice*, 97. For an extended argument that vouchers best serve democratic values, see Michael W. McConnell, "Education Disestablishment: Why Democratic Values Are Ill-Served by Democratic Control of Schooling," in *Nomos XLIII: Moral and Political Education* 87 (Stephen Macedo and Yael Tamir eds., New York: New York University Press, 2002). For replies, see Amy Gutmann, "Can Publicly Funded Schools Legitimately Teach Values in a Constitutional Democracy? " in Macedo and Tamir, *Moral and Political Education*, 170; Nancy L. Rosenblum, "Pluralism and Democratic Education: Stopping Short by Stopping at Schools," in Macedo and Tamir, *Moral and Political Education*, 147.

9. Coons and Sugarman, *Education by Choice*. So too, John Stuart Mill was suspicious of government schools. Mill, *On Liberty*, 98. For commentary on this aspect of Mill, see E. G. West, *Education and the Industrial Revolution* (New York: Barnes and Noble, 1975).

10. Joseph P. Viteritti, *Choosing Equality: School Choice, the Constitution, and Civil Society* (Washington, D.C.: Brookings Institution Press, 1999).

11. *Pierce v. Society of Sisters*, 268 U.S. 510 (1925).

12. See Tribe, *American Constitutional Law*, 1184 n. 38 ("Parents . . . have the right to educate their children privately"); Erwin Chemerinsky, *Constitutional Law: Principles and Policies* 654–55 (New York: Aspen Publishers, 1997).

13. For a thorough historical and perceptive analytical treatment, see Barbara Bennett Woodhouse, " 'Who Owns the Child?': *Meyer* and *Pierce* and the Child

as Property," 33 *William and Mary Law Review* 995 (1992). In the end, despite cogent criticism, Woodhouse believes that *Pierce* reached the right result. Barbara Bennett Woodhouse, "Child Abuse, the Constitution, and the Legacy of *Pierce v. Society of Sisters*," 78 *University of Detroit Mercy Law Review* 479, 484 (2001). Others take the criticism further. See, e.g., Meira Levinson, *The Demands of Liberal Education* 158, 161–63 (Oxford: Oxford University Press, 1999) (arguing for education within common schools and requiring heavy regulation of private schools to reach liberal public school ideals, including the prohibition of religious private schools); Abner S. Greene, "Civil Society and Multiple Repositories of Power," 75 *Chicago-Kent Law Review* 477, 489–92 (2000); Abner S. Greene, "Why Vouchers Are Unconstitutional and Why They Are Not," 13 *Notre Dame Journal of Law, Ethics and Public Policy* 397 (1999). For defenses, see, e.g., Martha Minow, "Before and after *Pierce*," 78 *University of Detroit Mercy Law Review* 407, 415 (2001); William G. Ross, "*Pierce* after Seventy-Five Years: Reasons to Celebrate," 78 *University of Detroit Mercy Law Review* 443 (2001).

Conservative scholars, who generally criticize decisions based on substantive due process, praise *Pierce* as it applies to the Society of Sisters but fall silent about the case's application to the Hill Military Academy. See, e.g., Michael W. McConnell, "The Selective Funding Problem: Abortions and Religious Schools," 104 *Harvard Law Review* 989, 992 n. 11 (1991) (discussing the substantive due process aspect of *Pierce*).

14. *Pierce*, 268 U.S. 534–35.

15. Is this a slip of the pen? Could the *Pierce* Court possibly believe that children belong to the state? See Minow, "Before and After *Pierce*," 415.

16. *Pierce*, 268 U.S. 534–35.

17. But see Chandran Kukathas, "Are There Any Cultural Rights? " 20 *Political Theory* 105, 126 (1992) (suggesting that the Amish have a freedom of association right not to send their children to public schools at any time). For the contention that the parents' rights aspect of *Pierce* is only an incidental part of the case, see Paula Abrams, "The Little Red Schoolhouse: *Pierce*, State Monopoly of Education and the Politics of Intolerance," 20 *Constitutional Commentary* 61 (2003).

18. For criticism of the teacher requirements, see Stephen L. Carter, "Parents, Religion, and the Schools: Reflections on Pierce, 70 Years Later," 27 *Seton Hall Law Review* 1194, 1195 (1997). States, of course, continue to regulate private schools in many details though not as extensively as public schools. Aaron J. Saiger, "School Choice and States' Duty to Support 'Public Schools,' " 48 *Boston College Law Review* 909, 916–18 (2007).

19. Although scholars typically do not distinguish on the basis of age, and although they arrive at different conclusions, many have suggested that there are problems with permitting parents to have a monopoly regarding the education of children. See, e.g., Amy Gutmann, *Democratic Education* 30 (rev. ed., Princeton: Princeton University Press, 1999) ("[N]either parents nor a centralized state have a right to exclusive authority over the education of children"); Bruce Ackerman, *Social Justice in the Liberal State* 160 (New Haven: Yale University Press, 1980) ("The problem with the public schools is *not* that they are insufficiently responsive to parental views, but that they are *already* overly concerned with reinforcing,

rather than questioning, the child's primary culture"); Harry Brighouse, *School Choice and Social Justice* 17 (Oxford: Oxford University Press, 2000); Richard J. Arneson and Ian Shapiro, "Democratic Autonomy and Religious Freedom: A Critique of *Wisconsin v. Yoder*," in *Nomos XXXVIII: Political Order* 365, 366, 379–82, 388–403 (Ian Shapiro and Russell Hardin eds., New York: New York University Press, 1996); Greene, "Why Vouchers Are Constitutional," 406–7; Macedo, *Diversity and Distrust*, 52–53. But see Stephen Gilles, "On Educating Children: A Parentalist Manifesto," 63 *University of Chicago Law Review* 93 (1996). For the suggestion that parents should be able to determine the religious complexion of the primary school, but not in the later years, see Deborah Fitzmaurice, "Liberal Neutrality, Traditional Minorities and Education," in *Liberalism, Multiculturalism, and Toleration* 50, 68 (John Horton ed., New York: St. Martin's Press, 1993); see also Will Kymlicka, *Politics in the Vernacular: Nationalism, Multiculturalism, and Citizenship* 305 (New York: Oxford University Press, 2001).

20. Regrettably, their agents include television programmers. See Edward L. Palmer, *Television and America's Children: A Crisis of Neglect* 12 (New York: Oxford University Press, 1988).

21. *Pierce,* 268 U.S. 534.

22. *Pierce,* 268 U.S. 535.

23. Cf. McConnell, "Governments, Families, and Power," 850–51 (arguing that public education indoctrinates children).

24. For some of the difficulties of achieving uniformity in an educational bureaucracy, see Yudof, *When Governments Speak*, 116–21. See also Rosenblum, "Pluralism and Democratic Education," 152–53:

> [I]n public education, the tug-of-war between federal and state, and state and local "control" (itself an abstraction that must be broken down into an array of legal requirements, funding schemes, curricular decisions, classroom organization, assessment, and so on) is a part of a larger field of competing authorities that includes professional educators' groups, teachers' unions, textbook publishers, and parenting (organized and disorganized). Localism, unionism, and housing patterns dilute unitary government "control." So do the many arrangements for student opt-outs, parental vetoes over aspects of the curriculum, charter schools, and so on. Even if there is one authoritative curriculum in each public school jurisdiction, every parent and student knows that variability from classroom to classroom is the rule. To say nothing of the fact that the substantive content of democratic education is a moving target.

25. Charles E. Larmore, *Patterns of Moral Complexity* 42–47 (Cambridge: Cambridge University Press, 1987); Ackerman, *Social Justice*, 11, 57–58, 166 n. 10; Ronald Dworkin, "Liberalism," in *Public and Private Morality* 113, 127 (Stuart Hampshire ed., Cambridge: Cambridge University Press, 1978). But cf. Ronald Dworkin, "Is There a Right to Pornography? " 1 *Oxford Journal of Legal Studies* 177, 210–11 (1981) (qualifying his view). For criticism, see Joseph Raz, *The Morality of Freedom* (Oxford: Clarendon Press, 1986); William A. Galston, *Liberal Purposes: Goods, Virtues, and Diversity in the Liberal State* (Cambridge: Cambridge University Press, 1991); Shiffrin, "Liberalism, Radicalism."

26. The National Institute on Alcohol Abuse and Alcoholism estimates that one in thirteen adult Americans abuses alcohol or is an alcoholic. "The National Institute on Alcohol Abuse and Alcoholism: Getting the Facts," http://www.hiaanih.gov/publications/booklet/html (last visited November 22, 2002).

27. A 1995 study estimated that sixty-one million Americans were in the smoking ranks. Centers for Disease Control, "1995 National Household Survey on Drug Abuse, Tobacco Related Statistics, SAMHSA," http://www.cdc.gov/tobacco/research_data/survey/samhsa.html (last visited November 22, 2002). The Surgeon General reports that the vast majority of smokers want to quit, but only 2 percent succeed each year. "1995 National Household Survey."

28. For the contention that many abstinence-only programs have emerged in contexts that violate the Establishment Clause, see Gary J. Simson and Erika A. Sussman, "Keeping the Sex in Sex Education: The First Amendment's Religion Clauses and the Sex Education Debate," 9 *Southern California Review of Law and Women's Studies* 265 (2000).

29. According to the National Center for Chronic Disease Prevention and Health Promotion, nearly three thousand young people a day under the age of eighteen become regular smokers. Nationall Center for Disease Prevention and Health Promotion, "Tobacco Information and Prevention source," http://www.cdc.gov/tobacco/issue.htm (last visited August 16, 2001).

30. The National Institute on Alcohol Abuse and Alcoholism reports that 21 percent of all eighth-graders state that they have used alcohol within the last thirty days; more than one hundred thousand twelve- to thirteen-year-olds binge drink on a monthly basis; three million fourteen- to seventeen-year-olds are regular drinkers. "Leadership to Keep Children Alcohol Free, Statistics," http://www.alcoholfreechildren.org/gs/stats/index.cfm (last visited November 23, 2002).

31. The Alan Guttmacher Institute estimates that some nine hundred thousand teenagers become pregnant each year. More than 75 percent of these pregnancies were not intended. Alan Guttmacher Institute, "Why Is Teenage Pregnancy Declining? The Roles of Abstinence, Sexual Activity and Contraceptive Use," http://www.agi-usa.org/pubs/ or_teen_preg_decline.html (last visited November 23, 2002).

32. National Center for Education Statistics, "Public and Private School Enrollment," http://nces.ed.gov/fastfacts/display.asp?id=65 (last visited November 23, 2002) (1999 statistics).

33. Nonetheless, the American consumer culture has become more homogenized. Paul Van Slambrouck, "There's more diversity but less . . . diversity," *Christian Science Monitor*, February 8, 2000, 1.

34. See Richard A. Baer Jr., "The Supreme Court's Discriminatory Use of the Term 'Sectarian,'" 6 *Journal of Law and Politics* 449, 465–66 (1990).

35. Ironically, some of the same people who worry that public schools turn people from religion point to the religious character of the American people. See Baer, "Supreme Court's Discriminatory Use," 463 (describing Americans as "incurably religious"; noting that 90 percent of Americans profess belief in God; church attendance approaches 50 percent of the population). Estimates differ as to the depths of religious conviction of American citizens, but religious beliefs are clearly more widespread and deep than is generally the case in western Europe.

See Fowler and Hertzke, *Religion and Politics*, 28–29; Alan Wolfe, *One Nation after All: What Middle-Class Americans Really Think about God, Country, Family, Racism, Welfare, Immigration, Homosexuality, Work, the Right, the Left, and Each Other* 44–45 (New York: Viking, 1998); cf. John Cornwell, *Breaking Faith: The Pope, the People, and the Fate of Catholicism* 2, 3 (New York: Viking Compass, 2001) (describing European Catholic practice as in "terminal decline"; in France, only 7 percent of the young ever attend church). This makes it all the more disturbing that this wealthy country filled with "incurably religious" people would house the largest percentage of poor children in the Western world. I think it an interesting question whether a commitment to religion on an institutional level is more likely to exhibit a correlation with moral behavior, however that might plausibly be defined, and to what extent and in which ways, than would be the case with persons who maintain no such commitment. For evidence that religious commitment makes a difference in some ways, see Eastwood Atwater, *Adolescence* 296–99 (3rd ed., Englewood Cliffs, N.J.: Prentice Hall, 1992). Those who maintain no institutional religious commitment, of course, includes those who see themselves as religious, see generally Robert Wuthnow, *After Heaven: Spirituality in America since the 1950's* (Berkeley and Los Angeles: University of California Press, 1988), and those who do not. In one sense, however, it might be difficult to make a sharp distinction between the two categories because many of the nonreligious have been influenced by cultural values strongly influenced by religious traditions. Küng, *On Being a Christian*, 30–31.

36. One might wonder whether Supreme Court decisions removing prayer and Bible readings from the public schools have had a significant impact in secularizing the schools. I am dubious. It seems unlikely that brief ceremonies of that character had any significant religious influence. Indeed, surprisingly, the historical evidence is that such ceremonies were far from universal in the nineteenth century and nonexistent in many states. Many in the nineteenth century argued that such ceremonies where they did exist were of doubtful value. Yet religious commitments were strong. R. Laurence Moore strongly argues that the "importance of religion to intellectual development in the Nineteenth Century had almost nothing to do with what happened in public school classrooms." Moore, "Bible Reading," 1598.

37. Josh Chafetz, "Social Reproduction and Religious Reproduction: A Democratic Communitarian Analysis of the Yoder Problem," 15 *William and Mary Bill of Rights Journal* 263, 284 (2006) (public schools do not stifle dissent).

38. Walter M. Pierce, "Brief of Appellant," in *Oregon School Cases: Complete Record, Pierce,* 268 U.S. 98.

39. Pierce, "Brief of Appellant," 103. "Redbaiting" was not confined to the proponents of the initiative. The *Portland Telegram* published a cartoon showing Lenin and a hooded Ku Klux Klansman holding a placard with the message: "State Monopoly of Schools is an Absolute Success in Russia." David Tyack Thomas James, and Aaron Benevot, *Law and the Shaping of Public Education, 1785–1954* 184 (Madison: University of Wisconsin Press, 1987).

40. Tyack, James, and Benevot, *Law and Shaping*, 115–16.

41. Seven percent of elementary students attended private schools in Oregon. Tyack, James, and Benevot, *Law and Shaping*, 179. Of the estimated 12,031 stu-

dents enrolled in such schools, 7,300 were in Catholic schools. M. Paul Holsinger, "The Oregon School Controversy 1922–1925," 37 *Pacific Historical Review* 327, 330 n. 14.

42. Woodhouse, "Who Owns the Child? " 998, 1026, 1032.

43. The Scottish Rite Masons were the official sponsors of the initiative, but Tyack maintains that "there is much evidence that the KKK was using the Scottish Rite as a front." Tyack, James, and Benevot, *Law and Shaping*, 180. In any event, the Klan, though not an official sponsor, was a prominent public supporter of the initiative. Holsinger, "Oregon School Controversy," 330. A Klan publicist made it clear that "the public schools were to replace immigrant cultures with 100% Americanism and wanted to Protestantize the Catholics by requiring 'their priests to marry and live normal lives' and by forcing Catholics to 'abolish the parochial grade school and join with other Americans in building up the Public School' " (Holsinger, 182). After the *Pierce* decision, the *New York Times* editorialized that the initiative was "born of prejudice." Although it "professed to be one of equality, [it] was one of the most hateful by-products of the Ku Klux Klan movement." E.g., Lloyd B. Jorgenson, "The Oregon School Law of 1922: Passage and Sequel," 54 *Catholic History Review* 455, 464 (1968).

44. Holsinger reports that Klan-supported candidates carried both houses of the Oregon legislature in 1922. Holisinger, "Oregon School Controversy," 335. Tyack reports that Klan-supported candidates had the "potential deciding vote" in the legislature. Tyack, James, and Benevot, *Law and Shaping*, 180.

45. Woodhouse, "Who Owns the Child? " 1032.

46. Woodhouse, "Who Owns the Child? " 1016–17.

47. Woodhouse, "Who Owns the Child? " 998, 1000, 1019.

48. Gutmann, *Democratic Education*, emphasizes this perspective, but she does not support compulsory education.

49. Brighouse, *School Choice*, 61. It might be argued that democratic education is good for the child wholly apart from any social consequences. For many, it may be an important part of the good life that they recognize and appreciate the just aspects of the society of which they are a part. On the other hand, many individuals live apparently full and rich lives without any such recognition or appreciation.

50. Brighouse, *School Choice*, 44 (maintaining that civic stability requires educating a large critical mass of citizens, but not more).

51. Even if they did not have obligations, citizens have rights of participation and need to be educated to exercise such rights, if they choose to do so. Arneson and Shapiro, "Democratic Autonomy," 379.

52. But see McConnell, "Education Disestablishment"; Viteritti, *Choosing Equality*, 19 ("There is nothing inherent in a religious education that is anathema to the ethos of democracy, whether it is paid for by parents or with the assistance of public funding"). Indeed, many argue that private schools do a better job of inculcating democratic values than public schools. After analyzing the studies on this issue, however, Brian Gill and others conclude that the studies are "inherently insufficient to the task methodologically and tell very little about the relative performance of public and private schools in producing students who will function well in the America democracy." Brian Gill et al., *Rhetoric versus Reality: What*

We Know and What We Need to Know about Vouchers and Charter Schools 211 (new ed., Santa Monica, Calif.: Rand Corporation, 2007). Similarly, Henry Levin criticizes the studies as "inconclusive." Levin, "Comprehensive Framework," 167. This is not surprising. First, many of the findings are plagued by selection effect difficulties. Parents who decide to send their children to private schools, usually making financial sacrifices to do so, may in the aggregate be more serious about education than the aggregate of their public school counterparts. Second, public schools are burdened with more "high cost" students than private schools. They educate students who present disciplinary problems (who would be expelled from private schools), students with handicaps (some of whose disabilities affect performance), and students on vocational tracks whose general academic performance might be expected to be less than others. They do not have admission requirements. And they educate nine times as many students. It seems clear that different school populations can play a significant role in affecting the results. If the private schools educated the public school population and the public schools educated the private school population, it seems obvious that the results would be different. It is not easy to account for all of these variables. Third, the studies do not distinguish between the types of private schools, and the one that does shows that the Catholic schools drive most of the comparisons. Compare David Campbell, "The Civic Side of School Choice: An Empirical Analysis of Civic Education in Public and Private Schools," 2008 *BYU Law Review* 487 (does account for the differences between private schools) with Jay P. Greene, "Civic Values in Public and Private Schools," in Peterson and Hassel, *Learning from School Choice* (does not account for the differences between private schools). This is problematic. At the time of the survey that Campbell relied upon, the overwhelming percentage of students who attended Catholic schools were Catholic. It is not clear whether the positive results were attributable to Catholicism or to Catholic schools. To know this, one would have to compare Catholics attending private schools to Catholics attending public schools instead of the entire public school population. One might also compare non-Catholics attending Catholic schools with Catholics. Neither of these comparisons were made.

Apart from the measures related to achievement, it is not clear that the measures on tolerance give much to rely upon. The Campbell study disaggregating the private school data was based on a survey asking only two questions relevant to tolerance: first, whether people should be allowed to speak against religion or churches. Eighty-eight percent of public school students said yes; 90.9 percent of private school students said yes; second, the survey asked whether a book stating that it was all right to take illegal drugs should be kept out of a public library. Forty-four percent of public school students said yes; 34.6 percent of the private school students said yes. See U.S. Department of Education, *The Civic Development of 9th through 12th Grade Students in the United States: 1996*, at 44 (1998). The answer to the first question does not sharply distinguish the two school systems. The second question is deficient. A majority of the United States Supreme Court might well conclude that such a book could at least kept away from children and not freely available in a public library. The answers might also have been influenced by the reluctance of children to admit to an adult that they thought a book advocating illegal drug usage should be in their library. Moreover, public schools at the time might have employed stronger antidrug programs influencing the results. In any event, the second question seems poorly calculated to arrive at any general conclusions about tolerance. See also note 92 *infra*.

Even if general conclusions about tolerance were warranted, implications for policy would be unclear. Non-Catholic religious schools performed less well on the tolerance measures than the public schools, and they are the fastest-growing segment of the private school community. If this empirical work were to ground policy, it would seem that some religious schools would receive vouchers and others would not. Apart from the constitutional difficulties, it would be a political nonstarter to make such distinctions.

53. For the claim that community control of schools is vital, see Michael Engel, *The Struggle for Control of Public Education* (Philadelphia: Temple University Press, 2000); Gutmann, *Democratic Education*, 70 ("[The] problem with voucher plans is not that they leave too much room for parental choice but that they leave too little room for democratic deliberation"). Of course, even substantial voucher programs would leave plenty of room for democratic deliberation both about the remaining public schools and about the conditions that should be placed upon the voucher schools.

54. This was one of the main goals of the common school movement. Macedo, *Diversity and Distrust*, 52–54.

55. For a deep discussion of the nature of autonomy and its connection to liberal education, see Levinson, *Demands of Liberal Education*, 14–41. On the connection between common education and autonomy, see Levinson, 100–169. For an argument that education for autonomy is consistent with education into a particular culture, see Ackerman, *Social Justice*, 139–67. For the claim that toleration is more important than autonomy, see Kukathas, "Cultural Rights," 121–23.

56. I would not suggest that understanding of the social and physical environment is exclusively important for its promotion of autonomy or for its contribution to democratic education. Contrary to the implications of some liberal and democratic theorists, a good education has value independent of autonomy and democracy. See, e.g., Brian Barry, *Culture and Equality: An Egalitarian Critique of Multiculturalism* 221–22 (Cambridge: Harvard University Press, 2001).

57. On the importance of these skills and habits to liberal theory—whether or not labeled as autonomy—see Will Kymlicka, "Two Models of Pluralism and Tolerance," in *Toleration: An Elusive Virtue* 81–105 (David Heyd ed., Princeton: Princeton University Press, 1996). For a similar perspective, see Arneson and Shapiro, "Democratic Autonomy," 388–403 (contending that an integrated education is a helpful but not sufficient condition for teaching such skills). Many evangelicals argue that their children should remain in the public schools precisely to show that their message is the preferred option. James Forman Jr., "The Rise and Fall of School Vouchers: A Story of Religion, Race, and Politics," 54 *UCLA Law Review* 547, 560 (2007).

58. Exposure to different lifestyles constrains autonomy at the same time that it enables it. If the parent of a child wishes to raise a child to be an illiterate farmer, compulsory reading instruction will forever foreclose that possibility, even though it opens many other possibilities at the same time. Public education is

neutral about many forms of the good life, but it is not and cannot be neutral about them all.

59. Cf. John Rawls, *Political Liberalism* 199–200 (New York: Columbia University Press, 1996).

60. Galston, *Liberal Purposes*, 253.

61. Galston, *Liberal Purposes*, 254.

62. Galston, *Liberal Purposes*, 255.

63. Even in that context, the argument that the state displays insufficient respect for the autonomous choices made by consenting adults is not a conversation stopper. The state could say, "We are required to respect you as persons, and we do, but we are not required to respect the choices you make, and we do not." Gays or lesbians could respond that "choices about sexual orientation, if they are choices, are choices about identity. Not to respect these choices or, alternatively, not to respect the way we are, is not to respect us as persons." The state could respond that, if so, the state is not required to respect them as persons in that respect. State attempts to prohibit same-sex sexual conduct can be appropriately condemned as iniquitous without walking into the respect quagmire. But whatever the merits of the respect argument in contexts of behaviors that are harmless to the state and important to the lives of individuals, it is out of place in the educational context.

64. Surely the overwhelming majority of parents value autonomy. Not to encourage autonomy because some parents are opposed would amount to accepting a "heckler's veto."

65. See Donald Arstine, *Democracy and the Arts of Schooling* 31 (Albany: State University of New York Press, 1995) (emphasizing the choices made even in the teaching of reading and writing); David C. Paris, "Moral Education and the 'Tie That Binds' in Liberal Political Theory," 85 *American Political Science Review* 875, 883–90 (1991).

66. Brighouse argues that schools should facilitate autonomy, but possibly should not promote it. Brighouse, *School Choice*, 64, 82. It is hard to see how one could effectively facilitate autonomy without promoting it.

67. See T. H. McLaughlin, "Parental Rights and the Religious Upbringing of Children," 18 *Journal of Philosophy of Education* 75 (1984).

68. Eamonn Callan, *Creating Citizens: Political Education and Liberal Democracy* 134 (Oxford: Clarendon Press, 1997).

69. Wayne C. Booth, *The Company We Keep: An Ethics of Fiction* 17 (Berkeley and Los Angeles: University of California Press, 1988) ("Each narrative, fictional or historical, provides an alternative story set in a created 'world' that is a itself a fresh alternative to the 'world' or 'worlds' previously serving as boundaries of the reader's imagination").

70. See generally Martha C. Nussbaum, *Cultivating Humanity* (Cambridge: Harvard University Press, 1997); see also Benjamin R. Barber, *An Aristocracy of Everyone: The Politics of Education and the Future of America* 5 (New York: Ballantine, 1992) ("Human association depends on imagination: the capacity to see in others beings like ourselves. It is thus through imagination that we render them sufficiently like ourselves for them to become subjects of tolerance and respect, sometimes even of affection").

71. Considerations such as these form a strong part of the case for multicultural education. See Bhikhu Parekh, *Rethinking Multiculturalism: Cultural Diversity and Political Theory* 226–27 (Cambridge: Harvard University Press, 2000). Cf. Callon, *Creating Citizens*, 8, 43; Terence H. McLaughlin, "Liberalism, Education and the Common School," 29 *Journal of Philosophy of Education* 239, 250 (1995) (referring to the "need for the development in pupils of imaginative engagement, understanding and sympathy with views with which they disagree").

72. *Cf.* Arstine, *Democracy*, 11 ("Socialization requires firsthand experience . . . you don't get socialized by reading about what others believe").

73. "Separatism denies the value, even the possibility, of such a dialogue. It rejects exchange. It is multiculturalism gone sour." Robert Hughes, *The Culture of Complaint* 84 (New York: Oxford University Press, 1993). But see Michael W. McConnell, "Multiculturalism, Majoritarianism, and Educational Choice: What Does Our Constitutional Tradition Have to Say?" 1991 *University of Chicago Legal Forum* 123, 150–51 (1991) (recommending separate education and calling it multicultural).

74. *Cf.* Levinson, *Demands of Liberal Education*, 65:

> [E]mphasis on common education, mutual toleration, and critical engagement ensures the development and maintenance of an interactive and mutually responsive plural society, as opposed to a society composed of separate, insular, and self-protective communities which, while formally part of a diverse and multicultural whole, are internally homogeneous and disengaged from other groups in their midst.

For criticism of separatist education in England, see Levinson, 110–16.

75. Cf. Alan Ryan, *Liberal Anxieties and Liberal Education* 181 (New York: Hill and Wang, 1988):

> One of the central purposes of education is to overcome the sense of being thrown into a "meaningless" world. Anyone who wants to connect liberalism as a set of cultural and political ambitions with liberal education as a commitment to a humanist and historical understanding of human culture hopes that the second will sustain the first and that the first will provide a proper shelter for the second.

76. Holsinger, "Oregon School Controversy," 334–35.

77. One might think that John Dewey would be persuaded by this argument. Not so. Dewey opposed the initiative on the ground that it struck at the "root of American toleration and trust and good faith between various elements of the population and in each other." See, e.g., Jorgenson, "Oregon School Law," 460–61. But cf. Viteritti, *Choosing Equality*, 158–59 (discussing Dewey's hostility to religion in general and to Catholicism in particular). Nonetheless, many, including Dewey, have subscribed to the view that integrated classrooms support toleration and respect. See, e.g., Rupert Brown, *Prejudice: Its Social Psychology* 236–69 (Oxford: Blackwell, 1995); Ronald Dworkin, "Affirming Affirmative Action," *New York Review*, October 22, 1998, at 99–100. This contention was a major part of the argument for the initiation of the public schools. Macedo, *Diversity and Distrust*, 52–54. That toleration is encouraged by integration is supported by

evidence from the racial context. Blacks and whites who attended desegregated schools are less likely to express negative views about members of the other race, are more comfortable in integrated work and social situations, are more likely to live in integrated neighborhoods, and are more likely to have personal relationships with persons of the other race. James S. Liebman, "Desegregating Politics: 'All-Out' School Desegregation Explained," 90 *Columbia Law Review* 1463, 1626–27 (1990); Jennifer Hochschild, "Public Schools and the American Dream," *Dissent* 35, 38 (Fall 2001). Cf. Gutmann, *Democratic Education*, 163 (pointing to reduction of prejudice in settings with cooperative learning and absence of tracking when integration is fully and carefully carried out). The experience with heterogeneous grouping discussed in the literature about tracking also supports this view. Arstine, *Democracy*, 142. See also Henry M. Levin, "The Theory of Choice Applied to Education," in Clune and Witte, *Choice and Control*, 247, 268 ("Research on political socialization has shown that tolerance for diversity is related to the degree to which different children are exposed to different viewpoints on controversial subjects in both the home and school").

78. Thomas F. Pettigrew and Linda R. Tropp, "A Meta-analytic Test of Intergroup Contact Theory," 90 *Journal of Personality and Social Psychology* 751 (2006) (meta-analysis of 515 studies in support of the conclusion). See also note 77 *supra.*

79. Thomas F. Pettigrew and Linda R. Tropp, "How Does Intergroup Contact Reduce Prejudice?" 38 *European Journal of Social Psychology* (2008), http://www3.interscience.wiley.com/search/allsearch?mode=quicksearchandproducts=journalandWISsearch1=1099-0992andWISindexid1=issnandcontentTitle=European+Journal+of+Social+PsychologyandcontextLink=blahandcontentOID=1823andWISsearch2=troppandWISindexid2=WISallandarticleGo.x=0andarticleGo.y=0 (last visited August 11, 2008).

80. Pettigrew and Tropp, "Intergroup Contact."

81. See Will Kymlicka, *Liberalism, Community, and Culture* 196–97 (Oxford: Clarendon Press, 1989); Susan Moller Okin, *Is Multiculturalism Bad for Women?* 9–24, 117–31 (Joshua Cohen, Matthew Howard, and Martha C. Nussbaum eds., Princeton: Princeton University Press, 1999); Joseph Raz, "Multiculturalism: A Liberal Perspective," *Dissent* 67, 74–75 (1994) (contending that respect for cultures does not include oppressive aspects); Peter Gardner, "Tolerance and Education," in Horton, *Liberalism, Multiculturalism, and Toleration*, 83, 94 (maintaining that dispositional tolerance does not lead people to care less about hunger, racism, or torture). Cf. Gutmann, *Democratic Education*, 44–45 (pointing to nonrepression and nondiscrimination limits on the democratic process). Lack of respect for the internal oppressive actions of groups, however, need not justify state intervention. See Rosenblum, *Membership and Morals*. See also Kukathas, "Cultural Rights," 133–34 (arguing for freedom of association, but demanding that the state assure exit rights).

82. David Heyd, "Introduction" to *Toleration*, 15.

83. Cf. Callan, *Creating Citizens*, 5, 51 (arguing that a pluralistic society depends upon the cultivation of independent criticism). As Callan observes, "[T]here can be no oppression in the molding of a character that would refuse to resort to domination or manipulation in dealing with fellow citizens and would resist those

measures when others use them. In fact, a more promising corrective to oppression is hard to imagine" (51).

84. Mill, *On Liberty*, 44. Brighouse, *School Choice*, 75–76. Cf. Callon, *Creating Citizens*, 177 ("[I]maginary interlocutors are a pallid substitute for the real thing").

85. Levin, "Theory of Choice," 268.

86. Oregon had a particular interest in this argument. See Woodhouse, "Who Owns the Child? " 1016–36.

87. The median income of parents with children in private schools exceeds that of those with children in public schools, and, of course, a substantial number of those parents are quite wealthy. But the distribution of income among private school parents is surprisingly broad, though less so if Catholic schools are excluded. See Gutmann, *Democratic Education*, 117. The evidence seems to suggest that the existence of charter schools actually strengthens the support for public schools. James Forman Jr., "Do Charter Schools Threaten Public Education," 2007 *University of Illinois Law Review* 839.

88. Official Pamphlet Distributed Among Voters Prior to Election November 7, 1922, *Oregon School Cases: School Cases: Complete Record, Pierce*, 268 U.S. 733.

89. Holsinger, "Oregon School Controversy," 332; Woodhouse, "Who Owns the Child? " 1016.

90. See, e.g., McConnell, "Governments, Families, and Power," 850 (speaking of a "leftist stew" in the public school, including race and gender egalitarianism among other things). Elsewhere, however, McConnell maintains that public schools teach our children to be "value-less, culture-less, root-less, and religion-less." McConnell, "Multiculturalism," 150. It is hard to recognize American children in this description, living as we do in an age of multiculturalism and persistent adherence to religion. See also *supra* notes 28–41 and accompanying text.

91. On the importance of this, see, e.g., Will Kymlicka, *Multicultural Citizenship: A Liberal Theory of Minority Rights* (Oxford: Clarendon Press, 1995); Charles Taylor, *Multiculturalism: Examining the Politics of Recognition* (Amy Gutmann ed., Princeton: Princeton University Press, 1994). For concerns about essentialism, see K. Anthony Appiah, "Culture, Subculture, Multiculturalism: Educational Options," in *Public Education in a Multicultural Society* 65–89 (Robert K. Fullinwider ed., Cambridge: Cambridge University Press, 1996); Jeremy Waldron, "Multiculturalism and Mélange," in Fullinwider, *Public Education*, 90–118.

92. One study asked students in public and private schools which group they liked the least, and found that students in public schools tended to pick the Nazis or the Ku Klux Klan (82 percent) while only 47 percent students in evangelical private schools selected those groups. Thirty-one percent of the latter students picked advocates of the rights of women or ethnic minorities as their least liked group; only 2 percent of public school students picked these groups. R. Kenneth Godwin, Carrie Ausbrooks, and Valerie Martinez, "Are Public Schools More Effective Than Private Schools in Teaching Political Tolerance," 82 *Phi Delta Kappan* 542, 544 (2001). The authors of the study found that students in public schools were less likely to permit their least liked group to speak than the private

school students were with respect to their least liked group. The authors use this data to compare the tolerance levels of the evangelical student population and the public school population. As comparative measures of toleration, this data is deficient. Legislative prohibitions on the speech of groups like the Nazis are common throughout Europe and in Canada. The question of whether Nazis should be protected by the First Amendment split the ACLU. To suggest that the populations of Europe, Canada, a sizable percentage of the ACLU, and many public school students are intolerant because of their attitudes on this question is farfetched. Indeed, the question whether the intolerant deserve toleration has been the subject of exquisite philosophical debate. On the other hand, no serious student of democracy maintains that advocates of the rights of women or of people of color should be silenced. That any significant segment of a student population thinks that those groups should be silenced suggests that the schools are weak in communicating basic principles of democracy. In fairness, the study attempts to show that the student views in the evangelical schools about the most disliked group was caused by the parents' view, not the schools. But the study does not show that the schools did anything to combat these views, and the parents chose these schools presumably because they thought the schools would be responsible agents for the parents' values. In the end, the study seems to show nothing of value with respect to public schools and a lot to worry about with respect to private evangelical schools. On the difficulties associated with studies comparing public and private schools on civic matters, compare note 52 *infra*.

93. There is some evidence, albeit dated, to suggest that Catholic girls in Catholic schools are less likely than their counterparts in public schools to have restricted views of the roles of women. See Andrew M. Greeley, *Catholic High Schools and Minority Students* 55 (New Brunswick, N.J.: Transaction Books, 1982).

94. This homogenization included a religious emphasis that sought to inspire or teach in ways that would offend no Christian religion. This did not succeed. Catholic objections to the reading of the Bible without commentary, for example, were deeper than objections to the particular Bible chosen. Reading without commentary suggested that it was up to the individual to interpret the scripture, but the Catholic Church taught that its hierarchy was to guide believers in the interpretation. Proponents of public schools thought the Catholics were unreasonable. The Catholics thought the Protestants were hostile (they were). The Catholic decision to maintain a private school system followed. See e.g., Macedo, *Diversity and Distrust*, 56–59, 64–76. Obviously, the "ecumenical" character of the public schools did not sit well with other more sectarian religions and was not well tailored to meet the values of non-Christian religions in general, though the numbers of the latter were not substantial enough to make for a political problem. In addition to the Catholic political problem, the objections of those who argued that the religious content of the schools was too thin to make a difference were not easily dismissed. See Moore, "Bible Reading."

95. Some schools recognize that saluting diversity is not enough. Building from the lived experience of poor people and people of color is necessary both from the perspective of self-respect and from the perspective of effective education. See Sonia Nieto, *The Light in Their Eyes: Creating Multicultural Learning Communi-*

ties 1–18 (New York: Teachers College Press, 1999). Cf. Arstine, *Democracy*, 14 (arguing that effective education requires proceeding from the learner's perspective). Progressive criticism of multiculturalism typically tries to privilege class considerations or universalism without exhibiting any understanding of the pedagogical considerations relevant to the socialization of children. See, e.g., Todd Gitlin, *Twilight of Common Dreams* (New York: Metropolitan Books, 1995). For pointed responses, attacking the critics on their own terms, see Judith Butler, "Merely Cultural," 15 *Social Text* 52 (1997); Henry A. Giroux, "Counter-Public Spheres and the Role of Educators as Public Intellectuals: Paulo Freire's Cultural Politics," in *Masses, Classes, and the Public Sphere* 251 (Mike Hill and Warren Montag eds., New York: Verso, 2000); Iris Marion Young, "Iris Young Responds to Todd Gitlin," *Dissent*, Spring 1997.

96. See Macedo, *Diversity and Distrust*, 122–23, 276.

97. Coons and Sugarman, *Education by Choice*, 22–23, suggest that a mature child should prevail over the parents if he or she should want to attend a public high school.

98. Coons and Sugarman, *Education by Choice*, 84–85; Fitzmaurice, "Liberal Neutrality," 68.

99. Cf. Callan, *Creating Citizens*, 158 (arguing that a premature understanding of ethical diversity could be harmful to the child). I do not believe, however, that parents of preadolescent children should have absolute control over their children. I support the power of the state to regulate private schools and would support very strict regulation of home schooling.

100. Paris, "Moral Education," 887, 893; Coons and Sugarman, *Education by Choice*, 85–86; John Janeway Conger and Nancy L. Galambos, *Adolescence and Youth* 103–5 (5th ed., New York: Longman, 1997); Joseph Adelson, "The Development of Ideology in Adolescence," in *Adolescence in the Life Cycle* 66–77 (Sigmund E. Dragastin and Glen H. Elder eds., Washington, D.C.: Hemisphere; New York: distributed by Halsted Press, 1975); Raymond Montemayor and Daniel J. Flannery, "Making the Transition from Childhood to Early Adolescence," in *From Childhood to Adolescence* 293 (Raymond Montemayor, Gerald R. Adams, and Thomas P. Gullatta eds., Newbury Park, Calif.: Sage, 1990). Cf. Coons and Sugarman, *Education by Choice*, 32, 63 (maintaining that as children gain maturity, they should be able to decide what school to attend).

101. Atwater, *Adolescence*, 285–87; Nancy Eisenberg, "Prosocial Development in Early and Mid-Adolescence," in Montemayor, Adams, and Gullatta, *From Childhood to Adolescence*, 243; Conger and Galambos, *Adolescence and Youth*, 105–6.

102. Conger and Galambos, *Adolescence and Youth*, 280–81.

103. Atwater, *Adolescence*, 139–40 (stating that adolescents show increased ability to make autonomous decisions largely because of stronger cognitive abilities, including ability to formalize, to consider different views simultaneously, and to "consider divergent views in light of other person's perspectives"); J. Roy Hopkins, *Adolescence: The Transitional Years* 245 (New York: Academic Press, 1983) ("[A]dolescents show increasing autonomy with age; they become somewhat less likely to conform to either parents or to peers as they grow older").

104. See Adelson, "Development of Ideology," 67.

105. Because the case for public education rests on the ideal of bringing children of all races, classes, and religions together, to the extent that privately operated schools are open to all, while requiring tuition payments no greater than the average per pupil expenditure in their school district (with modifications for special education students, see Barry, *Culture and Equality*, 206), providing free transportation and the like, and operating with the kind of curriculum that would be acceptable in a public school (for example, not teaching from a favored religious perspective that could skew the demographics of the students), it could be argued that they should be considered "public" schools for purposes of my analysis and for purposes of government funding. I do not see sufficient reason to favor state-operated schools just because they are embedded in an allegedly "democratic" framework, and certainly not because they are part of the state bureaucracy. But I would be concerned about the impact on the children left in the public schools in permitting such an exception. Even if such an exception might be appropriate in some limited circumstances (the overwhelming majority of private schools would not qualify for any such exception), I would not conclude that such an exception is constitutionally required. For policy discussion suggesting the treatment of some private schools as common schools, see Levinson, *Demands of Liberal Education*, 144–45.

106. Wolfe, *One Nation after All*, 19.

107. Cf. Barry, *Culture and Equality*, 211 ("Home schooling . . . is bound to be weak in developing the ability to cope with treatment as an equal among others and in fostering the realization that others do not share the beliefs and norms in which one has been raised").

108. Some might argue that courts could not handle this sort of inquiry even on a case-by-case basis. I recognize the difficulties but do not think that it is different in kind or degree from numerous other inquiries that courts handle on a case-by-case basis. In any event, as I have already mentioned, I do not believe any government is likely to enact a system of compulsory education, so this is unlikely to be a real-world problem. I do think it is important to indicate the limits of the argument.

109. Gilles, "On Educating Children."

110. Thanks to Seana Shiffrin for this argument. Cf. Seana Valentine Shiffrin, "What's Wrong with Compelled Association."

111. Cf. Yudof, *When Governments Speak*, 229 (explaining that *Pierce* promotes educational dissent).

112. Alternative forms of public education can achieve many of the same benefits. The school district where I was a board member has an alternative middle and high school (that to a large extent is democratically operated by the students), and the district has considered two other alternative schools.

113. Principle 7 of the United Nations Declaration of the Rights of the Child states:

> The child is entitled to receive education, which shall be free and compulsory, at least in the elementary stages. He shall be given an education which will promote his general culture, and enable him, on a basis of equal opportunity, to develop his abilities, his individual judgment and his sense of moral and social responsibility, and to become a useful member of society.

United Nations Resolution 1386, Principle 7 (1959).

114. This argument should make the so-called Blaine amendments (prohibiting aid to religious schools) somewhat vulnerable because anti-Catholic motivation played a strong role in their passage. Viteritti, *Choosing Equality*, 152–54.

115. Some might argue that serious administrative problems would be presented in implementing this argument. The free speech and freedom of religion arguments rest on the assumption that parental determinations to send their children to private schools are ideologically motivated, and in many cases no such motivation exists. But case-by-case determinations of whether parents are sincere in claiming ideological reasons for sending their children to private schools would be unreliable and unseemly. By the same token, many parents send their children to Catholic schools for nonreligious reasons, but I think case-by-case determinations of religious motivation would also be unreliable and even more unseemly because of the need to adjudicate the sincerity of allegedly sudden parental religious conversions. Unseemly case-by-case determinations might be the best alternative in some circumstances. Such determinations were probably justified in the Selective Service context.

116. Carter, "Parents, Religion," 1204.

117. David P. Baker and Cornelius Riordan, "The 'Eliting' of the Common American School and the National Education Crisis," *Phi Delta Kappa* 17, 18, 22, September 1998. Twenty-six percent of the American population is Catholic despite the relatively small percentage of those who attend Catholic schools. Adherents, "U.S. Demographics," http://www.adherents.com/adh_dem.html (September 9, 2001).

118. James G. Dwyer, "School Vouchers: Inviting the Public into the Religious Square," 42 *William and Mary Law Review* 963, 1002 (2001) (estimating 15 percent). I assume nine hours of sleep per night and six hours of school per weekday. As students grow older, more time is spent in school, but those hours are not compulsory. Even if those hours are included, the percentage of time spent in school is a minority of the child's waking hours.

119. Neal Devins, "Social Meaning and School Vouchers," 42 *William and Mary Law Review* 919, 943–44 (2001).

120. Some aspects of Catholic doctrine regarding sexuality are widely disbelieved among Catholics. See, e.g., Conger and Galambos, *Adolescence and Youth*, 281:

> [R]ightly or wrongly, approximately half of all adolescents believe that churches are not doing their best to understand young people's ideas about sex. Contemporary adolescents are more likely to state that God has understanding attitudes about sex than to attribute such attitudes to institutionalized religion. . . . A majority of Catholic youth disagrees with their church's position on birth control, annulment and divorce, and the right of priests to marry.

121. For evidence that the church hierarchy's position on various issues regarding sexuality is widely rejected by Catholics throughout the world and that this rejection has led to a general renunciation of church authority, including widespread defections from the clergy, see generally Cornwell, *Breaking Faith*. In particular, see 117–45.

122. In most circumstances, excusing such children seems the pragmatic course as well.

123. Most fundamentalists would forthrightly maintain that reason and science are on their side and that they are afraid of neither one. See Harvey Cox, *Religion in the Secular City* 50–51 (New York: Simon and Schuster, 1984). On the other hand, it is common for fundamentalists to want to keep their children away from views that they believe are contrary to those in the Bible. See Bates, *Battleground*.

124. For an excellent discussion, see Arneson and Shapiro, "Democratic Autonomy." For elaboration of the concept of basic interests, see Ian Shapiro, *Democratic Justice* 85–90, 92–96, 98–99, 104–9 (New Haven: Yale University Press, 2000). For a brief critique, see Shiffrin, "Liberal Theory."

125. *Wisconsin v. Yoder*, 406 U.S. 205 (1972). In defense of *Yoder*, see Shelley Burtt, "In Defense of *Yoder*: Parental Authority and the Public Schools," in Shapiro and Hardin, *Political Order*, 412; Steven D. Smith, "*Wisconsin v. Yoder* and the Unprincipled Approach to Religious Freedom," 25 *Capital University Law Review* 805 (1996).

126. Cf. Barry, *Culture and Equality*, 240 ("The education [or rather non-education] of a gypsy child fits it for nothing except to be a gypsy, whereas a conventional education opens up a potentially limitless range of occupations and ways of life"). But cf. Arneson and Shapiro, "Democratic Autonomy," 391–92 (criticizing conceptions of autonomy based on maximizing options).

127. Arneson and Shapiro, "Democratic Autonomy," 385.

128. Wuthnow, *After Heaven*, 67–68 (stating that fertility rate of 3.8 per woman in 1958 dropped to 1.9 in 1973).

129. College enrollments increased from 3.6 million to 8.6 million students. Wuthnow, *After Heaven*, 68. The number of women tripled. Wuthnow, 68.

130. Atwater, *Adolescence*, 247–48; Conger and Galambos, *Adolescence and Youth*, 156 ("Twice as many teenage women now engage in *premarital* sexual intercourse as in the 1950's").

131. Conger and Galambos, *Adolescence and Youth*, 156.

132. On the place of the family in the so-called culture wars, see James Davison Hunter, *Culture Wars: The Struggle to Define America* 176–96 (New York: Basic Books, 1991).

133. "[I]nformation now besieges people from all parts of the world, making particular religious traditions seem increasingly local and historically contingent." Hunter, *Culture Wars*, 11. At the same time this encourages many people toward postmodernism or, more narrowly, toward broader exploration of religious traditions; it threatens others and causes them to dig in their heels.

CHAPTER 6
VOUCHERS

1. Friedman, *Capitalism and Freedom*, 87.

2. For a thorough analysis of the issues surrounding this contention, see McConnell, "The Selective Funding Problem," 989. In the end, McConnell does not conclude that *Pierce* requires vouchers (1038).

3. For a powerful argument along these lines, influenced by McConnell, but taking a step beyond, see Levinson, "Some Reflections on Multiculturalism."

4. Jon Elster, "Self-Realization in Work and Politics: The Marxist Conception of the Good Life," in *Alternatives to Capitalism* 132 (Jon Elster and Karl Ove Moene eds., Cambridge: Press Syndicate of the University of Cambridge, 1989) (referring to epic Technicolor films).

5. As will be clear, although I subscribe to the distinction between negative and positive liberty, I do not treat positive liberty with the fear expressed by some liberals. See Isaiah Berlin, *Four Essays on Liberty* 173–206 (London: Oxford University Press, 1969).

6. I do not contend that the current Court supports such rights. For scholarship supporting such rights, see Robin West, *Progressive Constitutionalism: Reconstructing the Fourteenth Amendment* 111, 265–66 (Durham, N.C.: Duke University Press, 1994); Erwin Chemerinsky, "Making the Right Case for a Constitutional Right to Minimum Entitlements," 44 *Mercer Law Review* 525 (1993); Peter Edelman, "The Next Century of Our Constitution: Rethinking Our Duty to the Poor," 39 *Hastings Law Journal* 1 (1987); Frank I. Michelman, "Welfare Rights in a Constitutional Democracy," 1979 *Washington University Law Quarterly* 659.

7. One might argue that every child has a right to equal educational resources. This principle is overbroad. For example, children with disabilities might need more resources to get the same education. But it is hard to see why the children of the rich should get more educational resources than others. A program of compulsory public education speaks to this issue, but the equality of resources concern does not seem to justify vouchers. Money spent for vouchers could be spent improving the public school system, and one of the criticisms of vouchers is that they drain the public schools of needed resources. For rich discussion of the equality of resources issue, without reaching a conclusion on the voucher issue, see Brighouse, *School Choice*, 17.

A stronger argument might be founded by invoking an equal right to educate a child in the religion of the parent's choice, but that argument, at a minimum, runs into serious Establishment Clause problems. More generally, one might argue for the right to raise a child in the ideology of one's choice. Then, however, every parent could demand a voucher claiming ideological objections to the public schools, and, absent unseemly and unworkable administrative hearings about sincerity, the narrow right would amount to a universal offer of vouchers. More important, although there is unquestionably a right to raise a child in the ideology of one's choice, it does not follow that such a right extends to state-funded schooling.

8. See, e.g., G. A. Cohen, *If You're an Egalitarian, How Come You're So Rich?* (Cambridge: Harvard University Press, 2000).

9. To a large extent in this brief discussion, I pass over most of the details of the voucher programs, but the arrangements for financing, regulating, and providing information about the voucher schools can trigger quite different impacts. See Levin, "Theory of Choice," 256–60. But, for purposes of this argument, I assume, for example, that voucher schools could not refuse to admit special needs children; would, when oversubscribed, admit on the basis of a lottery; could not expel

children in circumstances where public schools would be disabled from doing so; and could not charge tuition beyond the voucher. In the absence of these conditions, the existence of vouchers would intensify some concerns or create new ones.

10. See Nicole Stelle Garnett and Richard W. Garnett, "School Choice, the First Amendment and Social Justice," 4 *Texas Review of Law and Politics* 301 (2000) (reviewing evidence of favorable academic effects); Viteritti, *Choosing Equality*, 82–86, 216; Paul E. Peterson, "School Choice: A Report Card," in Peterson and Hassel, *Learning from School Choice*, 3; see also R. Kenneth Godwin et al., "Comparing Public Choice and Private Voucher Programs in San Antonio," in Peterson and Hassel, *Learning from School Choice*, 275–392; John E. Chubb and Terry M. Moe, *Politics, Markets, and America's Schools* (Washington, D.C.: Brookings Institution, 1990).

11. The claim that vouchers particularly benefit disadvantaged children is contested on the grounds that parents and children tend to focus on nonacademic factors in making choices and low-income families tend to make decisions on less information than wealthier parents. Amy Stuart Wells, "The Sociology of School Choice," in Sugarman and Kemerer, *School Choice*, 31. See also Angela G. Smith, "Public School Choice and Open Enrollment: Implications for Education, Desegregation, and Equity," 74 *Nebraska Law Review* 255 (1995) (maintaining that there is a relative lack of information by low-income families and less-educated families, though parents of all backgrounds confront obstacles in making informed decisions); Levin, "Theory of Choice," 269 (attempting to provide information does not bridge the gap). But cf. David J. Armor and Brett M. Peiser, "Interdistrict Choice in Massachusetts," in Peterson and Hassel, *Learning from School Choice*, 182 (arguing that choice decisions are primarily based on academics, but choice families are "whiter, have higher SES, and score higher on achievement tests than the nonchoice population in the sending districts"). Moreover, low-income families tend to make choices that reinforce the class position of their children. Smith, "Public School Choice," 269–70 (concluding that vouchers are favorable to more advantaged families). These contentions are not necessarily in tension with the claim that those low-income families that do take advantage of voucher programs are particularly benefited, though that claim is also disputed.

12. Richard Rothstein, "Introduction" in *School Choice: Examining the Evidence*, 25 (Washington, D.C.: Economic Policy Institute, 1993) ("[A]s the evidence of this volume shows, there is no evidence that private schools do a better job of educating students than public schools do"); Henig, "School Choice Outcomes," 95 (stating that evidence is inconclusive).

13. Henig, "School Choice Outcomes," 90.

14. E.g., Macedo, *Diversity and Distrust*, 23 (stating that academic advantages of private schools over public schools "appear to be modest, perhaps even trivial"); Levin, "Theory of Choice," 275 (stating that differential academic effects are small).

15. Anthony S. Bryk, Valerie E. Lee, and Peter B. Holland, *Catholic Schools and the Common Good* 312 (Cambridge: Harvard University Press, 1993) (finding advantages in Catholic schools but warning that these advantages do not obtain in other private schools, thus raising "doubts about any blanket claim that a move toward greater privatization will ensure better consequences for students").

Cf. James S. Coleman Thomas Hoffer, and Sally Kilgore, *High School Achieve-ment: Public, Catholic, and Private Schools Compared* 179 (New York: Basic Books, 1982) (arguing that conclusions about private schools' effect may not hold for non-Catholic private schools); Greeley, *Catholic High Schools*, 122 (maintaining that the academic advantage of Catholic schools over public schools, particularly for low-income and African American students, is in substantial part because such schools have long been organized to help lower-class children, originally immigrants). On the other hand, Greeley indicates that more research is needed on the extent to which the success of Catholic schools is based on their ability not to admit or to expel students who present substantial disciplinary problems (109). Cf. Coleman, Hoffer, and Kilgore, *High School Achievement*, 193 (discussing whether public schools might find structures permitting greater discipline).

16. Baker and Riordan, "The Eliting" (changing demographics and the differ-ent message in Catholic schools throw doubt on the continuing relevance of the studies). Cf. Devins, "Social Meaning," 940–43 (describing changes in Catholic schools without reference to possible implications for the studies).

17. But cf. Forman, "Rise and Fall," 583 ("We do not know, with any certainty, the impact of vouchers on either the students who receive them or the public schools those students left behind").

18. Satisfaction with public schools is surprisingly high, though not as high as with choice schools. Rebecca E. Lawrence, "The Future of School Vouchers in Light of the Past Chaos of Establishment Jurisprudence," 55 *University of Miami Law Review* 419, 422 (2001).

19. See Helen Hershkoff and Adam S. Cohen, "School Choice and the Lessons of Choctaw County," 10 *Yale Law and Policy Review* 1, 19–22 (1992) (arguing that children left behind in the public schools are harmed). In accord are Raquel Aldana, "When the Free-Market Visits Public Schools: Answering the Roll Call for Disadvantaged Students," 15 *National Black Law Journal* 26, 36 (1997–98); and Richard D. Kahlberg, "The Voucher Wars," *The Nation*, November 26, 2001, 30, 32 (drawing on the experiences in Sweden, Chile, and New Zealand).

20. On the importance of further research on this point, see Gill et al., *Rhetoric versus Reality*, 126.

21. Gill et al., *Rhetoric versus Reality*, 94, discuss several ways in which expan-sion could damage private schools, concluding, "Even if the results of the voucher experiments are read in their most favorable light, they provide only weak guid-ance about the academic effects of a large-scale voucher program."

22. Aside from problems of declining clergy in teaching positions, 70 percent of Catholic schools have admission tests. Most voucher programs would require something close to open admissions. The experience in Florida and Milwaukee shows that "the more regulations placed on schools to qualify for vouchers, the fewer the number of schools that will participate." Kahlberg, "The Voucher Wars," 31.

23. See, e.g., Minow, "Before and After *Pierce*," 419.

24. Gutmann, *Democratic Education*, 70.

25. Concerns that the cost of vouchers would take needed funds from the pub-lic schools played a role in the defeat of vouchers in California. See Bulman and

Kirp, "Shifting Politics," 47 n. 11. A difficult dilemma confronts vouchers on this score. On the one hand, children might be permitted to attend schools with greater resources than their public schools. If so, financial incentives are in place for them to leave the public schools rather than providing more support for such schools. Alternatively, one might limit tuition payments to no greater than the average per pupil expenditure in their school district, with modifications for special education students, see Barry, *Culture and Equality*, 206, or the failure to provide free transportation and the like. If so, however, students in wealthier school districts would receive greater voucher funding than those in poorer school districts. Hershkoff and Cohen, "School Choice," 19. This alternative also seems perverse.

26. Private schools cost less per child than public schools. This in part is due to lower teacher salaries and donated time. Beyond costs, tuition fees are subsidized in most private schools in large part by donations from a wide variety of sources, including foundations. Caroline M. Hoxby, "Analyzing School Choice Reforms That Use America's Traditional Forms of Parental Choice," in Peterson and Hassel, *Learning from School Choice*, 133. Many of these contributions would dry up in an expanded voucher program. Assuming, however, that the state gains significantly from these offsets, because of the economies of scale, the public schools could be severely damaged if they lost revenue from children leaving public schools to attend private school. It might be possible to determine the true losses involved in particular cases, but confidence that a state accounting department would pull this off should be difficult to muster. If one assures that districts below the state average do not financially lose because of students leaving for private schools, incentives to change are diminished.

27. On the other hand, since middle-class and upper-class parents pick neighborhoods based in part on the quality of the public schools, they already have the advantage of choice to a large extent. Michael W. McConnell, "Governments, Families, and Power: A Defense of Educational Choice," 31 *Connecticut Law Review* 847, 851 (1999).

28. *R.A.V. v. City of St. Paul*, 505 U.S. 377 (1992) (protecting racist speech in circumstances not involving state subsidies).

29. Coons and Sugarman, *Education by Choice* (predicting that such a refusal would withstand constitutional challenge); Dwyer, "School Vouchers," 1000; Lupu and Tuttle, "*Zelman's* Future," 979. See Devins, "Social Meaning," 958 (stating that the Cleveland voucher system prohibits the teaching of hatred on religious grounds).

30. See Coons and Sugarman, *Education by Choice*, 41 (maintaining that state regulation of private schools is minimal, accomplishing little in educational terms); Dwyer, "School Vouchers" (arguing that the state's regulation of religious social service organizations and religious colleges and universities is haphazard); Stephen Monsma, *When Sacred and Secular Mix: Religious Nonprofit Organizations and Public Money* 63–108 (Lanham, Md.: Rowman and Littlefield, 1996).

31. Dwyer, "School Vouchers."

32. The statistics in this paragraph can be found in Robert K. Vischer, "Racial Segregation in American Churches and Its Implications for School Vouchers," 53 *Florida Law Review* 193, 196–97, 204–5 (2001). In addition to racial segregation, there are strong grounds to believe that vouchers would increase class segregation.

Hershkoff and Cohen, "School Choice." But see Garnett and Garnett, "School Choice," 353–54 (arguing that vouchers would lead to racial and economic integration); Coleman, Hoffer, and Kilgore, *High School Achievement*, 182–83 (questioning the extent to which private schools currently contribute to racial or ethnic discrimination, at least with respect to Hispanics).

33. Stephen Eisdorfer, "Public School Choice and Racial Integration," 24 *Seton Hall Law Review* 937, 944 (1993); Molly Townes O'Brien, "Private School Tuition Vouchers and the Realities of Racial Politics," 64 *Tennessee Law Review* 359, 399 (1997). Indeed, "many—probably most—of the natural constituents of the Republican Party oppose any voucher experiment that would bring poor urban students of color into 'their' schools." Hochschild, "Public Schools," 41.

34. Richard Elmore, "Choice as an Instrument of Public Policy," in Clune and Witte, *Choice and Control*, 285, 306; Viteritti, *Choosing Equality*, 117; Godwin et al., "Comparing Public Choice," 279.

35. I concede the possibility that this may be a good thing for many black children because of the racism they might confront at an early age, though I remain persuaded that segregation is bad for Anglos and for most African American children. For doubts about the value of integration for black children, see Robin D. Barnes, "Black America and School Choice: Charting a New Course," 106 *Yale Law Journal* 2375 (1997). One way to mitigate the segregation concern might be to require voucher schools to meet certain racially required mixtures. Aside from the practical difficulties with this approach, there may be constitutional difficulties as well. Michael Heise, "An Empirical and Constitutional Analysis of Racial Ceilings and Public Schools," 24 *Seton Hall Law Review* 921 (1993).

36. See Baer, "Discriminatory Use of 'Sectarian.' "

37. Coons and Sugarman, *Education by Choice*; Michael W. McConnell, "Education Disestablishment: Why Democratic Values Are Ill-Served by Democratic Control of Schooling," in Macedo and Tamir, *Moral and Political Education*; Godwin et al., "Comparing Public Choice," 9:

> Caution is recommended before suddenly dismantling a system that has been established over the course of 150 years. The very size of the public school system—over $300 billion a year[—] . . . stands as a warning against immediate, wholesale alterations . . . [B]efore dramatically restructuring American education, school choice reformers need to remember that the first rule is to do no harm. Reforms should be taken gradually, experimentally, focusing on the places of greatest need and urgency.

38. The question is of substantial practical importance. In 1977, 78 percent of private schools were religious. Lawrence, "Future of School Vouchers," 432 n. 108.

39. See Douglas Laycock, "The Supreme Court and Religious Liberty," 40 *Catholic Lawyer* 25, 48–54 (2000); Jesse H. Choper, "Federal Constitutional Issues," in Sugarman and Kemerer, *School Choice*, 235, 259.

40. For criticism of *Zelman*, see Gary J. Simson, "School Vouchers and the Constitution—Permissible, Impermissible, or Required?" 11 *Cornell Journal of Law and Public Policy* 553, 564–76 (2002); Note, "They Drew a Circle That Shut Me In: The Free Exercise Implications of *Zelman v. Simmons-Harris*," 117

Harvard Law Review 919 (2004) (claiming that the Cleveland system severely impaired free exercise values). But see Thomas C. Berg, "Vouchers and Religious Schools: The New Constitutional Questions," 72 *University of Cincinnati Law Review* 151, 220 (2004) (arguing that "once vouchers are made available for use at private schools, they must be made available for use at religious schools as well").

41. In fact, 96 percent of the voucher recipients used vouchers in religious schools.

42. These facts were mentioned in the opinion, but they were not relevant to the outcome except to show that Ohio could not reasonably be understood to have the purpose of advancing religion, or to be endorsing religion.

43. See also *Locke v. Davey*, 540 U.S. 712, 124 S. Ct. 1307 (2004). In *Locke*, the Court ruled that formal neutrality in postsecondary school aid was not required when the state funded scholarships, but refused to fund studies in devotional theology. The Court observed that the state's interest was not based on hostility toward religion, but rather was to avoid establishment of religion. Justice O'Connor's concurrence was mildly more demanding than that of the chief justice, but it is unlikely that those distinctions will make a difference, particularly given the new composition of the Court. On the differences, see Lupu and Tuttle, "*Zelman*'s Future," 926–46.

44. Forcing individuals to advance religious views they reject is the "primary vice of government support for private religious schools." Conkle, "Toward a General Theory," 1175.

45. Ninety-six percent of the voucher students attended Catholic schools.

46. Conkle, "Path of Religious Liberty," 22.

47. Cooley, *Treatise on Constitutional Limitations*, 967. See Green, "Private School Vouchers," 50 (describing how, from the second half of nineteenth century into the twentieth, state courts consistently invalidated financial aid to religious schools).

48. For criticism of the view that Madison's opinions are necessarily contrary to the constitutionality of vouchers, see Ira C. Lupu, "The Increasingly Anachronistic Case against School Vouchers," 13 *Notre Dame Journal of Law, Ethics and Public Policy* 375 (1999); Blasi, "School Vouchers."

49. But cf. Bryan C. Hassel, "The Case for Charter Schools," in Peterson and Hassel, *Learning from School Choice*, 45.

50. Proponents of vouchers and some justices argue that if parents are given money, and then give it to the schools, the constitutional connection between the state and the schools is broken. But it is hard to see why "the fact that money is laundered through 'private choice' under a state voucher plan" should make a constitutional difference. Laura S. Underkuffler, "The Price of Vouchers for Religious Freedom," 78 *University of Detroit Mercy Law Review* 463, 473 (2001); Laura S. Underkuffler, "Vouchers and Beyond: The Individual as Causative Agent in Establishment Clause Jurisprudence," 75 *Indiana Law Journal* 463 (2000); Green, "Private School Vouchers." On the other hand, I do not believe that financial aid to a religious school makes the message of the school a government message. But see Kathleen M. Sullivan, "Parades, Public Squares and Voucher Payments: Problems of Government Neutrality," 28 *Connecticut Law Review* 243,

256–57 (1996). It has been argued, see, e.g., Volokh, "Equal Treatment," that voucher programs should be upheld by analogy to the GI Bill, which permits veterans to use government funds to attend the college of their choice whether religious or secular. Voucher programs at the K–12 level would disproportionately go to religious schools, however. In addition, they would be employed at a stage of life in which children are more impressionable. These factors raise the stakes substantially, heightening the church-state concerns developed *infra*. See Frank R. Kemerer, "State Constitutions and School Vouchers," 120 *Education Law Reporter* 1, 1 (1997) (stating that some 85 percent of private schools are religious).

51. See Mark E. Chopko, "Religious Access to Public Programs and Governmental Funding," 60 *George Washington Law Review* 645, 653 n. 33 (1992).

52. For a brief period in the 1850s, California subsidized private schools, including Catholic schools. Nonetheless, religious books (except for the Bible) were banned from publicly funded schools. The archbishop of San Francisco "declared independence from the religious prohibitions in the law." Tyack, James, and Benevot, *Law and Shaping*, 90. Funding was withdrawn because of anti-Catholic protests. "The controversy over the funding of religious schools demonstrated how the state could seek to enlist religious groups as allies in garnering support for public education but then exclude them from benefits when protest arose." Tyack, James, and Benevot, 90–91.

53. It is still too early to know what the issues lying behind the events of September 11, 2001, might ultimately augur for religious divisions within this country. Other than the issues mentioned with respect to other values, I do not think the promoting community value described in chapter 3 is independently implicated with vouchers.

54. The percentage has declined substantially over the years. Catholics previously accounted for 87 percent of private school enrollment, but that percentage dropped to 64 percent in 1982. Viteritti, *Choosing Equality*, 81.

55. The Court has frequently maintained that such schools are "pervasively sectarian." For criticism of the use of the term *sectarian* to mean religious, see Baer, "Discriminatory Use of 'Sectarian,'" 449–60.

56. For an expression of concern about the power of religious lobbies from a Madisonian perspective, see Hamilton, "Power," 816–21. But see Steven H. Shiffrin, "Religion and Democracy," 74 *Notre Dame Law Review* 1631, 1646–52 (1999).

57. Cf. Laycock, "Benefits of Establishment Clause," 381 (arguing that religion is always part of politics, but theology, worship, and ritual are beyond the scope of government); Daniel O. Conkle, "God Loveth Adverbs," 42 *DePaul Law Review* 339, 345–46 (1992) (distinguishing between worldly and spiritual matters in terms of the political role of religions). It is possible that a constitutional decision against vouchers could fail to mitigate political interaction between church and state along these lines. The *Roe* decision hardly took the abortion issue off the political table. Although some religious institutions would have a stake in combating a decision against vouchers, I doubt that the people in the pews would muster the necessary intensity to give the churches any significant clout.

58. See Hamilton, "Calvinist Paradox."

59. See Macedo, *Diversity and Distrust*, 119 ("The unavailability of many forms of state aid reduces the incentives for religious schools to tailor their convictions in order to qualify for state aid"). One prominent religious leader maintains that the proposed charitable choice program in the current Bush administration is calculated to co-opt the black church and, to some extent, has already done so. Amos C. Brown Sr., "African American Political Empowerment," Panel Discussion, Cornell University (February 6, 2002). For a tracing of shifts by churches regarding their positions on financial aid to private schools and the role of religion in the public schools as guided by their perceived self-interest, see Jeffries and Ryan, "Political History." The history of church complicity with the state may be the most significant reason for the decline of religious commitment in much of western Europe. See Casanova, *Public Religions*, 29. But see Blasi, "School Vouchers," 899 (contending that denominations already receive financial benefits from the state, giving politicians levers for retaliation, but recognizing that the size of the voucher program could make a difference unless there is sufficient size and variety of schools to create multiple constituencies and a powerful alliance).

60. Understanding this requires rejection of the idea that a significant purpose of the Establishment Clause is to ensure that the polity is not divided politically along religious lines. Often accompanying this claim is the view that religious reasons should not be given in public life. Of course, pandering by politicians on religious lines is regrettable. Moreover, it is an unqualified outrage that George W. Bush's inauguration "for all the people" featured two ministers praying to Jesus Christ. But, as I will discuss more fully in chapter 7, the stability of our country does not depend upon keeping religious arguments out of public life.

61. For problems in the application of conditions to religious institutions, see Monsma, *Sacred and Secular*, 63–108.

62. For examples of voucher programs that do this, see Devins, "Social Meaning," 958; Marc D. Stern, "School Vouchers: The Church-State Debate That Really Isn't," 31 *Connecticut Law Review* 977 (1999) (maintaining that such rules, if enforced, would have "a substantial impact on the character of the schools"). For discussion of the constitutional issues regarding many forms of discrimination, see Michael Kavey, "Private Voucher Schools and the First Amendment Right to Discriminate," 113 *Yale Law Journal* 743 (2003).

63. Gutmann, "Publicly Funded Schools," 172–73 ("Private religious schools (or schools that teach atheism) are permitted to discriminate on grounds of religion precisely because they are not publicly funded"). Many proponents of vouchers argue that conditions should not apply to religious schools at the same time they are arguing that subsidies for education should flow neutrally to religious and to nonreligious institutions. Thus they favor neutrality—except when they don't. See Steven K. Green, "The Ambiguity of Neutrality," 86 *Cornell Law Review* 692, 715–16 (2001). But see Monsma, *Sacred and Secular*, 173–99 (abstaining from applying conditions is "positive neutrality"). For arguments that a wide variety of conditions are constitutional, see Dwyer, "School Vouchers," 980–1006. See also Stephen Macedo, "Constituting Civil Society: School Vouchers, Religious Nonprofit Organizations, and Liberal Public Values," 75 *Chicago-Kent Law Review* 417, 433–42 (2000).

64. Cf. Elliot Mincberg, "Vouchers, the Constitution and the Court," 10 *George Mason University Civil Rights Law Journal* 155, 158 (1999–2000) (claiming that subsidies to religious schools have diminished the autonomy of those schools).

65. Alan E. Brownstein, "Evaluating School Voucher Programs through a Liberty, Equality, and Free Speech Matrix," 31 *Connecticut Law Review* 871, 894–99, 908 (1999).

66. Cf. John H. Garvey, "What Does the Constitution Say about Vouchers," 44 *Boston Bar Journal* 14 (2000) (supporting the constitutionality of vouchers, but, nonetheless, concerned that schools "will be tempted to adjust their teaching in order to attract the maximum degree of public support"). Whatever state impositions on the content of education at religious schools—with or without vouchers—enforcing those impositions implicates concerns about entanglement. Cf. Nancy L. Rosenblum, "Pluralism and Democratic Education," 153 ("We know that in democracies where the establishment question is resolved in favor of government support for religious schools, the question of the *civic content* of religious education remains unresolved and produces fierce political conflict"). See also Rosenblum, 156 ("We can predict that the instability of public opinion would be amplified in the face of public funding for the wild array of private schools devoted to some secular ideology, schools established by and for ethnic and cultural groups, ideologues of many stripes, vegetarians, weird pedagogic experimentalists, and so on").

67. For very different reasons, I think the conditions that accompany the No Child Left Behind Act are bad for either public or private education. See Jonathan Kozol, *Letters to a Young Teacher* (New York: Basic Books, 2006). It is worth noting that fear of these conditions has deterred many conservative Christians from supporting voucher programs. Forman, "Rise and Fall," 547, 547, 591–96.

68. Blasi, "School Vouchers," 798. Blasi does not regard the corruption concern as necessarily dispositive, but he does think it should play a greater role in the voucher debate than it ordinarily has.

69. Blasi, "School Vouchers," 798.

70. Lupu and Tuttle, "Limits of Equal Liberty," 1251 (no interest-balancing is part of Establishment Clause methodology).

71. Shiffrin, *First Amendment*, chap. 1.

72. I do not mean to suggest that the arguments for balancing in the free speech context are noncontroversial. Controversy rages, and there is no reason to plow the ground again. It is odd, however, to make use of a methodology in the free speech context and foreclose it altogether in the Establishment Clause context.

73. For discussion of the voucher movement's decision to emphasize the poverty argument (particularly with respect to black children), see Forman, "Rise and Fall," 547, 567–73.

74. *W. Va. State Bd. of Educ. v. Barnette*, 319 U.S. 624, 642 (1943) (holding that a schoolchild cannot be forced to salute the flag).

75. Speech published in reckless disregard of the truth is subject to liability. But proving reckless disregard of the truth requires a showing of a high awareness of probable falsity or a showing that the publisher entertained serious doubt about

the truth and proceeded anyway. Gross negligence may be established without any showing of subjective awareness.

76. The number of children attending schools that are designed to address the collective needs of Protestants, Catholics, and other children has grown to slightly in excess of 5 percent. N. *Ireland Council for Integrated Educ., A Background to the Development of Integrated Education in Northern Ireland* 3 (September 2002). Even this small number of children attending integrated schools is a relatively new development. The first significant move to press for integrated education came in the late 1980s. N. *Ireland Council,* 2. Although these figures do not take into account the number of Catholic children attending Protestant secondary schools, religious segregation has been and continues to be the norm. Laura Lundy, *Education Law, Policy and Practice in Northern Ireland* 6–7 (Belfast: SLS Legal Publications, 2000). I do not mean to suggest that integrated education would be or would have been a cure-all in Northern Ireland. A history of colonialism and persecution against Catholics is not easily undone by sitting children in school together any more than racial problems in the United States are easily solved by integration. The extent to which integrated schools are good for civic purposes, good for Catholics, and good for Protestants in Northern Ireland turns out to be quite complicated. But at least one civic goal in Northern Ireland should be to reduce the palpable hostility and continuing violence between largely poor Protestants and Catholics. If that were the only issue, moves toward integrated education would seem to be constructive.

77. It has been somewhat bounded by the unwillingness of suburban schools to accept vouchers.

CHAPTER 7
RELIGION AND PROGRESSIVE POLITICS

1. There is no logical incompatibility between holding liberal theological views and politically conservative views, but that combination is not a significant part of the American scene. To the extent it were, I would still be questioning their theological attitudes toward church-state relations.

2. Andrew Greeley and Michael Hout, *The Truth about Conservative Christians: What They Think and What They Believe* 4 (Chicago: University of Chicago Press, 2006).

3. Greeley and Hout, *Truth about Conservative Christians,* 47.

4. Peter Gay, *The Party of Humanity* 44 (London: Weidenfeld and Nicolson, 1964).

5. *The Essential Marx: The Non-economic Writings* 287 (Saul K. Padover ed., New York: New American Library 1978)

6. Richard Rorty, "Anticlericalism and Atheism," in Richard Rorty and Gianni Vattimo, *The Future of Religion* 40–41 n. 2 (New York: Columbia University Press, 2005) (expressing the hope that institutionalized religion will eventually disappear); Richard Rorty, "Religion in the Public Square: A Reconsideration," 31 *Journal of Religious Education* 141, 142; Richard Rorty, *Contingency, Irony, and Solidarity* 45 (Cambridge: Cambridge University Press, 1989) (advocating a form of liberalism with "no trace of divinity" remaining).

7. Cf. Sullivan, *The Party Faithful*: "The problem for any progressive religious movement during the last fifty years has been that its most natural allies–the New Left and the future leaders of the Democratic Party–largely threw religion overboard in the countercultural revolution of the 1960's."

8. Harris Interactive, "The Religious and Other Beliefs of Americans 2003," *The Harris Poll* #11, February 11, 2003, http://www.harrisinteractive.com/harris_poll/index.asp?PID=359 (last visited March 6, 2007). Ninety percent of adults believe in God; 68 percent believe in the devil and 69 percent believe in hell. *Id.*

9. Although the majority of those who regularly attend church vote Republican, the gap between Democrats and Republicans shrunk to 12 percent in the 2006 elections. Indeed, 28 percent of white evangelicals voted Democratic in 2006, as did a majority of Catholics. Alan Cooperman, "Democrats Win Bigger Share of Religious Vote," *Washington Post*, November 11, 2006, http://www.msnbc.msn.com/id/15662295/ (last visited December 8, 2006).

10. I believe the political aspects of that subject need somewhat more discussion. See text accompanying notes 7 to 73 *infra*.

11. Carter, *The Culture of Disbelief*, 60 (referring to the "instinctive mistrust of God-talk by contemporary liberals"); Paul J. Weithman, "Introduction: Religion and the Liberalism of Reasoned Respect," in Paul J. Weithman, *Religion and Contemporary Liberalism* 1, 1 (Notre Dame: University of Notre Dame Press, 1997) ("It is a shibboleth of contemporary political analysis that religion and liberalism are mutually antagonistic").

12. "Liberalism is *par excellence* the doctrine of the Enlightenment. Brian Barry, "How Not to Defend Liberal Institutions," 20 *British Journal of Political Science* 1, 2 (1990). On the hostility of much of the Enlightenment to religion, the subtitle of Peter Gay's classic tells it all: *The Enlightenment: An Interpretation; the Rise of Modern Paganism* (New York: Knopf, 1966). See also Gay, xi (emphasis added): The philosophes' rebellion was a "paganism directed against their Christian inheritance and dependent upon the paganism of classical antiquity, but it was also a *modern* paganism, emancipated from classical thought as from Christian dogma."

13. Suzanna Sherry, "The Sleep of Reason," 84 *Georgetown Law Journal* 453, 456 (1996) ("The lasting accomplishment of the Enlightenment, then, was its development of an epistemological method. That method was a repudiation of the 'millennium of superstition, other worldliness, mysticism, and dogma known as the Middle, or Dark, Ages'"), quoting Ralph Ketcham, *Framed for Posterity: The Enduring Philosophy of the Constitution* 21 (Lawrence: University Press of Kansas, 1993).

14. "A . . . notable aspect of the Enlightenment thought is the emergence of a scientific way of thinking." James M. Byrne, *Religion and the Enlightenment* 10 (Louisville, Ky.: Westminster John Knox Press, 1996).

15. Voltaire's "secular philosophy was a formidable, almost irresistible rival of Christianity." Gay, *The Party of Humanity*, 5. See Byrne, *Religion and the Enlightenment*, 2 (Voltaire's criticism of Christianity and the church weakened the power of religion in French cultural life). On the other hand, Voltaire thought that it might be a good thing for the masses to remain religious despite his con-

tempt for the religion they held. Frank E. Manuel, *The Changing of the Gods* 66 (Hanover, N.H.: Brown University Press, 1983).

16. Dewey did not object to God talk, but he rejected any concept of the supernatural. Ryan, *John Dewey*, 273.

17. See note 6 *supra*.

18. Ronald Dworkin, *Sovereign Virtue: The Theory and Practice of Equality* 281–84 (Cambridge: Harvard University Press, 2000); Ronald Dworkin, *A Matter of Principle* (Cambridge: Harvard University Press, 1985); Dworkin, *Taking Rights Seriously*. I do not think Dworkin is generally hostile or favorable to religion in *Life's Dominion* (New York: Knopf, 1993). He argues that the right to procreative autonomy should be protected under the religion clauses (160–68), and he argues that the question whether to abort is morally serious (68–101), but he does not make remarks for or against religion generally. He does indicate that government could encourage women to take the question of the sanctity of life seriously (168), and he suggests that the question of the sanctity of life is an essentially religious question (163–64). One might argue that the latter commits him to a favorable view of religion (at least in this narrow area), but he recognizes that a belief in the sanctity of life could follow from traditional religion or from a belief in a godless nature that is not "conventionally religious" (82). And he argues that it is no business of the state to settle on one account or another (160–68).

19. Raz, *The Morality of Freedom*.

20. "In *Political Liberalism* and recent essays, the story Rawls tells us is that political liberalism [what I call cooperative liberalism] emerges out of the conflicts between opposing moral doctrines, specifically the early modern wars of religion and the debates about religious tolerance." James Bohman, "Public Reason and Cultural Pluralism," 23 *Political Theory* 253, 253 (1995).

21. Secular premises of comprehensive views would be excluded unless they were shared among other reasonable comprehensive views.

22. Rawls, *Political Liberalism*.

23. Stephen Macedo, *Diversity and Distrust*, 169 (view about public reason is consistent with what Rawls advocates).

24. Nussbaum explicitly identifies with political liberalism (Martha C. Nussbaum, "A Plea for Difficulty," in Okin with respondents, *Is Multiculturalism Bad for Women?* 105, 109–110), emphasizes the importance of respecting other comprehensive positions (109), and states that her own comprehensive vision as a Kantian reform Jew would not justify eliminating sex discrimination in the choice of Catholic priest or in abrogating various Jewish positions on sex equality (114) even though she repudiates the Catholic discrimination and the positions held by many Jews (114). But she might, consistent with the views she had previously stated, have had a more expansive conception of the role of religion in democratic life than Rawls. Nonetheless, her more recent work puts her in the Rawls camp, as I read her. Nussbaum, *Liberty of Conscience*, 43, 58. William E. Connolly, *Why I Am Not a Secularist* (Minneapolis: University of Minnesota Press, 1999) is a Nietschean leftist who believes in cooperation with the religious Left, but is not a cooperative liberal in the sense I am using here. He is entirely comfortable with religious discourse in the public sphere.

25. On the definition of reasonable comprehensive doctrines, see Rawls, *Political Liberalism*, 59. For explication of the reasonableness requirement, see Samuel Freeman, "Deliberative Democracy: A Sympathetic Comment," 29 *Philosophy and Public Affairs* 389, 399–405 (2000). Rawls's conception of the reasonable has been carefully criticized. Onora O'Neill, "Political Liberalism and Public Reason: A Critical Notice of John Rawls, Political Liberalism," 106 *Philosophical Review* 411 (1997).

26. Macedo, *Diversity and Distrust*, 85 (impact of the content of public schools wisely makes it harder for some religions to perpetuate their views).

27. In particular, see Mill, "Utility of Religion," 50–51 (belief in supernatural once served useful purposes, but is now dispensable). For commentary, see Linda C. Raeder, *John Stuart Mill and the Religion of Humanity* (Columbia: University of Missouri Press, 2002).

28. For an intriguing account of why a Catholic should be a cooperative liberal, see Leslie Griffin, "Good Catholics Should be Rawlsian Liberals," 5 *S.California Interdisciplinary Law Journal* 297 (1997).

29. Although she is not an indifferent liberal, Martha Nussbaum is a religious Kantian. See *Liberty of Conscience*.

30. Justice O'Connor's theoretical commitments in this area were generally liberal: "The Establishment Clause prohibits government from making adherence to a religion relevant in any way to a person's standing in the religious community." *Lynch*, 465 U.S. 687 (O'Connor, J., concurring).

31. *Lynch*, 465 U.S. 688 (repudiating endorsement because it sends a message to some that they are insiders and to others that they are outsiders). Regrettably the endorsement test was, for the most part, ignored in the Ten Commandments cases. Greg Abbott, "Upholding the Unbroken Tradition: Constitutional Acknowledgement of the Ten Commandments in the Public Square," 14 *William and Mary Bill of Rights Journal* 51, 54–55 (2005). For criticism of the endorsement approach, see Jesse Choper, "The Endorsement Test: Its Status and Desirability," 18 *Journal of Law and Politics* 499 (2002); Steven D. Smith, "Symbols, Perceptions, and Doctrinal Illusions: Establishment Neutrality and the 'No Endorsement' Test," 86 *Michigan Law Review* 266 (1987); William P. Marshall, "'We Know It When We See It': The Supreme Court and Establishment," 59 *Southern California Law Review* 495 (1986). For a modest modification of the endorsement test that speaks to some of the criticisms, see B. Jessie Hill, "Putting Religious Symbolism in Context: A Linguistic Critique of the Endorsement Test," 104 *Michigan Law Review* 491, 539–544 (2005). For an even more ambitious discussion of the concerns that have been addressed by the endorsement test, proposing a shift in focus, see Adam M. Samaha, "Endorsement Retires from Religious Symbols to Anti-sorting Principles," 2005 *Supreme Court Review* 135, 192 (2005) (focusing on the "strategic deployment of religious symbols" influencing religious demographics).

32. *County of Allegheny*, 492 U.S. 599–600 (striking down the display of a crèche in a county courthouse).

33. *Van Orden v. Perry*, 545 U.S. 677 (2005), considered the question whether the display of a monument 6 feet high and 3 feet wide on the grounds of the Texas State Capital violated the Establishment Clause.

34. Thomas B. Colby, "A Constitutional Hierarchy of Religions? Justice Scalia, the Ten Commandments, and the Future of the Establishment Clause," 100 *Northwestern University Law Review* 1097, 1097–1103, 1117–21 (2006).

35. Eisgruber and Sager, *Religious Freedom*, 8 ("The government has long been the primary funding agency for church-run charities in the United States").

36. There is a spectrum of charitable activities. At one end, it would be the rare liberal that would oppose the use of vouchers for medical care at a religious hospital. At the other end would be schools that are in the business of religious socialization. In between are a range of activities including soup kitchens and adoption agencies.

37. There is strong evidence that discrimination in favor of conservative Christian evangelical programs has been present in the Charitable Choice program. See Kuo, *Tempting Fate*, 213–16.

38. As I argued in chapter 6, this issue raises a dilemma. Either schools and religious organizations are not held accountable or they are held accountable and subject to potentially intrusive regulation leading to worrisome entanglement issues.

39. Another important view of many liberals is that public education is to be preferred on the ground that it brings people of all races, classes, and religions together and that a diverse student body promotes many important values. This argument may have special attraction to perfectionist liberals or cooperative liberals (whose perfectionism is limited to developing skills and attitudes for participation in democratic life), but it depends upon the facts on the ground as well.

40. DiIulio, *Godly Republic*. DiIulio, however, is not himself opposed to school vouchers (142). Presumably the presence of parental choice as an intermediary between government and the school makes a difference for him.

41. Eisgruber and Sager, *Religious Freedom*, attack the separation metaphor altogether (22–50), and maintain that religious organizations should not be discriminated against in the receipt of aid (24). Aid to religious organizations on their understanding should be permissible so long as government avoids "preferring, endorsing, or affiliating itself with a particular viewpoint about religion" (203). Nussbaum also criticizes the separation metaphor and emphasizes equality and neutrality in dealing with the question of financial aid. Nussbaum, *Liberty of Conscience*, 285–86.

42. *Employment Division v. Smith*, 494 U.S. 872 (1990).

43. Most supporters of *Smith* relied on conservative constitutional grounds. See, e.g., Gerard V. Bradley, "Beguiled: Free Exercise Exemptions and the Siren Song of Liberalism," 20 *Hofstra Law Review* 245, 248 (1991) (defending *Smith* by looking to the understanding of the Free Exercise Clause in the years 1789–91). Liberal groups, both religious and nonreligious overwhelmingly opposed the outcome in *Smith*. Bradley, 246.

44. Barry, *Culture and Equality*, 321 ("There is no principle of justice mandating exemptions to generally applicable laws for those who find compliance burdensome in virtue of their cultural norms or religious beliefs"). Although Barry supports *Smith* (320–21), he might permit exemptions on the basis of prudence or generosity (38–39). For an even broader defense of *Smith*, see Marshall, "In Defense of Smith." For a response to Marshall by a leading religious conservative,

see Michael W. McConnell, "A Response to Professor Marshall," 58 *University of Chicago Law Review* 329 (1991).

45. Almost invariably, this neutrality refers to neutrality toward particular forms of the good life in governmental justifications, not in consequences of government action, since most state arrangements could negatively impact some conceptions of the good life. Cf. Kwame Anthony Appiah, *The Ethics of Identity* 82 (Princeton: Princeton University Press, 2005). Notice further that liberals distinguish between the right (and wrong) and the good. The state is not neutral about murder, for example. For an early statement by Dworkin on the issue of the good life (that he has since qualified, see, e.g., Dworkin, "Right to Pornography"; Dworkin, "Liberalism"; see also Ackerman, *Social Justice*, 11, 57–58, 166 n. 10; Larmore, *Patterns of Moral Complexity*, 50–68. Some secular liberals are perfectionists and thus permit the state to favor some conceptions of the good life over others. Raz, *The Morality of Freedom*, Part VI. Even then, the perfectionist liberal typically favors a broad range of lifestyles so long as they are autonomously chosen. The favoring of autonomously chosen lifestyles over nonautonomous lifestyles need not lead to the view that the latter receive no protection, but they might well receive less weight in a constitutional balance, and they would not be encouraged by the state. Some perfectionists who identify as liberals place stress on diversity without privileging autonomy. Galston, *Liberal Purpose*. Other liberals emphasize the values of autonomy and diversity. John Stuart Mill, "On Liberty," in *The Spirit of the Age, On Liberty, and the Subjection of Women* (Alan Ryan ed., New York: Norton, 1996).

46. Forst, *Contexts of Justice*, 69 ("A person's religious conviction is worthy of protection because it is identity-determining, and not because it is religious"). Ronald Dworkin, *Is Democracy Possible Here: Principles for a New Political Debate* 61 (Princeton: Princeton University Press, 2006): "A tolerant secular community must . . . find its justification for religious freedom in a more basic principle of liberty that generates a more generous justification of the spheres of value in which people must be free to choose for themselves. It must treat freedom of religion, that is, as one case of a more general right not simply of religious . . . freedom." See also Dworkin, 61: "[A] tolerant secular society . . . does not, as a community, attach any special value to religion as a phenomenon."

47. These are permitted under *Smith*, 494 U.S. 890.

48. That is, they would be regarded as discrimination for favoring religious over nonreligious views. Dworkin, *Is Democracy Possible Here*, 61. For development of this argument, see Marshall, "In Defense of Smith." A strong theme in the legal literature is that such accommodations tend to favor majority over minority religions. Stephen L. Carter, "The Resurrection of Religious Freedom?" 107 *Harvard Law Review* 118, 122–23 (1993); Lupu, "Reconstructing the Establishment Clause"; James D. Gordon, "Free Exercise on the Mountaintop," 79 *California Law Review* 108 (1991).

49. For the argument that a contrary result in *Smith* would privilege faith over reason and that the American Constitution is an Enlightenment Constitution that favors reason over faith, see Suzanna Sherry, "Enlightening the Religion Clauses," 7 *Journal of Contemporary Legal Issues* 473, 477 (1996). Sherry maintains that reason is at odds with faith, but I think she would search hard to find believers

that concede this. Rather they might say that faith is a gift *supported* by or fully compatible with reason. Indeed, some religious traditions regard reason as an important source of religious understanding. Robert Audi, *Religious Commitment and Secular Reason* chap. 5 (Cambridge: Cambridge University Press, 2000). See generally, Tracy, *The Analogical Imagination*, 54–82 (describing the nature of reason in what he describes as fundamental, systematic, and practical theology).

50. For discussion of the depth of the religious foundations of Locke, see Waldron, *God, Locke, and Equality*.

51. John Locke, *Two Treatises of Government and A Letter concerning Toleration* 236–37, 243 (Ian Shapiro ed., New Haven: Yale University Press, 2003).

52. Concerns about religious division were expressed by several members of the Court in one of the Ten Commandments cases, *Van Orden v. Perry*, 125 S.Ct. 2854, 2868 (2005) (Breyer, J., concurring); *Van Orden*, 2875 (Stevens, J., joined by Ginsburg, J., dissenting). For the contention that concerns about religious division should not be taken into account by the Court, see Garnett, "Religion, Division."

53. For the suggestion that stability concerns with respect to many religious groups are out of place, see Ronald Dworkin, *Is Democracy Possible Here*, 68.

54. Their view was initially presented in Eisgruber and Sager, "The Vulnerability of Conscience," 1285–86. It has been developed more fully in Eisgruber and Sager, *Religious Freedom*, 89–100.

55. On the other hand, Eisgruber and Sager do not regard all liberties as alike. They maintain that deep commitments should be treated equally ("The Vulnerability of Conscience," 1255), though it is not clear how they determine which commitments are deep. Andrew Koppelman, "Is It Fair to Give Religion Special Treatment," 2006 *University of Illinois Law Review* 571, 583–87.

56. This would not cover many religious claims not based in conscience. Koppelman, "Is It Fair," 586. Indeed, important religious claims sometimes have nothing to do with voluntary actions of the claimants. Williams and Williams, "Volitionalism and Religious Liberty."

57. One could regard any invocation of conscience as "religious" regardless of whether the source of the obligation was thought to be based on a Supreme Being. *Seeger*, 380 U.S. 166 (conferring conscientious objector status to someone who declared a "religious faith in a purely ethical creed" finding that the faith occupies "a place in the life of its possessor parallel to that filled by the orthodox belief in God"). See Gutmann, *Identity in Democracy*, 154, 158–59, 168–69 (arguing that invocations of conscience should be similarly treated whether or not theologically based).

58. Barry, *Culture and Equality*, 34–35; cf. Dworkin, *Sovereign Virtue*, 154–55 (comparing the religiously intolerant to the person with expensive tastes).

59. Eisgruber and Sager, "The Vulnerability of Conscience," 1255–77.

60. Of course, it can be argued that state neutrality is a moral requirement.

61. Unlike garden variety liberties, a basic liberty may not be denied unless it interferes with another's freedom (Kant), or compromises another's "basic liberty" (Rawls) or "right" (Dworkin) or "harms the interests of others" (Mill), and even then a further showing would ordinarily need to be made. Freedom of religion in this respect would occupy the same plane as other basic liberties. One of

the problems for liberals is to explain how to distinguish garden variety liberties from more important liberties or rights.

62. Because of various characteristics, Eisgruber and Sager recognize government endorsement of sectarian views sends a "message of disparagement, of exclusion and subordination." Eisgruber and Sager, "Chips Off Our Block?" 1281. Ordinarily, true enough. But the use of symbols of minority religions may not disparage in many contexts. Does this mean there is no Establishment Clause issue? See Lupu and Tuttle, "Limits of Equal Liberty," 1254, 1258–59. Eisgruber and Sager also recognize that messages of racial, gender, or sexual orientation should be unconstitutional ("Chips Off Our Block?" 1281–82). I agree. But I doubt that such categories would exhaust those that disparage, and some government speech that has a disparaging effect is not unconstitutional. Consider the teaching of evolution. Consider also a setting in which a person sits in a government meeting where people are asked to rise for the "Star Spangled Banner." Most important, this argument makes the Establishment Clause superfluous. Any clause of the Constitution that can preclude these other forms of discrimination can also preclude religious discrimination.

63. Some secular liberals will recognize in the Free Exercise context that it is especially cruel to require someone to act or not to act when her conscience or sense of moral obligation demands otherwise. But that concern is remote in the Establishment Clause context. Government display of religious symbols does not invade religious conscience in a significant way. Religious citizens are not required to act or not act in a way that would violate their conscience.

64. For a well-articulated argument that religion should not be discriminated against in the financial aid area, see Eisgruber and Sager, *Religious Freedom* 198–239.

65. It may also be overinclusive because the concern about the autonomy of the state may be confined to some important issues, but not all issues.

66. One escape from this problem is to condemn government pronouncements on the good life generally whether of not religious in character. But this escape route leads to a minefield. See paragraph accompanying note 5 *infra*.

67. Those cooperative liberals who are religious, nonetheless, justify their conclusions in terms that can be shared by other reasonable forms of liberalism. This excludes religious reasons.

68. Locke, *Two Treatises of Government*; for discussion of the depth of the religious foundations of Locke, see Waldron, *God, Locke, and Equality*.

69. Michael Lerner, *The Left Hand of God: Taking Back Our Country from the Religious Right* (San Francisco: HarperOne, 2006).

70. Joan Chittister, *In the Heart of the Temple* (New York: BlueBridge Books, 2004).

71. *Dorothy Day: Selected Writings*, xv (Robert Ellsberg, ed., Maryknoll, N.Y.: Orbis, 1998) (Dorothy Day "wrote to give reason for a marriage of convictions that was a scandal and a stumbling block to many: radical politics and traditional, conservative theology"); see also Mel Piehl, *Breaking Bread: The Catholic Worker and the Origin of Catholic Radicalism in America* (Philadelphia: Temple University Press, 2006).

72. Richard Rohr and John Bookser Feister, *Hope Against Darkness: The Transforming Vision of Saint Francis in an Age of Anxiety* (Cincinnati: Saint Anthony Messenger Press, 2001); Richard Rohr and John Bookser Feister, *Jesus' Plan for a New World: The Sermon on the Mount* (Cincinnati: Saint Anthony Messenger Press, 1996).

73. Barry W. Lynn, *Piety and Politics: The Right Wing Assault on Religious Freedom* (New York: Harmony Books, 2006).

74. Charles Taylor, *A Secular Age* (Cambridge: Belknap Press of Harvard University Press, 2007)

75. Jim Wallis, *God's Politics: Why the Right Gets It Wrong and the Left Doesn't Get It* (San Francisco: HarperOne, 2005).

76. Ronald J. Sider, *Rich Christians in an Age of Hunger* (4th ed., Nashville: Thomas Nelson, 1997).

77. Martin Luther King Jr., *Why We Can't Wait* (New York: New American Library, 2000); Stewart Burns, *To the Mountaintop: Martin Luther King Jr.'s Mission to Save America: 1955–1968* (New York: HarperSanFrancisco, 2005); Taylor Branch, *At Canaan's Edge: America in the King Years, 1965–68* (New York: Simon and Schuster, 2006); Taylor Branch, *Pillar of Fire: America in the King Years, 1963–65* (New York: Simon and Schuster, 1999); Taylor Branch, *Parting the Waters: America in the King Years, 1954–63* (New York: Simon and Schuster, 1989); Anthony E. Cook, "Beyond Critical Legal Studies: The Reconstructive Theology of Dr. Martin Luther King," 103 *Harvard Law Review* 985 (1990).

78. Gustavo Gutiérrez, *A Theology of Liberation: History, Politics, and Salvation* (rev. ed., Sister Caridad Inda and John Eagleson eds. and trans., Maryknoll, N.Y.: Orbis Books, 1988); Leonardo Buff, *Saint Francis: A Model for Human Liberation* (John W. Diercksmeier trans., New York: Crossroad, 1982). Religious liberalism, as I use the term, may include political radicals as well. My usage is thus somewhat broader than that of Paul Rasor (see *Faith without Certainty: Liberal Theology in the 21st Century* 141–63 (Boston: Skinner House Books, 2005), but his book is an outstanding introduction to liberal theology.

79. *African American Religious Thought: An Anthology* (Cornell West and Eddie S. Glaude eds., Louisville: Westminster John Knox Press, 2003); Michael Joseph Brown, *Blackening of the Bible: The Aims of African American Biblical Scholarship* (Harrisburg, Pa.: Trinity Press International, 2004).

80. Among other things, Catholic social teaching is concerned about the economic injustice associated with poverty and ill treatment of workers. *Option for the Poor: A Hundred Years of Vatican Social Teaching* (Donald Dorr ed., Dublin: Gill and Macmillan, 1992); *Catholic Social Thought: The Documentary Heritage* (Jean Vanier ed., Maryknoll, N.Y.: Orbis Books, 1992); *Modern Catholic Social Teaching: Commentaries and Interpretations* (Kenneth R. Himes ed., Lisa Sowle Cahill et al. assoc. eds., Washington, D.C.: Georgetown University Press, 2005). Of course, concern for the poor is common among ministers of virtually all denominations. Robert Wuthnow, *The Crisis in the Churches: Spiritual Malaise, Fiscal Woe* 207 (New York: Oxford University Press, 2006), but the involvement of churches does not match the need. Wuthnow, 208.

81. For an excellent introduction to his thought, see *A Call to Fidelity: On the Moral Theology of Charles E. Curran* (Samuel Koranteng-Pipim ed., Washington, D.C.: Georgetown University Press, 2002).

82. Ronald Dworkin suggests that the argument for religious freedom must be encased in a more general theory of liberty. Dworkin, *Is Democracy Possible Here*. He argues in part that the willingness of religious conservatives and liberals to protect atheists shows that a more general theory is needed (67–69). But he recognizes that there are theological reasons to avoid forced conversions (68). This causes him to shift to the argument that the forced conversion argument does not explain the Establishment Clause (68). He is right about that, but as we shall see, religious liberals have different concerns regarding the Establishment Clause. Moreover, as we shall also see, his general liberty principle in the end is overly general. Finally, believing that religion is special does not remotely suggest that freedom of religion should be the only right. Dworkin would be correct if he said that any account of religious freedom must have an account of its relationship to more general liberties, but it need not be encased in a single theory of liberty.

83. Hostile liberals also believe that it would interfere with the autonomy of the state and undermine the public interest.

CHAPTER 8
THE POLITICS OF LIBERALISM

1. *Van Orden v. Perry*, 545 U.S. 677 (2005).

2. He cast the decisive vote in the case in part because he was concerned about divisiveness. This has been met with substantial criticism. "Quelling public strife has been the Holy Grail or, perhaps more aptly, the siren song of religious liberty jurisprudence. . . . I submit that suggestions of this kind are both misplaced and quixotic: They are misplaced because we betray our constitutional aspirations if we compromise our commitment to equal membership in exchange for a bit more serenity, and they are quixotic because no Establishment clause doctrine will stop religious groups from bickering with one another in the public sphere." Christopher L. Eisgruber, "Justice Stevens, Religious Freedom, and the Value of Equal Membership," 74 *Fordham Law Review* 2177, 2180 (2006); see also William Van Alstyne, "Ten Commandments, Nine Judges, and Five Versions of One Amendment–the First ('Now What')," 14 *William and Mary Bill of Rights Journal* 17, 25 (2005); Erwin Chemerinsky, "Why Justice Breyer Was Wrong in *Van Orden v. Perry*," 14 *William and Mary Bill of Rights Journal* 1 (2005). But see Richard A. Posner, "Foreword: A Political Court," 119 *Harvard Law Review* 31, 100 (2004) (agreeing with Breyer on the divisiveness concern).

3. *County of Allegheny*, 492 U.S. 655, 657.

4. *County of Allegheny*, 492 U.S. 655.

5. Ronald Dworkin, "Can a Liberal State Support Art? " in Dworkin, *A Matter of Principle*, 221.

6. Audi, *Religious Commitment*, 60–61.

7. Other secular liberals may well resist at least part of the doctrine of public reason. See Dworkin, *Is Democracy Possible Here*, 64–65. Dworkin thinks that

secular liberals must convince religious conservatives that their deep premises are the same as his, but this is nearly impossible. It would require convincing religious conservatives that religion should not be regarded as special for political purposes (Dworkin, 61). Heclo, *Christianity and American Democracy*, 130, thinks that it is "ironic that attention to idealized deliberative democracy should coincide in time with the post–World War II triumph of a professionally PR-managed anti-deliberative democracy." To the contrary, the rise of such management ought to inspire efforts to improve and theorize about public dialogue. As will be clear, I simply disagree with the cooperative liberals approach to theorizing about public dialogue in a pluralistic society.

8. Rawls, *Political Liberalism*, 215. I focus on John Rawls's writings because they have been the most influential and because they have tried to justify the doctrine in the circumstances where Rawls believed they were strongest (Rawls, 215). As I will discuss, his later writings on the subject sharply constrict an already limited set of claims.

9. Rawls, *Political Liberalism*, 214.

10. Rawls, *Political Liberalism*, 224–25.

11. Rawls, *Political Liberalism*, 224. Rawls even posits that controversial scientific (I assume including social science) positions may not be introduced in determining either constitutional essentials or principles of basic justice, or how they should be applied (224). Rawls believes that consideration of the case for public reason in dealing with constitutional essentials or principles of basic justice is the best place to start. If it fails there, it fails elsewhere. See Gerald F. Gaus, *Contemporary Theories of Liberalism* 198 (London: Sage, 2003) (raising questions about the distinction).

12. Rawls, *Political Liberalism*, 224.

13. Rawls, "Public Reason," 769.

14. Rawls, *Political Liberalism*, 215. Indeed, he was interpreted to mean that the doctrine of public reason applied to political discussions on these issues not addressed to the public at large. See David Hollenbach, S.J., "Civil Society: Beyond the Public-Private Dichotomy," 5 *Responsive Community* 15 (Winter 1994–95), cited in John Rawls, "The Idea of Public Reason Revisited," 64 *University of Chicago Law Review* 765, 768 (1997). Rawls, however, confined himself to political utterances about constitutional essentials and basic questions of justice.

15. Rawls, "Public Reason," 771.

16. Rawls, *Political Liberalism*, 217.

17. Rawls, *Political Liberalism*, 217.

18. Rawls, *Political Liberalism*, 390–92.

19. Although Rawls does not desire to use coercion to enforce the doctrine of public reason, they are not just "debating tips." Appiah, *The Ethics of Identity*, 81.

20. Christopher J. Eberle, *Religious Conviction in Liberal Politics* 113–15 (Cambridge: Cambridge University Press, 2002).

21. Cooperative liberals insist, however, that restrictions are necessary to achieve political consensus based on shared premises. This may be true. But this assumes a political consensus is in the cards. Political consensus among millions of citizens is a rare event. Nicholas Wolterstorff, "Why We Should Reject What

Liberalism Tells Us about Speaking and Acting in Public for Religious Reasons," in Weithman, *Religion and Contemporary Liberalism* 162, 174 ("There's no more hope that all among us who are reasonable and rational will arrive, in the way Rawls recommends, at consensus on principles of justice, than that we all, in the foreseeable future, will agree on some comprehensive philosophical or religious doctrine"); cf. Marci A. Hamilton, "What Does Religion Mean in the Public Square? " 89 *Minnesota Law Review* 1153, 1157 (2005) (not clear that all important controversies can be resolved in this way). The exclusions seem designed not to achieve consensus, but to channel the character of the disagreement.

22. One's reflective intuitions might well be different if the rationale for a constitutional essential were based on theological premises, but that would not justify ruling out constitutional essentials based on other comprehensive visions. It would simply demand an explanation as to why religion is special. From a secular perspective, why is it that secular comprehensive visions might not raise legitimacy concerns, but religious comprehensive visions do? One possibility is hostility: Religious views are regarded by many as unreasonable or irrational. That possibility, however, would surely not be open to a cooperative liberal.

23. For the suggestion that the presence of religion in democratic politics may have contributed to stability, see Eduardo Moises Penalver, "Is Public Reason Counterproductive," 110 *West Virginia Law Review* 515 (2007).

24. Although Habermas, like Rawls, is primarily focused on legitimacy, the specter of disintegration caused by religious struggles haunts his project as well. Jürgen Habermas, "Religion in the Public Sphere," 14 *European Journal of Philosophy* 1, 12 (2006). Robert Audi's major concern is protecting autonomy from illegitimate constraints (Audi, *Religious Commitment*, 67–68), but concerns about polarization and violence drive his work as well (39, 47, 103, 174). To some extent, for him, the concerns seem to run together (67–68, 123).

25. Rawls refers more than once to religious wars in Europe. Perhaps I am too cynical or have too many Marxist bones in my body, but I believe that much governmental action done in the name of religion has been a cover for economic advantage. European governments may have said they fought wars in the name of one religion or another; they may have said that they colonized in the interests of educating the uncivilized and spreading Christianity. Religion may well have been a contributing factor, but it is way too fast to look to religion as the major cause of instability. And, may I say, anyone who thinks that President Bush's belief in Jesus Christ had much to do with American entry into the Iraq war knows nothing of American politics.

26. Hamilton, "What Does Religion Mean," 1158 ("[T]here has never been a time in the United States when religion has not been a driving force behind public policy").

27. *Sullivan*, 376 U.S. 270.

28. Cf. Philip L. Quinn, "Political Liberalisms and Their Exclusions of the Religious," 69:2 *Proceedings and Addresses of the American Philosophical Association* 35 (no dangerous conflict despite the use of religious arguments on a massive scale). We have survived with a *modus vivendi* and that is all we have needed; Robert Merrihew Adams, "Religious Ethics in a Pluralistic Society," 93, 102–7 in *Prospects for a Common Morality* (Gene Outka and John Reeder Jr., eds., Prince-

ton: Princeton University Press, 1993). For concerns about instability stemming from religious intolerance, see Sullivan, "Religion and Liberal Democracy," 197.

29. See text accompanying note 12 *supra*.

30. Gutmann and Thompson, who are committed to mutual respect and the principle of reciprocity, recognize the need to resort to general philosophical and moral considerations when mutually agreeable premises are not available to resolve disputes. Amy Gutmann and Dennis Thomson, *Democracy and Disagreement* 76 (Cambridge: Belknap Press of Harvard University Press, 1998).

31. As David Tracy has argued, public reason is not just about arguments; public reason is about conversation. David Tracy, "Catholic Classics in American Liberal Culture," in *Catholicism and Liberalism: Contributions to American Public Philosophy* 204 (R. Bruce Douglass and David Hollenbach eds., Cambridge: Cambridge University Press, 1994). Conversation in Tracy's sense can take place between a citizen and a work of art or a classic in a religious tradition. Tracy, 206. The classic in a particular tradition communicates a public message (207–8). That message is not static. Hans-Georg Gadamer, *Truth and Method* 271 (New York: Crossroad, 1983). As Gadamer maintains, it must be interpreted in terms of the different horizons of time and place (269–74, 337–38). Just as Ralph Waldo Emerson repeatedly emphasized the extent to which the universal is to be found in the particular (Shiffrin, *First Amendment*, 143–44, so work such as the Bible may communicate a message that has force outside a particular religious tradition. Even if that is not the case on particular subjects, citizens learn more about each other if they understand what is important to them. But they cannot learn about each other if they cannot advance their comprehensive position in public life.

32. For a thoughtful theological perspective on euthanasia, see John B. Mitchell, *Understanding Assisted Suicide: Nine Issues to Consider* (Ann Arbor: University of Michigan Press, 2007).

33. Theda R. Skocpol, "Foreword," in Heclo, *Christianity and American Democracy*, viii.

34. See Quinn, "Political Liberalisms," 50 (only liberals would be tempted to accept the obligations of public reason).

35. After some earlier attempts to defend a middle-ground position, see Perry, *Love and Power*, 99–100, 139–41 (New York: Oxford University Press, 1991), this is the conclusion endorsed by Michael J. Perry, "Religious Morality and Political Choice: Further Thoughts—and Second Thoughts—on Love and Power," 30 *San Diego Law Review* 716 (1993). For a middle-ground position, see Robert Justin Lipkin, "Reconstructing the Public Square," 124 *Cardozo Law Review* 2025 (recommending that some forms of religious argument be considered inappropriate in the public square).

36. Rawls, "Public Reason," 765, 776. Habermas, "Religion in Public Sphere," 9, denies that there is any direct obligation of religious citizens to supply secular reasons or to be guided by them. On the other hand, in the view of Habermas, they must accept the fact that their religious reasons may gain legal force only to the extent that they are "translated" into secular language and arguments. Habermas, 10.

37. "[T]he liberal state has an interest in unleashing religious voices in the political public sphere, and in the participation of religious organizations as well. It

must not discourage religious persons and communities from also expressing themselves politically *as such*, for it cannot know whether secular society would not otherwise cut itself off from key resources for the creation of meaning and identity. Secular citizens . . . [may] recognize in the normative truth content of a religious utterance hidden intuitions of their own." Habermas, "Religion in Public Sphere," 10.

38. Even before Rawls, Robert Audi, *Religious Commitment*, 86–87, maintained that citizens could ethically introduce religious arguments in the public sphere so long as they introduced adequate secular arguments to support coercion. In addition, he required as a prima facie matter that such citizens believe that the secular argument or arguments were sufficient to motivate them to support coercive policies even apart from their religious reasons. Audi, 96–100. Unlike Rawls, Audi did not place any restrictions on the introduction of most nonreligious comprehensive views in support of coercive policies (90). Nonetheless, wholly apart from their wisdom *vel non*, Audi's views are obviously far afield from the realities of American politics.

39. Habermas introduces variations on Rawls's utopia. He would require, for example (to use my terminology), that hostile liberals not dismiss religious arguments out of hand as superstition, but "be willing to enter and engage in a discussion of the content of religious contributions with the intention of translating, if there is such a content, morally convincing intuitions and reasons into a generally accessible language." Habermas, "Religion in Public Sphere," 15. Habermas has his own doubts whether citizens can bring appropriate attitudes to the public sphere (18–20).

40. Rawls, "Public Reason," 767.

41. Rawls, "Public Reason," 769.

42. For a nuanced discussion of the varying contexts in which the limits of public reason should or should not apply, see Kent Greenawalt, *Private Consciences and Public Reason* (New York: Oxford University Press, 1995). For a partial critique, see Shiffrin, "Religion and Democracy."

43. Rawls, "Public Reason," 768.

44. The question turns on the standards for determining the purpose of legislation. Legislation, under the Establishment Clause, must have a secular purpose. If the statements of legislators can be used to establish purpose, then the announcement of religious purposes by a legislator would be inappropriate.

45. See text accompanying note 12 *supra*.

46. I do not believe that this calls upon legislators to be deceptive. There is a difference between being deceptive and not engaging in full disclosure. Greenawalt, *Private Consciences*, 139, 165; Steven D. Smith, "Augustinian Liberal," 74 *Notre Dame Law Review* 1673, 1683 (1999) (in accord with Greenawalt). Moreover, from at least one religious perspective, the inability to engage in full disclosure is consistent with the understood conflict between the kingdom of God and the kingdom on earth. See Smith, "Augustinian Liberal," 1684–89.

47. This does not exhaust the content of the Establishment Clause. Government might have secular reasons for promoting religion, but this would not justify the promoting of religion. For a different reading of the Establishment Clause, see

Linker, *The Theocons*, 51 (both clauses promote religion, but favoring one religion over another is not permitted).

48. This assumes that legislative history is relevant to determining the purposes of a statute.

49. Habermas, "Religion in Public Sphere."

50. Habermas, "Religion in Public Sphere."

51. Rawls, *Political Liberalism*, 249.

52. Rawls, *Political Liberalism*, 250.

53. For the claim that the exception for abolitionists and for Martin Luther King would stimulate many others to think that they are similarly excepted, see Elizabeth H. Wolgast, "The Demands of Public Reason," 94 *Columbia Law Review* 1936, 1944 (1994).

54. Rawls, *Political Liberalism*, 251.

55. The Catholic Church has historically been attacked in the United States as "hierarchical, authoritarian, foreign, European, and hostile to intellectual inquiry." Jenkins, *The New Anti-Catholicism*, 33. Richard Rorty hopes that ecclesiastical organizations will wither away because they foster contempt for nonmembers. Rorty, "Religion in Public Square," 146.

56. The argument, however, has most frequently been directed at Catholics. As Rorty puts it: "Protestantism has often, and rightly, been thought to be more congenial to liberal democracy than Catholicism. This is because the idea of the 'priesthood of all believers' encourages the believer to interpret Scripture, theology, and devotional literature on his own, rather than simply waiting to be informed by church officials about what is required to be a member in good standing of a given denomination. The latter attitude does seem to be the sort of thing democratic societies have a right to discourage." Rorty, "Religion in Public Square," 147.

57. Both pertained to Mary, the mother of Jesus. She was said to be born without sin (the feast of the Immaculate Conception) and she was assumed into heaven (the feast of the Assumption).

58. Pope John Paul II in his encyclical *Veritas Splendor* stated that the Magisterium "teaches the faithful specific particular precepts and requires that they consider them in conscience morally binding." Veritas Splendor, in *The Encyclicals of John Paul II*, 654 (J. Michael Miller ed., Huntington, Ind.: Our Sunday Visitor, 1996). See also U.S. Conference of Catholic Bishops, "'Happy Are Those Who Are Called to His Supper': On Preparing to Receive Christ Worthily in the Eucharist," 10–11, November 14, 2006, http://www.usccb.org/dpp/Eucharist.pdf (last visited, November 21, 2006) (Catholics who knowingly and obstinately repudiate definitive moral teachings of the church should not receive communion). Although there is precedent for this view in the Catholic tradition, there is a countertradition that makes it the right and the duty of Catholics to follow their conscience when it is contrary to the Magisterium. Richard McBrien, *Catholicism* 972–75 (new ed., San Francisco: HarperSanFrancisco, 1994). For exploration of the two traditions, see Linda Hogan, *Confronting the Truth: Conscience in the Catholic Tradition* (New York: Paulist Press, 2001); *Conscience*, Readings in Moral Theology, No. 14 (Charles Curran ed., New York: Paulist Press, 2004). Even if the former view of conscience is accepted, there are technical questions as to what counts as

a teaching of the Magisterium or as levels of authority within the Magisterium. See generally *Magisterium and Morality*, Readings in Moral Theology, No 3 (Charles E. Curran ed., New York: Paulist Press, 1981).

59. Richard Rorty, "Religion as a Conversation-Stopper," 3 *Common Knowledge* 1, 2 (1994).

60. Habermas maintains that religious arguments are not accessible, but does not explain why. "Religion in Public Sphere," 12. Of course, it would be possible for a religious argument to be inaccessible. Imagine a citizen who claims to be following the directions of an angel who appeared to him. Arguments in the public forum are rarely of this type, and if introduced in a public forum, they would not likely be effective.

61. On the problems associated with the conservative interpretation frequently employed regarding what should be rendered to Caesar, see Ched Myers, *Binding the Strong Man: A Political Reading of Mark's Story of Jesus* 123, 310–12 (Maryknoll, N.Y.: Orbis Books 2006).

62. Fowler and Hertske, *Religion and Politics*, 38–39. Kenneth J. Heinman, *God Is a Conservative: Religion, Politics, and Morality in Contemporary America* 7 (New York: New York University Press, 1998): "During the civil rights revolution, Falwell had criticized King for politicizing the church. God and politics did not mix. By the seventies, Falwell had a change of heart. . . . Falwell followed King in becoming a crusader against government tyranny." On the two kingdoms theory, see Linker, *The Theocons*, 17–18.

63. Francis Schaeffer was a key player in this move. Heclo, *Christianity and American Democracy*, 113–14. Evangelicals, however, were not united on this score. Bob Jones called Jerry Falwell "the most dangerous man in America." Heclo, 39.

64. Until the 1970s, the main religious lobbies in the United States were liberal. See Michael Corbett and Julia Mitchell Corbett, *Politics and Religion in the United States* 97 (New York: Routledge, 1999).

65. "The Third Stage: New Frontiers of Religious Liberty," in Dionne and DiIulio, *What's God Got to Do*, 116 . See also Randall Balmer, *Thy Kingdom Come: An Evangelical's Lament*, chap. 2 ("Where Have All the Baptists Gone? ") 35–69 (New York: Basic Books, 2006)

66. Harris Interactive, "The Religious and Other Beliefs of Americans 2003," *The Harris Poll* #11, February 11, 2003, http://www.harrisinteractive.com/harris_poll/index.asp?PID=359 (last visited August 20, 2006). Sixty-eight percent believe in the devil and 69 percent believe in hell. At the same time, the religiosity of the American people is frequently exaggerated. As Heclo, *Christianity and American Democracy*, 139, puts it, "It seems that in America the frequency of going to church is roughly matched by the frequency of lying about going to church."

67. Consider Bill McKibben, "The People of the (Unread) Book," in *Getting on Message: Challenging the Christian Right from the Heart of the Gospel* 13 (Rev. Peter Laarman, ed., Boston: Beacon Press, 2006): "Only 40% of Americans can name more than five of the Ten Commandments, and a scant half can cite any of the four authors of the gospels." On the general problem of religious illiteracy,

see Steven Prothero, *Religious Literacy: What Every American Needs to Know—and Doesn't* (New York: HarperOne, 2007).

68. Greeley, *The Catholic Revolution*, 39.

69. Greeley, *The Catholic Revolution*, at 34–40.

70. It is not simply the Vatican to which Catholics are told to conform. The American Catholic bishops seem to maintain that their statements must be followed as well (at least when they teach "in communion" with the pope). U.S. Conference of Catholic Bishops, "Happy Are Those," 10 n. 18, citing *Second Vatican Council, Dogmatic Constitution on the Church* (Lumen Gentium) No. 25. Virtually all Catholics believe that some level of deference should be given to the teachings of church leaders (as opposed to occasional statements even in a papal encyclical). But so-called cafeteria Catholics, or, as I prefer, Catholics of conscience, are more comfortable in rejecting some church teachings than church leaders think they should be. This comfort flows from the recognition that the church has changed its position about some important moral issues (see, e.g., John T. Noonan Jr., *A Church That Can and Cannot Change: The Development of Catholic Moral Teaching* [Notre Dame: University of Notre Dame Press, 2005]), that the arguments put forward by church leaders on some issues seem quite unconvincing, that millions of other Catholics have rejected such positions (on the potential theological importance of this, see Francis A. Sullivan, S.J., *The Magisterium: Teaching Authority in the Catholic Church* 167–69 [New York: Paulist Press, 1983]), and that, in the area of sexuality, deference seems inappropriate because of the lack of personal experience of church leaders, the all-male character of the leadership, the lack of pastoral experience, and the failure of process in arriving at such decisions (most particularly the failure to involve lay Catholics). For a variety of views on the propriety of public dissent by Catholics from teachings of the church, see *Dissent in the Church*, Readings in Moral Theology, No. 6 (Charles E. Curran and Richard A. McCormick, S.J., eds., New York: Paulist Press, 1988).

71. Damon Linker maintains that a " 'culture of dissent' . . . is, in fact, the Catholic norm in modern America." Linker, *The Theocons*, 201.

72. "America's Ever-Changing Religious Landscape," in Dionne and DiIulio, *What's God Got to Do*, 17–18.

73. See note 59 and accompanying text *supra*.

74. Jim Wallis has been an important leader in promoting social change among evangelicals on these issues.

75. See text accompanying notes 30 to 32 *supra*.

76. It also discriminates between Jews, Catholics, and various Protestant denominations. See text accompanying notes 88 to 91 *infra*.

77. On Buddhist life and thought in the United States, see Diana L. Eck, *A New Religious America*, chap. 4, 142–221 (San Francisco: HarperSanFrancisco, 2001); Robert Wuthnow, *America and the Challenges of Religious Diversity* 47–56 (Princeton: Princeton University Press, 2005).

78. On Hindu life and thought in the United States, see Eck, *A New Religious America*, chap. 3, 80–141; Wuthnow, *Challenges of Religious Diversity*, 38–47.

79. Owen, *Religion and the Demise*, 168–69.

80. Consider the implications of Richard Rohr's statement: "Jesus always enters the imperial city on a donkey." Rohr with Feister, *Jesus' Plan*, 13.

81. See Myers, *Binding the Strong Man*. See also Obery M. Hendricks, *The Politics of Jesus: Recovering the True Revolutionary Nature of the Teachings of Jesus and How They Have Been Corrupted* (New York: Doubleday, 2006). I would submit that American Christians have the task of determining their responsibilities as they live in the American Empire. It is hard to believe that religious institutions should seek close ties with this regime. See Hendricks, *The Politics of Jesus*; John Dominic Crossan, *God and Empire: Jesus against Rome, Then and Now* (San Francisco: HarperSanFrancisco, 2007).

82. Fritz Detwiler, *Standing on the Premises of God: The Christian Right's Fight to Redefine America's Public Schools* 104 (New York: New York University Press, 1999).

83. See http://www.catholicleague.org/annualreport.php?year=2002andid=72 (last visited August 13, 2008).

84. *The New American Bible 75*, translating Exodus 20:17 (1987).

85. *McCreary County v. American Civil Liberties Union of Kentucky*, 545 U.S. 544 (2005) (striking down displays in county courthouses).

86. *Van Orden v. Perry*, 545 U.S. 677 (2005) (upholding display on grounds of Texas State Capital). One prominent conservative judge has pointed to the Ten Commandments cases as an example of the Court's turn to "split the difference" jurisprudence (J. Harvie Wilkinson, "The Rehnquist Court at Twilight: The Lures and Perils of Split-the-Difference Jurisprudence," 58 *Stanford Law Review* 1969, 1973–74 (2006), a phenomenon he speculated may have been influenced by a reaction to the criticism of *Bush v. Gore* (Wilkinson, 1971).

87. The translation used in *Van Orden* referred to a neighbor's manservant or maidservant rather than a slave.

88. Even if Christians, Jews, and Muslims were united, the displays discriminate against Hindus, Buddhists, atheists, and agnostics, among others.

89. Paul Finkelman, "The Ten Commandments on the Courthouse Lawn and Elsewhere," 73 *Fordham Law Review* 1477, 1489–90 (2005).

90. Finkelman, "Ten Commandments," 1489, 1491.

91. The dispute over the wording of the Ten Commandments regarding graven images does not precisely line up Protestants against Catholics. On one side of the divide are Lutherans and Catholics. On the other side are Jews and the rest of the Protestant denominations, including the Anglican community. Dairmaid MacCulloch, *The Reformation: A History* 145–46 (New York: Penguin, 2003). The monument in *Van Orden* favored the Lutheran version. Finkelman, "Ten Commandments," 1486–87. In response to the arguments about the various translations, Justice Scalia argues in *McCreary*: "The sectarian dispute regarding text, if serious, is not widely known. I doubt that most religious adherents are even aware that there are competing versions with doctrinal consequences (I certainly was not). In any event, the context of the display here could not conceivably cause the viewer to believe that the government was taking sides in a doctrinal controversy." It is hard to understand why Justice Scalia thinks the government was not taking sides when it chose the King James version of the Ten Commandments in *McCreary*. Nor is it easy to understand the relevance of the undoubtedly correct

assertion that most people are unaware of the textual difference in the Ten Commandments or the doctrinal disputes associated with them. If Justice Scalia, a Catholic, walked into a Texas courthouse and a Ten Commandments display said, "Though shall not murder," he would quickly learn that the Catholic version was not on display.

But the question in Establishment Clause law is not what Justice Scalia knows. It is what a hypothetical reasonable observer armed with all of the relevant facts would know and whether that knowledge would inform the observer that he or she was an outsider or an insider. For establishing purpose, this test makes sense. Suppose the Kentucky counties drew lots and picked the relevant text out of a hat. This would tell the reasonable observer that the counties were not endorsing one text over another. On the other hand, attributing knowledge an ordinary person is unlikely to have to a hypothetical observer is not appropriate if one is trying to determine the effects of a religious display. People entering courthouses with Ten Commandment displays in the absence of recent publicity are likely to know nothing about how the Commandments got there. The reasonable Jew will reasonably conclude that the Torah is not being employed because of the views of a religious majority reinforcing his or her outsider status.

92. In *McCreary*, one of the earlier resolutions calling for a prominent display of the Commandments acknowledged Christ as the "Prince of Ethics." The Commandments were then surrounded by other documents with a religious theme. After a court injunction against the display, the counties surrounded the Commandments with documents such as the Bill of Rights and the Declaration of Independence. The lawyers advising the counties presumably thought this might help cover over the religious purpose. But the Court emphasized that the purpose test was not a "pushover for any secular claim." The idea that the Court should ignore the religious purpose so obviously present in earlier displays was cast aside: "[T]he world is not made brand new every morning." *McCreary*, 545 U.S. 866.

93. The religious purpose of the Eagles screams out from their presentation of the Ten Commandments. The words "I Am the Lord Thy God," are in substantially larger print than the rest of the displayed text. *Van Orden*, 545 U.S. 707 (Stevens, J., dissenting opinion). The Commandments were referred to by the Eagles as the "foundations of our relationship with our Creator." *Van Orden*, 545 U.S. 714 (Stevens, J., dissenting).

94. For the suggestion that commercial motivation should count in favor of the display, see Posner, "Foreword," 101 n. 216 (2004).

95. Although Justice Breyer joined the majority's opinion in *McCreary*, he thought the display in *Van Orden* met constitutional standards. Justice Breyer realized that the display communicated a religious message, but he thought a secular message predominated. He was impressed by the placement of the monument in a large park containing seventeen monuments and twenty-one historical markers, all of them secular. He concluded that the setting contributed to the view that the message was primarily about a historical effort to tie the law to morals. But see Chemerinsky, "Breyer Was Wrong," 11 (the closest other monuments were thirty feet away and blocked by hedges). The fact that a group (Breyer characterized it as primarily secular) contributed the monument to the state further distanced the state from the religious aspects of the message in his view. The

forty-year history of the monument without litigation suggested to him no serious objections had been taken. Any other conclusion in this case Justice Breyer argued would show hostility toward religion and lead to the kind of divisiveness the Establishment Clause was designed to forestall.

This is not nonsense, but it is ultimately unpersuasive. As suggested previously, the text of the Ten Commandments emphasized the religious aspects. The lettering of "I am the Lord thy God" was substantially larger than the parts of the commandments compatible with secular morals. No theme tied the monuments together. The other monuments could not be seen from the area in front of the Ten Commandments. The memorial *was* sectarian. The "primarily secular" Eagles organization designed the memorial to combat juvenile delinquency (not as a history project) and "recognized that there can be no better . . . program . . . than the laws handed down by God himself to Moses more than 3000 years ago. . . . They are a fundamental part of our lives . . . the foundation of our relationship with our Creator." The forty-year history is not surprising since Establishment Clause claims are difficult (and would have been especially difficult forty years ago) and not financially rewarding. It provides no warrant for the proposition that the memorial was experienced by visitors as consistent with religious equality. As to hostility to religion and divisiveness, Justice Breyer does not explain how an emphasis on hostility or divisiveness can distinguish the Kentucky cases from the Texas case, how divisiveness can be avoided by any outcome, how judges are qualified to determine divisiveness in individual cases, or how it is consistent with their constitutional duties to decide such cases on the basis of such determinations.

96. Blasi, "School Vouchers," 798–99, recites the progressive role that religion has played in American politics and notes that Madison saw "religion as a crucial oppositional force in politics and a vital check on the tyranny of the majority." Elsewhere he states that religion "remains a distinctly dangerous political force." Vincent Blasi, "Vouchers and Steering," 18 *Journal of Law and Politics* 607, 613–614 (2002). Religion in my view has been progressive, reactionary, and divisive. On balance in American history, in my view, it has been progressive. But the dangers are there. In any event, it is not going away.

97. Heclo, *Christianity and American Democracy*, 22: "The danger to Christianity from entanglement with official state power is obvious. Worldly power, being worldly, is always ready and willing to use religion to win fights with political opponents. . . . Following their God's example, Christians are called to the unworldly ideas of loving their enemies and of defending the truth of their religion by suffering and dying, not by ruling and dying." At the same time Heclo recognizes that orthodox Christianity does not call for a "spiritual existence apart from the world" but for active democratic citizens (66–68).

98. See generally Walden Bello, *Dilemmas of Domination: The Unmaking of the American Empire* (New York: Metropolitan Books, 2005); David Ray Griffin, John B. Cobb Jr., Richard A. Falk, and Catherine Keller, *The American Empire and the Commonwealth of God: A Political, Economic, and Religious Statement* (Louisville: Westminster John Knox Press, 2006).

99. From the perspective of the Left, the notion that churches should be associated with the violent and oppressive policies of the U.S. government is a nonstarter.

100. Nicholas Atkin and Frank Tallett, *Priests, Prelates, and People: A History of European Catholicism since 1750* 324 (Oxford: Oxford University Press, 2003) (explaining that, in return for benefits from the state, the church preached submission to the temporal authority, though it practiced extensive charitable work).

101. Berg, "Church-State Relations," 1635–36.

102. Blasi, "School Vouchers," 783, 798.

103. Lupu and Tuttle, "Zelman's Future," 944, maintain that "the Establishment Clause does not protect religious institutions from becoming slothful through dependence on government support. Why should the indolence or energy of religious institutions be a legitimate matter for government concern–or, at least, any more a matter of concern than indolence of nonreligious voluntary associations." As I maintained in chapter 4, the Constitution favors religion and for the most part favors it by staying away from it.

104. On the appeal to conservatives of the claim that government action in support of an objective actually undermines it, see Albert O. Hirschman, *The Rhetoric of Reaction*, 1–42 (Cambridge: Belknap Press of Harvard University Press, 1991).

105. MacCulloch, *The Reformation*, 107, 109 (referring to Augustine's view of the worthlessness of humanity).

106. Wallis, *God's Politics*, 9–10. For an excellent and often surprising discussion of the role of religion in the politics of the Democratic Party over the past few decades, see Sullivan, *The Party Faithful*.

107. A part of what has contributed to that impression is the frequent failure of many Democrats explicitly to acknowledge that abortion presents a moral issue.

108. "The best selling of all evangelical books in recent years, Rick Warren's *The Purpose Driven Life* . . . has all the hallmarks of self absorption (in one five page chapter I counted eighty-five uses of the word *you*), but it also makes a powerful case that we're made for a mission." Bill McGibbon, "People of the Book," 24.

109. On the other hand, according to one poll, approximately 17 percent of Christians believe in the "prosperity gospel," the view that God brings wealth to those who pray. http://www.usnews.com/articles/news/national/2008/02/15/behind-the-prosperity-gospel.html (last visited August 21, 2008).

110. Thomas Frank, *What's the Matter with Kansas: How Conservatives Won the Heart of America* 6 (New York: Metropolitan Books, 2004). On the appeal of the Republican message, see Frank, 157–58.

111. Eighty-four percent of white regular churchgoing evangelicals voted for Bush. Kuo, *Tempting Fate*, 133.

112. Linker, *The Theocons*, 174.

113. For an excellent brief review of the data involving the role of Christian conservatives in the 2004 presidential election, see Mark J. Rozell and Debasree Das Gupta, "'The Values Vote'? Moral Issues and the 2004 Elections," in *The Values Campaign? The Christian Right and the 2004 Elections* (John C. Green, Mark J. Rozell, and Clyde Wilcox eds. ,Washington, D.C.: Georgetown University Press, 2006).

114. In response to the 2004 elections, "Democrats have been eager to 'get it' and craft new narratives to get their policy priorities before voters." Greeley and

Hout, *Truth about Conservative Christians*, 39. In the 2006 elections, Barack Obama, Hilary Rodham Clinton, and Howard Dean pressed Democrats to more openly confront religious issues of concern to voters. Lambert, *Religion in American Politics*, 238.

115. Barack Obama's reflections on religion and politics are especially insightful. Barack Obama, *The Audacity of Hope: Thoughts on Reclaiming the American Dream* 195–226 (New York: Crown, 2006).

116. Although the Democrats carried both houses in the midterm elections, it is widely believed that the vote was against Republicans, not for Democrats. In addition, few would suppose that any major alignment could be realized without a great deal of work.

117. The religious sensibilities of Gore and Lieberman in the 2000 election were clear, prompting Daniel Conkle to remark, "If the 2000 campaign has no other effect on the debate about religious values and governmental policymaking, it should dispel the impression that the Republican Party is uniquely connected to religious values and that such values are uniquely 'conservative' in a political sense." Daniel O. Conkle, "Religion, Politics, and the 2000 Presidential Election: A Selective Survey and Appraisal," 77 *Indiana Law Journal* 247, 255 (2002). This was forgotten by the 2004 election.

118. Pew Forum on Religion and Public Life, "Public Support Falls for Religion's Role in Politics," http://pewresearch.org/pubs/930/religion-politics, August 21, 2008 (last visited Nov. 5, 2008). The Democratic figure of 38 percent was up from 26 percent in 2006.

119. Stephen Prothero, "An Election That Is, and Isn't about God," *USA Today*, November 3, 2008, 15A/

120. See Frank, *What's the Matter*, 243 (appealing to corporations is the "criminally stupid" strategy the Democrats have pursued since the 1970s).

121. David Brooks, "A Matter of Faith," A19, *New York Times,* June 22, 2004 (Americans want to be able to see their leaders' faith).

122. Conkle, "2000 Presidential Election," 256.

123. See David E. Campbell, "A House Divided? What Social Science Has to Say about the Culture War? " 15 *William and Mary Bill of Rights Journal* 59, 69 (2006).

124. The role that religion should play regarding the state is much debated within Catholic, Protestant, Jewish, Muslim traditions, among others. For a helpful survey of the positions, see *God's Rule: The Politics of World Religions* (Jacob Neusner ed., Washington D.C.: Georgetown University Press, 2003).

125. Rawls, "Public Reason," 795–97.

126. Although Weber saw a rational worldview as a main causative factor in making the magical views of religion less attractive (see *The Protestant Ethic and the Spirit of Capitalism* [Stephen Kalberg trans., Los Angeles: Roxbury, 2001]), by the 1950s sociologists mainly focused on the rise of the industrial society and the functional differentiation associated with it as contributing to religious decline. See, e.g., Bruce, *God Is Dead*.

127. In the late 1990s, Peter Berger, one of the strongest proponents of the secularization thesis, recanted. Berger, "Desecularization of the World," 2.

128. The subtitle of Grace Davie's book on religion in England puts it well: *Religion in Britain since 1945: Believing without Belonging.* See generally Andrew Greeley, *Religion in Europe at the End of the Second Millennium* (New Brunswick, N.J.: Transaction Publishers, 2003).

129. The view that the rise of science and the decline of religion are associated is not supported by the sociological data. "Societies with greater faith in science often have *stronger* religious beliefs." Pippa Norris and Ronald Inglehart, *Sacred and Secular: Religion and Politics Worldwide* 67 (New York: Cambridge University Press, 2004).

130. These events also caused significant rethinking in modern theology. *The Twentieth Century: A Theological Overview* (Gregory Baum ed., Maryknoll, N.Y.: Orbis Books, 1999). On the theological reaction to World War I, see William R. Hutchison, *Religious Pluralism in America: The Contentious History of a Founding Ideal* 150–69 (New Haven: Yale University Press, 2003).

131. Cf. Chris Hedges, *I Don't Believe in Atheists* 13, 16 (New York: Free Press, 2008).

132. See generally Smith, *Why Religion Matters.*

133. Consider Michael Novak, *No One Sees God,* June 24, 2008, http://www.firstthings.com/: "In these matters, no one has knockdown proof. We make the most reasonable judgment we can, but practically everyone can see how easy it would be to come to the opposite conclusion. In actual life, many believers become atheists, and many atheists become believers. Each does this on the basis of evidence that makes a new and powerful impression on her."

134. For discussion of James's position, see Taylor, *Varieties of Religion Today,* 33–60.

135. Hans Küng, *Why I Am Still a Christian* 54 (David Smith et al. trans, Nashville: Abingdon Press, 1986).

136. Taylor, *Varieties of Religion Today,* 59–60.

137. Perhaps most often it is, however. Consider Dionne, *Souled Out,* 14: Faith "can be a psychological comfort (for many, it's easier to live in a world with a loving God at the center and with a promise of everlasting life)."

138. It is questionable whether the traditional doctrine of hell is psychologically productive for anyone, let alone children. In the absence of religion, a family that threatened its children with eternal torture would presumably be guilty of child abuse. Cf. Hans Küng, *Eternal Life?* 131 (Edward Quinn trans., Garden City, N.Y.: Doubleday, 1984) ("The problem of hell may not be dismissed in silence if only because the *fear of hell*—which has become a proverbial expression—has done immense harm over the course of centuries"). There are alternatives to the literal interpretation. Indeed, as Ellen Badone observes, "[S]ince the 1950's Catholic teachings on Hell and Purgatory have changed dramatically." Ellen Badone, "Introduction," in *Religious Orthodoxy,* 7; see McBrien, *Catholicism,* 1176–77 (suggesting that it is not clear that persons actually go to hell and conceiving hell as separation and isolation or as nonbeing). For a subtle discussion about the possibility of eternal damnation, see Karl Rahner, *The Content of Faith: The Best of Karl Rahner's Theological Writings* 634–37 (Karl Lehmann and Albert Raffelt eds., Harvey D. Egan, S.J., trans., New York: Crossroad, 1994).

139. Kung, *Why I Am Still a Christian,* 53–69.

140. Taylor, *A Secular Age*, 286, 364–65.

141. Taylor, *A Secular Age*, 286.

142. Taylor, *A Secular Age*, 303.

143. Taylor, *A Secular Age*, 768–69.

144. Until the 1970s, the main religious lobbies in Washington were liberal. Corbett and Corbett, *Politics and Religion*, 97.

145. On the religious character of the abolitionists, see Lawrence J. Friedman, *Gregarious Saints: Self and Community in American Abolitionism* (Cambridge: Cambridge University Press, 1982); Elizabeth B. Clark, "'The Sacred Rights of the Weak': Pain, Sympathy, and the Culture of Individual Rights in Antebellum America," 82 *Journal of American History* 463 (1995).

146. Charles Dunn, *American Political Theology: Historical Perspective and Theoretical Analysis* 31–34 (New York: Praeger, 1984). Conservative religious groups were involved in the movement against alcohol that led to Prohibition (though progressive groups dominated), but after the repeal of Prohibition, religious conservatives retreated from politics. Fowler and Hertzke, *Religion and Politics*, 23. The belief in an afterlife and the desire for salvation unquestionably has dulled participation in politics by many churches. At the same time, church organizations have been a major training ground for political action. Sidney Verba, Kay Lehman Schlozman, and Henry E. Brady, *Voice and Equality: Civic Voluntarism in American Politics* (Cambridge: Harvard University Press, 1995). Indeed, churches play a significant role in providing civic skills to those who otherwise would lack the resources. Verba, Schlozman, and Brady, *Voice and Equality*, 18, 519.

147. For an international perspective on the role of religion in violating the rights of women, see Martha Nussbaum, "Religion and Women's Human Rights," in Weithman, *Religion and Contemporary Liberalism*, 93. For a valuable examination of feminist protest with the Catholic church, see Mary Fainsod Katzenstein, *Faithful and Fearless: Moving Feminist Protest Inside the Church and Military* 105–76 (Princeton: Princeton University Press, 1998).

148. Gerda Lerner, "The Meaning of Seneca Falls: 1848–1898," *Dissent*, Fall 1998, at 35, 37.

149. Lerner, "Meaning of Seneca Falls," 98.

150. For commentary on its relative importance, see R. H. Tawney, *Religion and the Rise of Capitalism* (New York: New American Library, 1958); Weber, *Protestant Ethic*. See also Niebuhr, *Does Civilization Need Religion?* 67, 95–97, 103.

151. For an intriguing argument in support of this contention, see Seymour Martin Lipset, *American Exceptionalism: A Double Edged Sword* 53–76 (New York: Norton, 1996).

152. See Sanford Levinson, "Abstinence and Exclusion: What Does Liberalism Demand of the Religiously Oriented (Would Be) Judge?" in *Religion and Contemporary Liberalism*, 82 (citing Al Gore's linking of his environmental views to God and Christ); Wolterstorff, "Why We Should Reject," 180 (referring to views of the Christian Environment Council).

153. Fowler and Hertzke, *Religion and Politics*, 7; Ryan, *Liberal Anxieties*, 74, 78–79.

154. Liberal intellectuals have generally been slow to credit the role of religion in liberal movements. Consider Wolterstorff, "Why We Should Reject," 167: "Many of the movements in the modern world which have resulted in reforms and revolutions that the liberal admires have been deeply religious in their orientation: the abolitionist movement in nineteenth-century America, the civil rights movement in twentieth-century America, the resistance movements in fascist Germany, in communist Eastern Europe, and in apartheid South Africa. These movements are regularly analyzed by Western academics and intellectuals as if religion were nowhere in the picture."

155. For many decades in the twentieth century, the American Catholic Church's emphasis on loyalty and patriotism, rocking the boat only in areas of special interest for religious freedom, may have had political effects similar to the dominant strain of Protestantism (though Catholicism was socially segregated from the modern culture). For an excellent description of Catholic culture in the first sixty years of the twentieth century and the factors that caused it to change, see Morris, *American Catholic*, 113–281. For a view of the various Muslim perspectives, see L. Carl Brown, *Religion and State: The Muslim Approach to Politics* 175–80 (New York: Columbia University Press, 2000) (cautioning against an assumption that Muslims share uniform beliefs about engagement with political processes).

156. See Niebuhr, *Does Civilization Need Religion?* 11–18. On the relationship between Protestantism and economic attitudes, see Weber, *Protestant Ethic*; Tawney, *Religion and Rise of Capitalism*, 227–53, 277–87.

157. See generally Zagorin, *Religious Toleration* (detailing the religious arguments supporting religious violence and the arguments leading away from it).

Conclusion

1. See generally, William R. Hutchinson, *Religious Pluralism in America* 219–40 (New Haven: Yale University Press, 2003).

2. Hutchinson, *Religious Pluralism*, 226.

3. Charles H. Lippy, *Pluralism Comes of Age* 157 (Armonk, N.Y.: M. E. Sharpe, 2000).

Index